THE EXPERT SUCCESS SOLUTION

Praise For

THE EXPERT SUCCESS SOLUTION

What an eclectic and interesting collection of worthwhile knowledge and insight from a collaboration of experts. This is a gem of a book that seeks to be bought and delved into, delivering just the right information at just the right time. I have no hesitation in recommending this book to anyone who is looking for inspiration. I am happily giving a copy a permanent home on my bookshelf!

— **Dr. Jane Cox**—International Human Performance Specialist
www.newlevels.co.uk

How many times have we heard the well-worn phrase, 'thinking outside the box'? The Expert Success Solution *puts this phrase into action. It helps guide innovative solutions by providing simple questioning techniques and shows us how easy outside the box thinking can be!*

— **Dr. Patricia Dues**, Government IT Manager

What a fun and energizing read! The Expert Success Solution *contains fresh, concise, inspiring nuggets of wisdom on the topics that really matter. It's a modern and sometimes highly entertaining reference book.*

— **April Norris**, mult-sensory healer at Hyp. www.April-Norris.com

This book is a must read for anyone that truly wants to live life on their terms. It is packed full of countless ideas that can be implemented from the moment you read it.

— **Peggy McColl**, NY Times Bestselling Author
and Achievement Coach

The Expert Success Solution *will elev8hope in your community.*

— **Rina Shpiruk**, founder Elev8hope
www.elev8hope.com

I love making a difference in the lives of men and women. This book offers 22 top expert solutions to many life situations! Twenty-two innovative and powerful experts reveal how to live an extraordinary life. Whether you

seek a career change that reaches out to help others or you desire a healthy happy life for yourself, this book is a "must read"!

— **Jackie Harvey**—President and CEO of MaxxAlive Inc.
and www.HelpForHormones.com

This powerful book is the result of collaborative work of leading experts. In a simple and friendly manner, it provides the powerful strategies that will enable you to empower yourself whether it's in business or your personal life. This book is offering real help and is very inspiring.

— **Dr. Karen Sherman**, Psychologist/Speaker/Author/Radio Host
www.DrKarenSherman.com

With this book you may be inspired to recognize the many ways you can make a difference for others as well. If you are seeking to resolve an issue, with 24 experts sharing their wisdom in one book, your personal solution is likely in these pages.

— **Leslie McIntosh**, BCHt, founder of Coastal Academy
of Hypnotic Arts and Science

This book is packed with practical time tested wisdom on how to enhance your business and personal life. As a time management expert, I know first hand the kinds of issues that can steal your time and prevent you from accomplishing your mission. Learn from these experts how to quickly work through barriers to your success and finally achieve the outcomes you desire for your personal and professional mission.

— **Shari McGuire**: Consultant, Speaker and Author of
*Take Back Your Time: 101 Simple Tips to
Shrink Your Work-Week and Conquer the Chaos in Your Life*
www.ShrinkYourWorkWeek.com

I'm thrilled to endorse **The Expert Success Solution**, *because I believe this book is both timely and essential. This group of seasoned and respected experts offer life-changing ideas that will motivate and escalate a successful, fulfilling journey for those readers who are genuinely interested in getting to* *the heart of personal progress. There are a lot of books available that make beneficial claims, but few that deliver.* **The Expert Success Solution** *is the real deal.*

> — **Tamra Nashman**, image consultant, marketing coach, and author of *The Extra-Ordinary Image, Creating Your Unique Personal Style.*
> www.Extra-OrdinaryImage.com

Many books cross my desk but **The Expert Success Solution** *caught my eye because of the uniqueness of the collaborative style and the impressive caliber and expertise of the contributors. Real and lasting success is multi-faceted and requires balance and alignment is every part of our lives. Within the pages of this interesting and informative book, lie the solutions to so many of the problems and challenges which hold us back, preventing us from achieving our potential. And, as if that wasn't enough, it's also a great read!*

> — **Stephanie J. Hale**, The Oxford Literary Consultancy and founder of The Millionaire Bootcamp for Authors.
> www.millionaireauthorsbootcamp.com

I know what Einstein would do if he were to write a book today—he would buy this book! It has information from the industry experts that can stimulate one's imagination to find new ways to be successful in publishing. And it's all in the WRIST. I highly recommend it.

> — **Brian Jud**, Executive Director of the Association of Publishers for Special Sales and author of *How to Make Real Money Selling Books*

Dr. Lupe-Rebeka Samaniego has a beautiful conception of what it means to be alive and the collaboration of these 22 experts in **The Expert Success Solution** *fulfills the commitment to life.*

> — **Dr. Ralph I. Fisch**, co-author of *The Impact of Trauma on Development*, Retired Clinical Associate Professor, Graduate School of Professional Psychology, University of Denver.

This book is written by passionate people generously sharing their insights. It is difficult to condense your knowledge into a kernel of wisdom which would fit into one chapter, yet each of the 22 experts did it successfully. This is a fast track to learning.

— **Sky Blossoms**, Speaker and Author of *Best Thing Ever*
www.BestThingEver.com

This book is a good read for those that want to be in touch with who they are and where they want to be in both their personal and professional world.

— **Thomas Bahler**, Composer, Producer, Consultant
and Author of *Anything is Possible*

If you are looking to be the master of your own destiny, **The Expert Success Solution** *is the treasure map to get you there. This book is packed full of incredible ideas and suggestions for anyone that strives to be a personal and financial success. Once you read this book you will realize that nothing can ever hold you back again.*

— **Smiljan Mori**, Coach, Speaker and
Author of *MotivAction for Life.*
www.SmiljanMori.com

As a holistic nurse and founder of Trillium Wellness Consultants I am aware that millions of people want to create the conditions for health and happiness in their lives. In **The Expert Success Solution**, *22 experts share invaluable advice, tools and techniques that we all will benefit from. I highly recommend this book.*

— **Susan Krautter**, RN, BScN, Holistic Nurse, Trillium Wellness
Consultants www.UnderstandingHormones.com

The Expert Success Solution *is a must read for anyone who is looking for a practical, step-by-step guide to improve your professional and personal life. I have the pleasure to work with…many of these authors and I am confident that you will gain unique insights from each of these authors on ways to overcome obstacles and find the most efficient path to the life you have always desired.*

— **Tom Antion**, www.GreatInternetMarketingTraining.com

If you want your visions and dreams to come true, **The Expert Success Solution** *is the book to energize your life.*

    — **Mary Morrissey**, Bestselling Author and Speaker

Founder of a consultant referral firm, my goal is to make our clients' lives easier by matching them with the right consulting resources. The **Expert Success Solution** *provides the reader not only with a variety of outstanding resources, but also with strategic solutions from diverse areas of expertise. Short chapters, inviting writing styles, and practical advice around challenges that all of us face in our personal and professional lives, make this book impactful and motivational without being heavy handed. I also applaud the book's unique cross-referencing approach that models the benefit of networking and partnering. A great read and some very useful information!*

    — **Pat Schneider**, President, Expert-Access, LLC – Your One-Source Resource for Expert Consultants. www.Expert-Access.com

I'm sure we have all read a self-help book or two, but never have we had the opportunity to find wisdom and guidance from so many experienced, educated professionals in so many different fields, all in one book. The **Expert Success Solution** *might very well replace your entire bookshelf. Read, learn and enjoy. It's a gem.*

    — **Lili Bosse**, Vice Mayor, City of Beverly Hills, CA

The Expert Success Solution *is a book I wish I could have read more than 50 years ago when I began my career right out of law school. It is filled with wonderful insights that are clear, practical and simple, but never simplistic. It is a "how to" book that is powerful while also being written from a compassionate point of view. A "must read" no matter at what stage one's life is found.*

    — **Mary Libby Payne**, lawyer, founding dean and professor of Mississippi College School of Law, first woman elected to serve as Mississippi Appellate Court Judge, public speaker and author of *A Goodly Heritage, a Memoir of Mississippi College School of Law*

Kris Landry has been a supporting force in my life for over 20 years. She has shown through the example of her work how she has lived a life of love and compassion for all sentient beings. I offer high praise and many blessings for Kris and her colleagues with their book, The Expert Success Solution. *It will help many people.*

— **Geshe Chongtul Rinpoche**, Lama of the Tibetan Bon Tradition, Spiritual Director of Bon Shen Ling www.bonshenling.org

Having it all means reading this insightful book written by professionals for seekers of professional advice. The Expert Success Solution *offers a sound roadmap to success in both personal and business life and answers many questions that we have about why and how. A worthwhile read and learning experience.*

— **Carole Pumpian**, Immediate Past President, Hallandale Florida Chamber of Commerce. www.CPumpianPR.com

The Expert Success Solution *is both simple and elegant. These experienced professionals offer words that are guiding lights for people who want to improve the way they relate to themselves and each other.*

— **Jessica Kizorek**, Founder, www.BadassBusinessWomen.org

22 experts. 22 disciplines. 22 topics. 1 book. The Expert Success Solution *does what no book has done before: it brings together seasoned professionals who have combined their unique areas of expertise to make a significant difference for people worldwide. I applaud this creative, simple and much-needed approach. If you dream of better health and happiness for yourself and those you love, pick it up. You'll be happy you did.*

—**Melanie Bragg** Esq., Speaker, Coach and Author of *Crosstown* www.MelanieBragg.com

If you only buy one book, get The Expert Success Solution. *Offering inspiring strategies from 22 different experts, it delivers practical actions you can implement immediately to move forward in your personal life and in your business.*

—**Susan Adler**, LCSW

This is definitely one book I will keep handy and refer to over and over again! Every chapter is relatable at some point in everyone's life. A great combination of expert advice we can all use. After reading The Expert Success Solution I was so motivated to apply what I learned I have already started to apply these suggestions to improve my management skills and have noticed a tremendous difference. Thank you for helping me realize and achieve the true priorities in my life!

—**Stefanie Downes**, Regional Director, 18+ years in management and sales for healthcare and government retirement plans

Lisa Gibson is passionate about the power of forgiveness and letting go of anger. In The Expert Success Solution, the unique story Lisa shares illustrates how the art of conflict resolution transcends cultural barriers. She and her fellow co-authors have inspired me to examine all aspects of my life and business and take action using their simple questions even taking the principles they teach to other cultures I work in.

— **Anja Wynne**, Global Perspectives Consulting, www.gpcolorado. com

This book is important because it's a work of a partnership of people giving truth and simple perception to complex problems. As an actor for over 50 years, I have had to reinvent myself multiple times, and I now understand that help was always there—all I had do was ask. There's no shame in asking for help—only humility. You'll find humor and wisdom in this book from seasoned professionals who have been-there-done-that. I wish I had this book earlier - I might be competing for Brad Pitt's or Denzel Washington's roles!

— **George Hamilton**, Actor and Bestselling Author

The Expert Success Solution is a bright, genuine, fierce, and compassionate straight shooter of a book. The authors have created an expert guide to help you navigate the unknown waters in your business and life. If you want more happiness, success and fulfillment, the wisdom imparted by these authors needs to be part of your strategy. They address questions you would be crazy not to want answered. Truly brilliant!

— **Lisa Lane**, Founder www.TheInsideLane.com

I highly recommend this book for its spot-on practical intelligence. As one who helps people find and hone their expertise I applaud this collection of experts who have done just that. What is provided in this book is a wide-ranging array of useful information that will propel our business and personal lives."

— **Carol Mortarotti**, Founder, Expert Niche Academy
www.ExpertNicheAcademy.com

Success in life means great performance, at work, at home, and in the community. This is a book rich with insights and education on how to achieve what you want and be the best you in all arenas.

— **Lisa Parrelli-Gray**, President, Westport-Weston Chamber of Commerce (Westport, CT) www.WestportChamber.com

The contributing authors in The Expert Success Solution really get to the heart of the matter—and what matters to each one is different. These people have survived good, bad and ugly in matters of both head and heart, and have lived another day to share the mountains of wisdom gained. How lucky are we to learn from them. My advice to you is this: pick up the book and read, read, read! The Expert Success Solution is filled with not just pearls of wisdom but brilliant diamonds of insight. You will see yourself in this very helpful mirror.

— **Marilyn Mitzel**, Emmy Award-Winning broadcast journalist and news anchor www.MarilynMitzel.com

THE
EXPERT
SUCCESS
SOLUTION

*Get Solid Results
in 22 Areas of Business and Life*

WENDY LIPTON-DIBNER
and RICK FRISHMAN

with 22 LEADING EXPERTS

NEW YORK

THE EXPERT SUCCESS SOLUTION
Get Solid Results in 22 Areas of Business and Life

Published in New York, New York, by Morgan James Publishing. Morgan James and The Entrepreneurial Publisher are trademarks of Morgan James, LLC. www.MorganJamesPublishing.com

The Morgan James Speakers Group can bring authors to your live event. For more information or to book an event visit The Morgan James Speakers Group at www.TheMorganJamesSpeakersGroup.com.

FREE eBook edition for your existing eReader with purchase

PRINT NAME ABOVE

For more information, instructions, restrictions, and to register your copy, go to **www.bitlit.ca/readers/register** or use your QR Reader to scan the barcode:

ISBN 978-1-61448-938-2 paperback
ISBN 978-1-61448-939-9 eBook
Library of Congress Control Number:
2013948908

Cover Design by:
Rachel Lopez
www.r2cdesign.com

Interior Design by:
Bonnie Bushman
bonnie@caboodlegraphics.com

In an effort to support local communities, raise awareness and funds, Morgan James Publishing donates a percentage of all book sales for the life of each book to Habitat for Humanity Peninsula and Greater Williamsburg.

Get involved today, visit
www.MorganJamesBuilds.com.

This book is dedicated to all the experts who work alone. May you soon discover the power of collaboration so you can make a greater impact in your family, your community and around the globe.

CONTENTS

PREFACE   xvii

1   Get People to Do What You Want Them to Do!   1
Wendy Lipton-Dibner, MA

2   The Extra Step   9
Rick Frishman

3   Four Senseless Partnership Mistakes
and How to Avoid Them   15
Patty Soffer

4   Keep Conflict from Derailing
Your Organization's Mission   21
Lisa Gibson, JD

5   What Would Einstein Do?   28
Cheryl Lentz, DM, MSIR

6   Do You Secretly Hate Going to Work?   34
Donald Burns

7   Innovative Reinvention   40
Michael Harris

8   Live a Life That's Free, Fun
and Fabulous—at Any Age!   45
Babs Kangas, PhD

9   Three Styles of Retirement: Which is Best for You?   51
Suzanne Nault, MPs PCC

10   Big Bold Ambitions   57
Randy Stanbury

11   ESS—Feel Like a Kid Again   64
Jeffrey Kurtz

12   Do This, Don't Do That:
     Simple Steps For Your Quality of Life   70
     Jennifer Rosenwald

13   Life-Auditing for the Overwhelmed   76
     Lupe-Rebeka Samaniego, PhD

14   Flip Your Switch—It's Time to Shine Again   82
     Janet Swift

15   I Love My Journey   88
     Bonnie Goldstone, CHT, NLP

16   My Spirit Does Not Live in a Box   93
     Tina Sacchi

17   Join the PAC (Parents of Adult Children)
     and Never Lose Your Connection!   98
     BJ Rosenfeld, MA, MS, COGS

18   A Lasting, Exciting Love Relationship   104
     Dianne Flemington

19   Stop Getting Old: 3 Simple Steps to Get You Started   111
     Elizabeth Phinney

20   Break Through to Your Healthier and Happier Life   117
     Irina Koles, MD

21   Survivin' to Thrivin' Through Financial Distress   123
     Lorie A. L. Nicholas, PhD

22   Die Without Regrets   129
     M. Kris Landry, MRE

     Meet The Experts   137
     Connect with the Experts!   161
     Get Help From the Experts!   163

PREFACE

Welcome to *The Expert Success Solution*. The book you hold in your hands is the result of a carefully crafted collaboration of 22 experts in personal and professional development. The book took 9 months to create and represents a combined 300+ years of experience in our respected fields.

While there are many books available that offer a one-stop-reading-experience with a wide array of authors, this is the first book[1] where 22 independent experts from entirely different industries sat in a room together to bring you a solid solution for your business and your life.

Our goal was heartfelt: To help you get more success in every area of your life!

Our plan was deliberate: To introduce you to proven strategies and tools you can use right away to get solid results.

Our plan is complete and now we need your help to achieve our goal. So permit us to give you the short cut:

To increase your success in every area of your life, read each chapter and follow the how-to advice you find there.

---

1   To our knowledge as of this publication, this book is the first expert collaboration in personal and professional development.

Within the pages of this book you will find simple, powerful success tips on business development, marketing, business partnerships, financial health, spirituality, relationships, goal achievement, strategic thinking, work-life balance, family communications, retirement, reinvention, transformation, healthy eating, fitness, conflict management, career transition, relaxation, self-hypnosis, finding the 'kid' in you and dying without regrets.

The benefits you reap from *The Expert Success Solution* will depend on how you use it. So let's talk about that…

How to Get the Most from The Expert Success Solution

By design, the book you hold in your hands is strategically crafted to help you grow your success. Every area of your life is covered within the pages of this book with proven shortcuts to help you find more success faster. *We will help you in every way we can—we've even set up a Facebook community where you can come to ask us questions[2]!*

While there are many suggestions here you can use to grow your results, there is a secret to getting the most from our experts' contributions:

The raw truth is if you want your results to change, you will have to change.

We are providing amazing resources you can use to get where you want to go easier and faster. But these resources will only help you if you use them.

We've done everything we can to make that easier for you. Simply do 2 things:

(1) READ EACH CHAPTER

We're delighted you've purchased a copy of this book, but our goal for you depends on you actually *reading* the book.

---

2 Search *The Expert Success Solution* at Facebook.com

Far too many people buy books with great intentions. The book starts out on their desk or nightstand and then, inch-by-inch, it ends up on the shelf.

In our industry, we call that "shelf-help."

Don't be that person.

Start reading Chapter 1 and just keep on going until you finish Chapter 22. One chapter per night and in 3 weeks you'll have your Expert Success Solution.

And *please*…don't make the mistake of thinking,

Well, I don't have my own business so I'm not going to read that chapter!

-or-

I'm comfortable with my life, so I won't read that chapter!

-or-

I'm too young to think about that, so I won't read that chapter!

-or-

I'm too old to think about that, so I won't read that chapter!

Within each chapter you'll find wisdom and expertise that goes way beyond the written words. You will come up with new ideas simply by reading ours.

And even if you don't need a certain strategy in this book, someone you know might need it desperately! Be the messenger of hope and information for that person by sharing what you've learned here.

(2) IMPLEMENT THE ACTION STEPS

Each expert offers next steps for you to take so you can grow your success faster. You've got the tools in your hand, all you need to do is use them. And to make sure you get and stay motivated and never lose momentum, begin here by asking yourself the following questions[3] (write your answers right here in this book):

---

3   Reprinted here with permission from *Shatter Your Speed Limits®: Fast Track Your Success and Get What You Truly Want—In Business and in Life* (2010) Wendy Lipton-Dibner. All rights reserved.

Question 1: If you woke up tomorrow morning and magically found you had everything you truly want—in your business and your life—how would your life be different?

_____

_____

_____

Question 2: If your life looked as you've described it, what would that get for you? (Hint: be specific)

_____

_____

_____

_____

_____

Question 3: If you got what you described in Question 2, then what would _that_ get for you?

_____

_____

_____

_____

Question 4: What would you need to know, get and do to be able to make happen what you described in Questions 1-3? (Hint: you'll find many of the answers within the pages of this book.)

_____

_____

_____

_____

Question 5: How will you stop yourself from letting yourself have what you truly want?

_____

_____

_____

_____

_____

Question 6: What will you tell yourself so you'll give yourself permission to do what it takes to get what you want?

_____

_____

_____

_____

Now Make it Happen!

It is our sincere hope you will use this book to help you get everything you want and that you will in turn, share these tools with those you love. Because true success comes when you help others.

It is our profound privilege to help you in your life. Thank you for honoring us with your trust.

Wendy, Rick, Patty, Lisa, Cheryl, Donald, Michael, Babs, Suzanne, Randy, Jeffrey, Jennifer, Lupe, Janet, Bonnie, Tina, BJ, Dianne, Elizabeth, Irina, Lori and Kris

1

GET PEOPLE TO DO WHAT YOU WANT THEM TO DO!

Wendy Lipton-Dibner, MA

You're sleeping soundly when suddenly your eyes pop open and just like that—you're wide awake.

You lay in the dark staring at nothing, drenched in sweat while your heart pounds in your chest and your mind races from thought to thought without completion.

Now begins the familiar routine…

Half asleep, you roll out of bed and shuffle through the dark… one foot in front of the other…

Arms and hands outstretched, touching walls that aren't there, you find your way to the kitchen where you promptly stub your toe and whisper words that will never appear in a children's fairy tale.

Welcome to *2:00 a.m. Hell*—the loneliest place on Earth.

If this sounds familiar, please know you're not alone in your aloneness.

In a national research study of thousands of doctors and executives[4], 100% of respondents reported waking in the middle of the night, consumed with thoughts about work and/or home problems.

The really fascinating finding in the study was this:

All respondents reported their *2:00 a.m. Hell* could be summarized by one question...

The Universal Question

I've had the privilege of meeting hundreds of thousands of people in my work as a professional speaker, media guest, coach and trainer. From Akron to Australia in industries ranging from healthcare to hair care, people always ask me the same question:

How do I get people to do what I want them to do?

I'm guessing you're not surprised. Nearly everything that leads us to *2:00 a.m. Hell* finds its beginning in something someone else did or didn't do[5].

What would life be like if everyone would just do what you want them to do?

At home, dishes would get washed *and* put away, dirty socks would land inside the hamper, the remote control would *always* be in your hands and no one else would even think about taking that last piece of pizza.

At work? Well, if everyone would just do what you want them to do, things would get done faster and easier, you'd make more money and you could spend more time doing what you love instead of battling the things you wish would disappear.

---

4   Study conducted by the author in cooperation with Greenbranch Publishing.

5   Of course sometimes, that "someone" is ourselves, but for now, let's point the figure at other people. It's so much more fun!

Whether you're a doctor, an entrepreneur, an executive or non-profit volunteer…in a relationship or living single…mother, father or grandparent… no matter what your age, occupation or gender…

The simple truth is: life is better when you know how to get people to do what you want them to do.

But you can't really get people to change—can you?

They say we can't change other people. They even say we ourselves can't change—that we are creatures of habit, born to be who we are and nothing anyone else says or does can change us.

In my experience, those statements are myths. There are proven formulas you can use to get people to do what you want them to do *and more importantly,* to get them to actually *want* to do what you want them to do!

I first discovered the magical formulas at age 2 (yes, that's me in the photo).

I loved those private moments with my mom, so I figured out how to get her to stay there with me for as long as I wanted!

All I had to do was *not* … well, you get the idea.

As I grew older, I became a dedicated student of human behavior. From graduate school forward, I studied what makes people do what they do and continually searched for strategies to get people to change.

I certainly wasn't the only person fascinated with finding the secrets to move people to action. The fact is everyone tries to get someone else to change at one point or another.

- Mothers use tricks to get their children to eat broccoli.
- Teachers use persuasion to get students to sit quietly.
- Employers use threats and incentives to get employees to be more productive.
- Advertisers use tactics to get customers to buy products and services.

- Entrepreneurs use strategies to get new customers to choose them over their competition
- Professional speakers use stories to get a rise from their audiences
- And teenagers…ah they are the masters of manipulation!

Let's face it—at some point everyone tries to get someone else to change. It's in the minds and conversations of men and women in bedrooms and boardrooms all over the world.

- *How can I get him to tell me what he's thinking?*
- *How can I get her to stop asking me what I'm thinking?*
- *How do I get my boss to give me a promotion?*
- *What do I need to do to get people to come to my business?*
- *How do I get my employees to stop texting on the job?*
- *How do I get more traffic to my website?*
- *How do I get people to LIKE, SHARE, CLICK and BUY everything I offer online?*

And the list goes on and on.

After studying, testing, refining and teaching formulas to move people to action, I can tell you it all boils down to 5 simple steps.

5 Steps to Move People to Action!

Step 1: Identify the precise actions you want people to take. Most change initiatives fail right from the get-go because we don't clarify what we really want from people.

Yeah ok, but I just want people to come to my website.

Really, is that all you want? Or do you want them to actually DO something when they get to your website?

- Do you want them to read the words on your site?
- Do you want them to give you their contact information?
- Do you want them to buy what you offer?
- Do you want them to use what they buy?

- Do you want them to get amazing results from what you gave them?
- Do you want them to come back and buy again and again?
- Do you want them to refer others to your door?

Be specific. Break it down, focus on each piece and then move to Step 2.

Step 2: Develop a true connection with the person/people you want to influence by finding out everything you can about them. The more you understand about people, the more quickly you can discover precisely what they need you to do so they'll be open to change[6].

Do your research. Read their blogs, visit them at their business and local hangouts, attend their conferences, search their websites and find out all you can. Get to know the people you want to move to action. Once you truly get them, move to Step 3.

Step 3: Obtain 3 critical pieces of information[7]:

1. How will doing what *you* want help them get what *they* want?
2. What would keep them from being *able* to do what you want?
3. What would keep them from being *willing* to do what you want?

People always ask, "*How do I get that information?*"
The answer is: "*Ask them.*"

---

6   Rick Frishman is a master at Step 2. What's his secret? As soon as he meets someone, the first thing he asks is, "*How can I help you?*" and then he does his research to find out how best to help that person. In a world where people try to get away with doing less, Rick always takes the extra step to make an impact. Read Chapter 2 to find out what that looks like in the business world. I've been privileged to be on the receiving end of Rick's "Step 2" and I can tell you from experience—it's amazing.

7   These questions are the external version of the 6 questions provided for you in the Preface of this book. While the Preface questions invite you to look at what will move *you* to action, the questions listed here are what you need to use so you can gather the information to move *others* to action (professionally and personally). All of these questions find their foundation in my internationally acclaimed *Action Formula*©*TM*.

I'm a firm believer in surveys and personal interviews. You'll be amazed what you can discover over lunch with a set of strategically crafted questions.

Step 4: Use the data you collected in Step 3 as the foundation for all communications with those you want to influence (in personal conversations, business meetings, all written communications, in marketing copy and in speeches—on stages and online in podcasts and video).

Connect the dots for people so they understand how giving you what *you* want will give them what *they* want. Help them get the resources they need so they are *able* to take action and then help them get out of their own way so they are *willing* to make the necessary changes that will lead to effective results.

Step 5: Once you get people to change, the key is to help them *sustain* the change by providing practical action steps they will take immediately. *Implementation is the key to success*, so use Steps 1—4 to move them to actually *use* the action steps you provide.

When you apply these 5 steps consistently and effectively, people will do what you want them to do. My clients have used these steps in hospitals to get patients to follow treatment recommendations, in non-profit organizations to get greater visibility and increase donations, in executive and company-wide meetings to enroll and engage employees, on stages worldwide to get audiences to implement how-to training, and in marketing and sales conversations that enabled users to increase revenues exponentially.

Why do these steps work so well?

Because all 5 Steps are based on helping other people get what *they* want.

Zig Ziglar had it right: *If you help other people get what they want, you'll get what you want.* So focus on finding out what people truly want, find the connection between what you want and what they want, help them see that connection and then help them get what they need so they are able and willing to take action.

It just doesn't get any simpler than that.[8]

The Plot Twist

Is it really this simple?

Yes.

And no.

Yes, people really will change if you use the 5 Steps to Move People to Action effectively.

But there's a twist.

- You've got to do the research.
- You've got to align with their needs.
- You've got to communicate differently.
- You've got to put total focus on helping them get what they want.

You see, it turns out the biggest secret of getting people to do what you want them to do is:

You've got to do what *they* want *you* to do.

I know—it's a stinker. But it's really quite fair when you think about it.

Move people to action. You'll make a positive impact on the loves of others and make your life a whole lot easier.

Start now and make an impact on every life you touch…because life is far too short to settle for less than you truly want—in your business or your life!™

WENDY LIPTON-DIBNER, MA is a two-time bestselling author, world-renowned keynote speaker and founder of the internationally acclaimed Move People to Action System for Experts, Executives and Entrepreneurs™. President of Professional

---

8   The information in this chapter goes beyond business skills. Men and women worldwide are taking the Move People to Action steps beyond the workplace and into their homes to strengthen their family and get their kids engaged in school and away from drugs. Once you know how to move people to action, there's no limit to the difference you can make for people.

Impact, Inc., she's touched millions of lives, helping people make a greater impact on the lives of others. For more information, see Wendy's bio in *Meet The Experts.*

›2‹

THE EXTRA STEP

Rick Frishman

Sam Walton, founder of Wal-Mart, said, "*There is only one boss: the customer…and he can fire everybody in the company from the chairman on down, simply by spending his money somewhere else.*"

Businesses are created to serve customers and ultimately offer value to each and every one of them. The more value you can create, the better chance you will find success.

Henry Ford was extremely accurate when he stated, "*The man who will use his skill and constructive imagination to see how much he can give for a dollar, instead of how little he can give for a dollar, is bound to succeed.*"

Fundamentally, the realm of business is cutthroat and enormously competitive. There may be dozens of companies in the marketplace that offer the same service or product as you do, yet one company may consistently lead the charge in both sales and success.

When studying the underlying reason why one company fails and another excels, the difference is in the details. Actually, the difference is in the last step, which is often the extra one. It is the step few people have the innate desire to take.

Flying High

If you look at all the airlines, it may seem like they're all alike. Southwest Airlines may not seem to offer a different product than Delta, American Airlines, or even British Airways. They all get you where you need to go. However, upon further examination, we find out Southwest Airlines is consistently the most successful Airline in the world. Why?

Southwest Airlines takes extra steps so they can differentiate— stand out from competitors. They focus their energy on customer service and ensuring the customer receives the best experience possible. That is why today, Southwest is the safest airline in the world and ranks number one in the industry for service, on-time performance and lowest employee turnover rate. Customers vote with their wallet and those votes are cast for Southwest more than any other Airline because Southwest puts forth the extra effort and takes more steps than others are willing to take.

If you want to get new business, you have to get the customer to love you, believe in your product and trust you. Once you get them you have to *keep* them. To do that, you have to over-deliver time and time again. It is the little things that show that you are different from your competition and are willing to go the extra step.

Fifteen years ago, Ray Bard founded Bard Books. A brand new publisher, they set out to launch their first book, knowing that would either make or break the company. This book was entitled *Nuts!* by Kevin and Jackie Freiberg.

Nuts! is the true story of the out-of-the-box business plan and history of Southwest Airlines. My publicity company was one of ten

PR firms contacted to interview with Ray and his team. Ray came to New York and when he walked into our office, our receptionist was waiting for him. We'd never met Ray, but he was welcomed with open arms. We created a wonderful presentation on what differentiated us, but the most important thing was that we showed how much we cared about him. When he left that day, he felt 100% loved.

After meeting with Ray and before he flew back to Dallas, we sent him an enormous box of nuts. Since Southwest was all about giving out nuts on flights, we felt it only appropriate. My PR firm received a prompt response to our symbol of appreciation. It came in the form of a handwritten letter from Ray that said, "*We would be nuts if we didn't work with you.*" It started a great relationship that led to a huge success and landed the book *Nuts!* on the *New York Times* bestseller list.

From the moment Ray walked into our office to following up in a thoughtful manner, we took the extra steps to align our company with both Ray and Southwest Airlines. And it paid off for everyone.

Success in life is a game of inches. That one step can be the difference between landing a million dollar account or losing it. But you should always strive to be defined by what you do, not by whether or not your competitors outdo you.

Taking the Extra Steps

So with this example in mind, how can you take the extra steps to separate yourself from your competitors? Luckily, creating a business known for taking the extra steps is not complicated or difficult. In fact, it just takes attention to detail and a touch of effort.

Consider some of the most powerful ways to distinguish your company from your colleagues:

Be Authentic

People know and feel deep in their soul if you are real or not. From the moment they meet you, their gut will quickly delineate if you are the type of person that will work hard for their business. For example, recently we had to order new closets for our home. As a good consumer, I called numerous companies. One came highly recommended from multiple people and I called them. After a week, I hadn't heard back so I continued my search. Another company sent a woman to our home who made us feel like we'd known her forever. She had already done research about our house and had with her every type of closet option imaginable. She was knowledgeable, direct, honest, and completely connected with us. We hired her on the spot and cut a check that day.

This may seem like a small example, but it outlines an important concept. Being authentic is not something everyone does, but when they do, it has gigantic potential. Oprah Winfrey smartly said, "*I had no idea that being your authentic self could make me as rich as I've become. If I had, I'd have done it a lot earlier.*"

Do Your Research

So many times, a little bit of time and effort on the front end can separate you from the competition. Knowing your clients and understanding their origin and goals can offer powerful insight into how they think and how they connect. Harvey McKay writes books about this and is famous for researching client's favorite beverage, candy, or deli food. He then orders it and has it readily available at the initial meeting. Besides the fact that people are happier on a full stomach, it shows he cares and is attentive to details. Do every bit of homework you can on a potential client's website, social media pages, and mutual connections. Sprinkle this information into your presentation to show you know their company inside and out.

Demonstrate You're Different

Everyone wants to work with a company that thinks out of the box. You know, those special and unique companies that are different than everyone else. To do this, think of one small change you can make to your company or your employee manuals that will blow people away.

One way we did this at my old company was with our voicemails. Most people would call us and reach our voicemails. Knowing that, I instituted a company wide policy to update voicemails on a daily basis. Now, I know that sounds difficult and slightly crazy. But it only takes a few minutes and creates an amazing reaction. For thirty years, I changed my voicemail virtually every day. It went like this: *"Hi, this is Rick Frishman. I'm so happy you called. Today is Monday. I'm in the office until 5:30 today. Leave a message and I promise I'll get back to you within 24 hours. If you need something right away, hit STAR+0 and Amanda will help you right now. Thanks a lot."*

This small distinction became a huge difference-maker. First of all, people were excited to leave voicemails because they were invested in the process. If I took the time to change my voicemail everyday, they felt they could take the time to leave me a message. Furthermore, when I called back, the first thing I often heard was how unique my voicemail was. It allowed me a nice transition into telling people that is just how we did business.

Don't Sell the House, Build the Foundation

Finally, people don't want to be sold, they want to build a relationship. People work with those they like and trust. At this high level, most everyone is an expert. So what distinguishes your company from the other experts out there? Relationships.

Rather than selling your product or your company, focus on building a foundation for a strong relationship. You will find yourself much more likely to succeed.

Speaker, Author, and Consultant Wendy Lipton-Dibner says, *"You never, ever, ever have to sell. Just be focused on helping others get what they want, be vulnerable and real and share your message from your heart whenever you speak or write. Do those things and people will be driven to ask for your help and buy whatever you have that's right for them."* [9]

---

9   See Wendy's Chapter 1 for information on how to move people to action.

Getting the business should be an ancillary effect of building the relationship. People can sense when you are overly invested in the sale, and not the person. In business, we are mistakenly taught to hit the ground ready to sell. However, the extra step is being patient and building the relationship, understanding that the sale will become the byproduct of the trust you've built.

Leading the Pack

We all want to be known as "a game-changer." Whenever our company is mentioned, we want the words that come before and after our business's name to be powerful and inspiring. Each of us wants to be remembered, even defined, as the leaders of the pack; the monumentally intriguing and fascinating company that offers its customers something different; something special. This is accomplished through taking the extra steps and understanding where other companies say "enough."

The most riveting companies of our lifetime are those that find another company's line in the sand and go just a little farther.

It is not difficult to be the best if you are willing to dedicate your business or brand to doing so. Your mantra should sound something like:

*"Be the best, even if it takes more work,
more dedication, and more patience."*

Once you adopt this vantage point and then inject it into the way you build business, you will find those extra steps just become part of your company's pillars. And that is when success will find you!

RICK FRISHMAN is a publisher at Morgan James Publishing in New York and founder of Planned Television Arts (now called Media Connect). He has been one of the leading book publicists in America for over 35 years. For more information, see Rick's bio in *Meet The Experts*.

›3‹

FOUR SENSELESS PARTNERSHIP MISTAKES AND HOW TO AVOID THEM

Patty Soffer

I n 2009, my business partnership blew up, scattering debris like trash in a tornado and polluting every part of my life—family, health, money, friendship, self-worth, security, happiness, ego and ultimately the business itself.

What I had thought was the best partnership since Rogers and Hammerstein turned into the worst of Sonny and Cher without the romance (we were business partners, not lovers).

During the ensuing legal, financial and emotional sh*tstorm, I had plenty of time to think about how this could happen. What had gone so wrong that we would blow everything we'd busted our humps to create? And was it just us or was this common in partnerships?

On the surface, all looked good, as it often does. We'd worked together for nearly 12 years, eight as partners. We liked each other. Had monster success. Great employees. Great energy. Intense creativity. Relentless confidence. Happy clients. Kudos. Awards. Respect. Fun.

Yet here we were. There had to be fierce cracks somewhere.

I was furious as a cornered rattlesnake, spewing what I now know to be predictable post-breakup blame-venom. It was not my finest moment. While I was not completely clueless as to cause, I had to clear this up before I could put my toe in any waters again, let alone business. It took awhile, but figure it out I did. I also discovered that what happened to us was not just common but pervasive. Worse, most parting partners don't bother with the forensics. They just move on to the next thing and stay angry.

FYI: Anger doesn't bode well for any next thing.

What led to our downfall? Stuff that happens every day. Simple, stupid, senseless, thoughtless human stuff. There doesn't have to be a big drama or trauma or even a defining moment, and it's rarely about someone robbing the bank account, 'tho that does happen. Partnerships turn into Partnersh*t because we take our eye off the human ball and it rolls right over us.

What is Partnersh*t?

- You stop caring what the other thinks.
- You stop asking because you assume (bad word; yes, it does make an a** of you and me) you know the answer.
- Listening disappears.
- You talk business to employees and spouses instead of each other.
- You blame and point the nasty finger.
- You have no clue how to manage growth spurts.
- There is no respect for life changes—marriages, aging and ill parents, child issues and so on.

- You become pseudo-talkers, making chatter but saying nothing.

There's more (how much time do you have to dissect thoughtless human behavior?), but you get the gist.

The good news? Most Partnersh*t is preventable.

Co-owners fixate on the business and forget about each other; it's the nature of business. However, the nature of Partnersh*t is like that cornered snake: nasty and aggressive. You get bit and the poison spreads until it eventually kills you.

Don't risk all you've built over this nonsense. A great partnership will be your best business asset. Build it and care for it. Nobody should ever let a good partnership go bad. Plus, two's more fun than one.

Here are four of the most senseless mistakes that, given an inch, will pulverize a partnership. This isn't Vegas, so there is no right amount of wrong. You must stop this stuff cold.

Senseless Mistake #1:
Not Understanding It's All About People.

Partnership and business = people. All business problems are people problems. All people problems become business problems. Don't deify the business. Focus on each other.

Harvard Review writer Dan Pallotta says, *"Only humans could routinely overlook human beings as an important part of the mix in the discussion about business. It should come as no surprise. These issues a) aren't as fascinating as corporate ethics and finance, b) are messy, and c) often hit too close to home. It's no wonder they get pushed aside."* [10]

You gotta love those darn humans; they miss what's right in front of them. You'd better get fascinated—and aware—fast, because one thing is for sure: human is as human does.

---

10   Dan Pallotta, *People Problems Masquerading as Business Problems,* Harvard Business Review Blog Network, Jan 6, 2011. http://blogs.hbr.org/pallotta/2011/01/diseases-of-the-psyche-masquer.html

Instead, Do This: <u>Become a Jedi about awareness—self and</u> <u>other.</u> Know what you and your partner feel, see, think, love, hate, want and so on. Use all your faculties including intuition. Learn to spot the Lance Armstrongs of the world. (C'mon, we all knew. We just didn't want to believe.)

Therapist Lee Schiller, MFT (CA Lic. MFC43554) says, "*What we convey to ourselves and others as well as how it is understood,*" he says, "*is the basis for everything past, present and future. That's what partnership is about. That's what business is about. That's what people are about.*"

Get to know as much about the character and background of the person you've chosen to partner with as you would someone you marry. Turn off the cell phones, shut the door and start talking. Ask good questions. And listen to the answers.

Senseless Mistake #2: Not Listening.

Here's a cool Maya Angelou-ism: *People will tell you who they are. All you have to do is listen.*

Partners get into the "*I know*" rut when it's time to listen and ears slam shut like a door on a vacuum cleaner salesman. Of the 70 to 80 percent of the waking hours we spend communicating, 9 percent is spent writing, 16 percent reading, 30 percent speaking and 45 percent listening, says a University of Missouri study that also confirms most of us are poor, inefficient listeners.[11] Think we have some work to do in this area? Our minds travel faster than any mouth. We get bored, critical, judgmental, hear via our filters and generally check out. Bottom line is we're not present.

Instead, Do This: <u>Get present. Silence the judge.</u> You are going to hear things you don't like; that's not the point. The point is to listen. You'll hear, "*I hate it when you take over every meeting,*" or "*You share too many business secrets with your wife.*" Nobody has the right to

---

11 Dick Lee and Delmar Hatesohl, *Listening, Our Most Used Communication Skill,* University of Missouri Extension CM 150, Reviewed October 1993. http:// extension.missouri.edu/publications/DisplayPrinterFriendlyPub. aspx?P=CM150

make anyone wrong, and anyway, when you judge it's you who's on the stand. Take the time it takes to ask. Listen. Absorb. Understand. Accept. Or reject. If differences emerge that are just too huge, you'll be able to make an informed decision to leave the partnership like an adult, not a two-year old.

Senseless Mistake #3: Not Being Accountable

Dr. Bruce Lipton, Pd.D. will tell you, *"You are personally responsible for everything that happens in your life once you realize you are personally responsible for everything that happens in your life."* Everything. So put down the nasty finger. Blame has no place. It's a weakness and will call you out. Be accountable. You chose it; now own it.

Accountability gets your head in shape so you can keep your partnership in shape. As business coach Jennifer Rosenwald says, *"Everything with your name on it is your responsibility."*[12]

Instead, Do This: <u>Start each and every meeting by declaring your intention.</u> Declaration is the very core of accountability. You might say, *"My intention is to solve the problem I am having regarding your tardiness every day."* (Don't make your problem your partner's problem. For them, it might not be a problem.) Your partner might say, *"My intention is to explain why I choose to come in at 1pm."* From the get-go, you have both created a mindset of **breathe/discuss/ solve**, rather than **constrict/blame/fight**. This formula will work for any issue that crops up with anyone in your life. Make this a habit. Intention is the red carpet to problem solving.

Senseless Mistake #4: Not Being Grateful.

The era of the greedy oinker exited with Gordon Gekko. The best partners are strong and soft; they are that way because they're grateful. Take a look at the magic of Warren Buffet and his partner of nearly 50 years, Charlie Munger. This is no accident. They got it a long time ago. More and more, you hear the words business and gratitude

---

12   See Chapter 12.

together. Also no accident. It signals an important shift; head and heart are intersecting. This is good news for all.

Instead, Do This: <u>Be grateful. Be nice.</u> Yes, it's that simple. Imagine the respect between Buffet and Munger; imagine how grateful they are for all they have built. So are their employees, shareholders, customers and families. Gratitude runs like a river through your life, creating fertility, abundance and strength. So when the sky is falling, and it will, you won't need to become Chicken Little. Instead, ask yourself, *"What am I grateful for?"* It will shape your approach to finding a solution. Ask your partner this same beautiful question when they're having a bad day; it will defuse even the most jacked-up monster.

Business is tough; it's also fun. Things go wrong, yet much goes right. We make mistakes and hit home runs. So take the time to prevent what is preventable. Even the best partnership goes off the rails now and again. Don't throw the baby out with the Partnersh*t bathwater. It's worth saving. Fight for it. And be grateful that you did.

PATTY SOFFER consults with new, established, family and stalemated small business co-owners to develop partnership and business strategies that position them for success. For more information, see Patty's bio in *Meet The Experts*.

4

KEEP CONFLICT FROM DERAILING YOUR ORGANIZATION'S MISSION

Lisa Gibson, JD

Hajer had been working as a doctor at the Benghazi Medical Center in Benghazi, Libya for several years. She had lived through the corrupt and oppressive regime of Muammar Gaddafi, and was relieved to see her country and its organizations moving forward. But change came slowly and the ever-present conflicts between hospital staff members who had once supported Gaddafi's regime and those who had consistently opposed him began to escalate. There was no trust between these two groups and that put patient care at risk.

In a brash tone, Hajer proclaimed her feelings boldly *"I hate Gaddafi and I hate those people who supported him. Everyday I see them walking through the halls of this hospital. They may have switched sides but I know what they have done!"*

Hajer's statement reflected the sentiment of others in the hospital as well. There was constant backstabbing, gossip, arguing and grudge holding. There was no teamwork and patient care was being negatively impacted.

The situation in Benghazi Medical Center may seem to be a unique situation, but the fact is every organization has unique situations that can lead to conflict. Mergers, buyouts, culture changes and even every day challenges like inadequate supplies and go-nowhere meetings can cause disagreements that escalate into major conflicts that cause tremendous stress and loss of productivity. That stress doesn't end at work. It gets brought back to the home, where families are impacted every day.

So what can be done? Is it really possible to let go of the hurts and resentments we hold on to? Are there ways for an organization to become productive and harmonious despite disagreements? What if it really were possible to keep small conflicts from escalating to big ones by helping employees quickly talk about, forgive and resolve conflicts with their coworkers?

As Hajer shared her anger and frustration toward her coworkers she had not even considered that her resentment toward her coworkers was affecting her work and the health and productivity of the hospital as a whole. The prospect of letting go of her hurts and offenses seemed like a sign of weakness rather than a sign of strength.

When she gave herself permission to feel the pain of the loss and begin to let go of the anger and resentment for the wrongs that she had experienced, Hajer's whole countenance softened and she began to weep. She realized that the resentment within her and the corresponding resentment of other staff in the hospital had combined to create a toxic work environment. It was only through making a decision to let go of the resentment, that she could begin to find the peace she desired. As she began to find her personal peace, that brought the organization one step closer to the harmony throughout the organization as a whole.

The Cost of Conflict

Conflict is defined as a condition between two people who are task interdependent. The pattern is that one or more of the parties feel angry and find fault with the other. They then start using behaviors that cause a problem for the team and the business. The reality is conflicts are destructive to individuals and organizations. So why are so many organizations filled with unresolved conflict?

Too often managers and leaders think they don't have time to deal with conflicts within their teams. In fact, studies have shown that 30-40% of a manager's time is spent dealing with conflict, taking away from time that could be spent on the vital organizational mission. As a result, most managers ignore the conflicts within their organization until they reach a crisis. Unfortunately by then the issues escalate to the point where there is a need for costly legal intervention or worker turnover, leading to costs anywhere between 75-150% of an employee's annual salary.

Workplace conflicts can cause tremendous stress for employees and impact morale[13]. In some situations, individuals have contributing mental or emotional health issues that contribute to the conflicts.[14]

In most conflicts, the outward behavior and issues are often just the tip of the iceberg. It is the hidden cancer in the organization and is all waste and no value. The cost of conflict includes:

- Wasted Time
- Opportunity cost of wasted time
- Lowered job motivation and productivity
- Lost performance due to conflict related absenteeism
- Loss of investment in skilled employees
- Conflict incited theft, sabotage and vandalism and damage
- Restructuring around the problem

---

13   To learn more about how to use fun to decrease stress and improve organizational health, see Chapter 11 by Jeffrey Kurtz.

14   Employees and employers often need the assistance of a therapist to help them work through their stress. See Chapter 13 by Dr. Lupe-Rebeka Samaniego.

- Health costs
- Degraded decision quality

The bottom line is conflict costs an organization a lot of money and prevents the people who work there from fulfilling their mission.

What Can be Done?

Businesses cannot afford to ignore the conflicts. By helping employees quickly and efficiently work through their conflicts, the business can not only save money, but also increase their productivity, service and revenues.

Imagine working in an organization where individuals are able to sit face-to-face with each other, talk through their conflicts when they arise and let them go.

The most effective way to resolve conflicts quickly is to help employees forgive the offenses of their coworkers. Just like in our story about Hajer, unresolved offenses and issues with coworkers can develop into deep bitterness. This bitterness becomes like a cut that never heals. Instead, it just continues to fester and eventually becomes infected. That is the effect of unwillingness to forgive.

When we aren't willing to forgive a hurt or offense it tends to consume our thoughts. People can forget about it for a while, but it will quickly resurface when they run into their coworker in the hallway or have to work with that person. The best example of this is to use a legal analogy. It is as if the injured person is litigating the case of what happened to them in the inner courtroom of his/her heart, but can find no relief.

They desire justice, but cannot seem to attain it. So, they will likely engage in one of two types of behavior: Power-plays (Fight) or Walk-aways (Flight). Neither of these behaviors is healthy or appropriate. If left unresolved, the offense will continue to escalate. Every thing the offending party does will be perceived as an offense. It continues to escalate into a retaliatory cycle that includes a trigger, a perception of threat, anger, and acting out. Forgiveness is the only way to stop the retaliatory cycle.

There are five stages in the forgiveness cycle.

Step 1. Identification of the Issue or Hurt

The first step is figure out what the offended party is angry about. This requires asking questions to really get to the root issue. It is not uncommon to have a person come to the table saying s/he is angry about one thing, but when you dig deeper you realize it is something very different. In addition, often individuals can have layers of hurts with the person who has offended them. So it is necessary to figure out what the root offense is and help the injured party forgive that offense before working your way forward to the other offenses.

Step 2. Validation

One of the most often overlooked steps in the forgiveness process is validation. People need to hear from other people that what happened to them was wrong or that they are justified in being angry. When people are injured emotionally, they will often go to others in the office to talk about what happened. When they do this, they are looking for validation. But validation should be done constructively, with the expectation of the injured party eventually letting go of the offense.

Step 3. Grieving

The next step in the forgiveness process is grieving the loss. Most often this would be grieving the loss of the ideal, whether it be a promotion, how they are viewed by other people, etc. At the heart of grieving is feeling the pain and being allowed to express your anger, sadness, fear in a healthy and productive way. If people are not able to grieve the loss, this is where they are most likely to get stuck in coping behavior (medicating the pain or stuffing it). This can have serious affects on their emotional and physical health.

Step 4. Confrontation

The most often overlooked phase in the forgiveness process is the confrontation phase. Too often people just perceive forgiveness as a personal thing, rather than a step toward reconciliation with the person who offended. If the person still feels anger, the problem and the offending party has not been forgiven. So, in that situation, the offended party must confront the offender in a gentle and humble way. He should communicate how he felt hurt and let the other person know what he needs in order to be able to forgive.

This can be a very scary prospect to most people. It is best to assume the person did not intend to hurt you. When done effectively, especially with the assistance of a third party, this can be very honoring to both people. In the end the expectation is there will be an expression of sincere regret about the wrongdoing and a commitment to change directions. In many situations, there will be a level of wrongdoing on both sides that needs to be dealt with.

Step 5. Pardon the Offense

The last step in the process is to pardon the offense. If there has been a true expression of regret, commitment to change or apology by the parties, then pardoning the offense should be easy. It doesn't mean the employees will become best friends, but they must commit to not bring up the issue again. It cannot and shouldn't be allowed to resurface as an issue between them again or affect their work. However, should the injuring party engage in the same offensive behavior again, he should be held accountable by organizational leadership.

If you use these 5 steps, you can help your employees resolve conflicts quickly and easily and prevent conflicts from escalating to catastrophic proportions.

Maybe you are struggling with whether it is necessary to talk about feelings or forgiveness in the workplace. The bottom line is just talking about facts will only get you far so in conflict resolution. Conflicts in a workplace are not resolved unless employees are encouraged to express their feelings about conflict in an appropriate and constructive manner. If this isn't done effectively, employees get stuck in fight or flight behavior which ultimately effects productivity and organizational revenue. Allowing your employees to express their emotions in a controlled environment can create a cathartic release, facilitate quick conflict resolution and restore workplace harmony.

Organizational success depends on effective teamwork and the leaders who manage conflict effectively consistently see increased productivity, reduced stress and improved morale. When the organization's mission includes helping employees maintain a good work environment, everyone wins.

LISA GIBSON, JD is an attorney, internationally acclaimed conflict and forgiveness expert, mediator, and certified trainer in managing workplace conflict. For more information, see Lisa's bio in *Meet The Experts*.

5

WHAT WOULD EINSTEIN DO?

Cheryl Lentz, DM, MSIR

As Jim and Diane tinkered away, they just weren't getting anywhere.

"This thing-a-ma-bob or whatever-it-is just doesn't work!"

Jim turned to Diane and let out a big sigh as he threw his hands up in anger.

"Do you think this thingie will ever work? We've been trying for weeks now. What are we missing?"

Diane turned away to think for a moment. *"Maybe …"* she said, tapping her finger on her chin, *"Maybe we just need a new way of looking at things, you know? Maybe we're just not asking the right questions."*

Her voice trailed off as she stared out of the window, deep in thought. A smile slowly formed on Jim's face as he raised an eyebrow, stroked his chin and asked, *"What would Einstein do?"*

Asking the question: "*What might Einstein do?*" offers a different way of finding possible solutions, "*What might happen if?*" or "*Could we do it this way?*" Learning to ask the right questions offers the possibility of discovering new answers.

During my 13 years of teaching, thousands of students have asked why they need to take a course in thinking. When we begin a class with a few problems the students cannot solve, they soon see why. Learning to think critically is an important skill to master. From problem-solving in the office to our personal lives, learning to ask the right *questions* leads to finding the right *answers*.

Carolyn, a high school teenager, suffered from bad headaches for years. Her parents took her to the doctor yet after many tests, they still didn't have an answer. Even though she was still in pain, the doctor gave up. He simply couldn't find a medical cause for Carolyn's headaches. With a quick swipe of the pen, the doctor simply offered yet more medication and sent her on her way. Distressed, Carolyn turned pleadingly to her mother, saying: "*Why can't they just find the problem, Mom, and stop this pain? I don't know how much more I can take.*"

Sadly, the pain continued all through Carolyn's college years, making life difficult for her. Several years later, Carolyn shared her story with a colleague. Immediately, her co-worker asked: "*Didn't anyone think to send you to a Dentist?*"

What a simple question. Why hadn't the headache doctor thought around the problem? Instead, he'd stopped asking questions and prescribed tablets while the pain and the underlying problem remained. Carolyn endured years of suffering because the doctor failed to ask the right questions. Happily, Carolyn did see a dentist who found that she suffered from a jaw problem called "TMJ." Finally, the right questions had been asked and the cause of years of pain and distress was found AND fixed.

Carolyn had never given up asking the questions, "*Why did her head still hurt?*" and "*What could be done to stop it?*" By asking the right questions to the right person, the problem was finally found and fixed, freeing her from severe and incapacitating headache pain for the first time in decades.

Case in point: Carolyn's headaches. How many people are living with this misdiagnosis as a result of poor thinking? According to Rod Moser, PA, PhD, TMJ affects some 10 million people within the United States alone. One researcher estimated that 75% of the U.S. population experiences one or more symptoms in their lives, yet despite being suffered by so many, the condition is not well understood and misdiagnosis is common.

This is only one example of the problem that occurs when we don't stop to ask the right questions.

The Magic of Asking Why: Do you Know What the Problem is?

I invite you to go back to when you were about four years old. Do you remember your favorite question? If you remembered constantly asking "**Why?**" you'd be spot on! Remember questions like *"Why is the sky blue?"* *"Why is the grass green?"* or *"Why is the man on the moon smiling?"* Why? WHy? WHY?

Parents tell me they find this endless list of questions difficult and often give up with a dismissive, *"Go ask your mother"* after the fourth round of 'whys.' Asking questions isn't easy; however the doors they open to our creativity are well worth the processes we learn to dig deep and follow the trail in pursuit of answers.

As a teacher, my goal is to turn all of my students back into 4-year olds so they can rediscover this love of asking questions in order to rediscover their inner curiosity. Little do they know that returning to the age of 4 holds the secret to *adult* thinking and problem solving!

According to Janet Swift [15], a child needs to feel the thrill of seeing a rainbow to experience the sheer joy and happiness of remembering the excitement an exhilaration of being curious.

---

15   See Chapter 14.

Like Jim and Diane, in continually asking *'why?'* you'll be unlocking the process leading you to the right answers. The goal is to keep asking questions until you are sure you are getting to the heart of the problem—but begin by making sure the problem is truly the one you want to solve.

Perhaps you're wondering how you know you've arrived at the correct problem. The answer is quite simply: when you no longer have to ask the question *'why?'* When we don't give ourselves either permission or the time to ask the right questions, we often get stuck just like Jim and Diane. We go round and round in circles constantly arriving at the starting point again and not moving forward.

Einstein spent a lot of time thinking about a problem and looking at it from many, many, MANY viewpoints. He would seek others' opinions to ensure he was solving the problem and not being sidetracked by only going as deep as the symptom. If we only solve the *symptom*, the *problem* will always remain.

The WRIST Method

To change your thinking, simply remember that help is at the end of your WRIST [**W-R-I-S-T: W**ords, **R**ules, **I**magination, **S**pace, and **T**ools].

Step 1: Change our Words

One way to change our thinking is to change the **words** we use. If you speak more than one language, you can simply change things up. Instead of thinking with your primary language, learn something new. For example, if your primary language is English, change to Spanish, French, or Italian. Einstein spoke several languages, sometimes thinking in a different language just to change his focus. Every language uses different patterns, different meanings, and different ways of thinking. For example, I struggled to come up with a name for one of my book imprints. When I got stuck in English, I simply translated the word *thinking* into a different language. Voila—this imprint is called *Pensiero* Press— which simply means *thinking* in *Italian*.

In addition to foreign languages, there are also differences in words spoken in specific fields or industries. An accountant will use different words than an engineer and an airline pilot's language will differ from that of a schoolteacher. The longer we work in one industry, the more we think in that specific way. When we use the same terms over and over, we lose our creativity and get stuck in old patterns just like Jim and Diane. By changing the **words** we use, we can change how we think when we use them.

At a conference, Lisa Gibson[16], was looking for a new way to say *forgive*. We spent time together consulting different languages and discovered in French, Italian, and Spanish, the word meant *to pardon* which offered just the right meaning Lisa was looking for to describe the conflict resolution skills she used. By experimenting with words, we can expand how we think to see through the language of another country.

Step 2: Change our Rules

Working for the same company for many years sometimes leads our thinking to get stuck inside the box. Like Jim and Diane, we're bogged down in thinking by the **rules.** Often I hear people say, *'that's the way we've always done it'* or *'this is how we do things here'* which offers rules, restrictions and boundaries. What would happen if I gave you a magic wand and took away all the rules? What if there was no box? What if you were free to think in any way you like? What might this look like? When we change our **rules**, we can change how we think.

Step 3: Change our Imagination and Play

When we get stuck in our thinking, it's really helpful to look at our creative side. Perhaps we need to spend time playing? What makes you happy? What makes you silly?

---

16 See Chapter 4

Perhaps put a jigsaw puzzle together, build a castle made of bricks (Legos), or play with bubbles. Jeffrey Kurtz[17] also explores the benefits of play as part of the importance of the learning process. When we change our **imagination** and **play**, we can change how we think.

Step 4: Change our Space

By changing our **space**, we can change how we look at the problem. Imagine Jim and Diane stopped for the day and simply went out for a walk, perhaps taking a new path this time. Maybe when they came back, they changed office, chairs, floors, buildings.

The goal here is to change the **space** around you. Just by moving to a different part of the room or a different chair, our perspective changes and we physically change what we see, which changes how we think. When we change the **space** we are in, we change how we think in it.

Step 5: Change our Tools

Sometimes we need to change *what* we are using, our **tools**. Perhaps we need to change what we write with. Instead of typing into your computer, try using a pen. If you are using a pen, try a pencil; if you are using a pencil, change to a new color of pencil, try a marker or highlighter or better still—try a crayon! Think about the actual experience of the **tool** for a moment. When we change the **tools** we use, we can change how we think when we use them.

When you change your thinking, you get what you want. So how will you make that happen? By using the WRIST Method, we can simply change little things that will change how we think when we use them.

DR. CHERYL LENTZ, DM, MSIR helps her clients think beyond limits when facing problems in their personal and professional lives. For more information about Cheryl, see her bio in *Meet The Experts*.

---

17   See Chapter 11

6

DO YOU SECRETLY
HATE GOING TO WORK?

Donald Burns

On October 12, 1989, while en route to a meeting with a top customer, I finally realized I had a problem.

As my train rolled to a stop in Grand Central Station, something inside me just snapped. I'd made this trip at least a dozen times, but suddenly the very idea of negotiating another pre-sales agreement made me sick.

A year earlier, age 37, I'd felt successful, even unstoppable. I had just earned my dream job—significantly more money and prestige—a big promotion into senior sales management. But within a year I was restless, bored and could not stomach the idea of another year of sales management or, God forbid, another 30 years.

I stepped off the train, walked halfway across the glorious lobby of Grand Central and stopped in front of the famous Clock Tower. I stood there paralyzed for five minutes, just watching all the other commuters run rings around me, eager to get where they were going.

Happy on the outside but miserable on the inside, I was trapped in a dream job I was starting to hate. And the more I hated that job, the more the money kept rolling in. My worst fear was that I'd be exposed as flaky and quickly replaced by somebody who really wanted the job.

I was wasting everybody's time, especially my own, unlike those commuters hustling and bustling around me—all of them obviously happy and productive at work. Or so I thought at the time.

Ever felt trapped in an awful job?

A bad employment situation is like a bad marriage. Every waking minute feels like wasted time. You are trapped, the clock is ticking and paranoia and fear interfere with normal life.

Can you imagine running out of money? According to the Washington Times (8/06), *"Many women fear they'll lose their income and end up a bag lady, forgotten and destitute."*

Will you run out of money? Will you run out of time and get pushed out before leaving on your own terms? Why would anybody hire you?

Maybe you know someone who has asked the question I hear every day, *"How did I get into this mess in the first place?"*

Maybe it's a classic case of *"Be careful what you wish for."*

Maybe you were just minding your own business but the world around you changed—or blew up—due to circumstances beyond your control.

Maybe you're making a "natural" transition, a separation from the military or a planned retirement, o maybe some combination of the above.

It doesn't matter how or why you're trapped at work. As soon as you hear that clock ticking, start planning your exit!

A better perspective

Instead of focusing on worst-case scenarios, why not focus on the best? A client of mine—a high-level consulting partner, making over a quarter million a year—said he hated the nonstop travel of his job. In fact, he hated his job, period.

Fast-forward two years, and now he's loving life as a baseball coach. In college he had been scouted by Major League Baseball—who knew? He loves what he's doing, feels like he's got his life back, and now he's working on a financial comeback via baseball camps.

Poll: Over half are unhappy at work

Just Google any phrase like "*people who hate their jobs*" and you'll see that roughly 55% are unhappy at work—a statistic that was trending worse every year, even before the big crash of 2008 (1/10 NY Post).

If so many people don't like their jobs, why don't they change? Many reasons, for example:

- Fear they'll land in an even worse situation.
- Fear that they're not marketable enough for something better.
- Fear that another crash is imminent, so "opportunities don't exist anyway."

Three things that might be stopping you

First, tune out all of the Mainstream News" on this topic. Opportunities always exist for qualified people—yes, that means YOU. But you must meet the following three prerequisites (in this order):

Burning Desire: You must be on fire and passionately eager to reach a clearly defined goal.

Courage: Are you willing to keep pushing forward despite naysayers who make you feel foolish or embarrassed? In 1989, people told me I was acting crazy and going through a midlife crisis. Remind yourself that a little short-term embarrassment today is better than another 30 years of slavery in employment hell.

Resources: Time, money, and information. If you are contemplating a job change or career transition, resources are available to you that did not exist for me in 1989. The Internet, for example. Don't reinvent the wheel. Educate yourself online and, ideally, hire a career coach to show you the shortcuts!

Your 3-Step Action Plan to Break Free

Since the great crash of 2008, I've advised over 1,200 people on their job transitions. All of my success stories actively used some variation of this three-step plan:

Step 1: Feel the Heat

Find a job target that turns you on—the same "burning desire" described above—don't leave home without it! This is the master step and a prerequisite that drives a successful job search.

If you're passionate about your goal, you'll blow past all of the inevitable indifference and rejection. In my experience, weak desire is the #1 reason that job searches crash.

Step 2: Share Your Vision

People can't help you if they don't know what you want. Show them a compelling bio, resume, CV, LinkedIn profile, brand, tagline, Twitter stream, website, portfolio or whatever else it takes to translate the dream inside your head into a computer screen or printed page.

- Be ready to show potential employers, networking contacts, and recruiters a crystal-clear idea of what you're trying to do.
- Forget the "elevator" speech. Can you write a compelling pitch on the back of a business card? When you approach people who don't know you, assume you've got only 5-10 seconds to make your case.

Step 3: Ask People to Help You

You must ask other people to help you. Many people recoil from this step, so break through any reluctance to reach. Eventually you'll reach real people who reside in or near your job target (real people—not pixels on Facebook).

- Another name for this is "targeted networking." Most people I know say they hate networking, which they confuse with time-wasting meetings *("let's exchange business cards")*. If you hate networking, just call it "connecting."
- Get active on LinkedIn or Switchboard. These are great tools for finding the right people if you use them effectively.

If you persist with this process, I promise you'll eventually achieve great results. Maybe not the results you originally intended, because each search takes on a life of its own. Surprises and serendipities are inevitable—happens all the time.

Don't Do What I Did!

In 1989, standing at the Clock Tower in Grand Central Station, watching "happy" people rushing to work—I was clueless about the art and science of career transitions.

I had a vague idea that I wanted to jump-start myself into a writing career, but no idea how to do it. I did not even have the prerequisite "burning desire" mentioned above. Instead of burning desire, the white-hot flames of Employment Hell forced me to leap into the unknown world of writing and advertising. It all worked out, but I didn't know what I was doing.

I figured it all out the hard way and then chose to spend the rest of my life helping others avoid the pain I experienced. Here are four pieces of wisdom I learned along the way:

1. You might decide that you don't want to work in another job at all—maybe you'd rather be working for yourself in your own business. Just ask my friend Michael Harris[18] how to do this—he specializes in this type of career transition and I wish I'd known somebody like him way back in 1989.

---

18 See Chapter 7

2. Maybe you're approaching retirement age and like my own father, 20 years ago, you are fearful and clueless about cutting the corporate umbilical cord. Suzanne Nault[19] is expert at easing people into retirement—total, partial, or reinvention.

3. Focus on **what's working now** in the area of career transitions. Let people do that work for you so you don't have to reinvent the wheel.

4. Assess some important factors that career coaches rarely talk about, for example: family, stress, physical fitness, sense of humor, mental toughness, spirituality, and faith. This book you are reading integrates expertise in all these areas[20]

Leaving my dream job in 1989 was one of the best decisions of my life and I've seen it work for hundreds of people since then. If you can imagine a better life—a better career, a better job—you can succeed by following the three-step plan in this chapter.

Start by deciding what you really want to do, because once that engine starts you'll inevitably succeed. If you have no idea what you really want to do, then imagine what you do NOT want to do.

If you are 70 years old and reasonably healthy, you probably have another 10 or 15 productive years. That's a long time, so find something you'd really enjoy doing. If you're 40 and feeling stuck, hire a coach and take the shortcuts ASAP. You can start living your heart's desire as soon as you figure out what it is! So start now!

DONALD BURNS—Executive Career Coach—has helped hundreds of people transition into better jobs and more fulfilling careers through coaching, consulting and video training. For more information, see Donald's bio in *Meet The Experts*.

---

19   See Chapter 9
20   For example, see Chapter 18 by Diane Flemington and Chapter 19 by Elizabeth Phinney.

7

INNOVATIVE REINVENTION

Michael Harris

Not being happy in your job is one of the most disheartening feelings in the world. Each day hearing the alarm clock ring and having to get ready to work—just for the sake of working. Oh, how painful. Yes, getting a paycheck is good, but just working at the expense of living your life can kill your personal spirit.

Are you in a dead end job? Are you doing what you really want to do? Well there is hope. Read on to hear Sally's story of a new life and how you can reawaken your dreams too.

College had been good to Sally. She had received a degree in marketing and a bright future was ahead. When Sally first got married she was pregnant. She loved her husband Don—yet wasn't sure she wanted to be with him the rest of her life. Sally got married for her unborn child. She was afraid to be a single mom without any help or support in raising her child.

For the first year after her child was born Sally stayed at home while Don went to work each day. Sally was grateful that she was able to spend so much time loving and nurturing her child. At the end of the day Don would come home and Sally would be happy that her new family was together. Yet even though she loved her family, Sally still felt like she had compromised herself by marrying a man that just wasn't right for her.

Sally returned to work when her child was two and built a career in marketing. Just like the famous song, in the blink of an eye 10 years had gone by. Over the years the marriage had deteriorated and Don was drinking way too much. Sally felt that she was living her life in a downward spiral. She had had enough.

Sally now knew that to be an example to her now 12-year-old daughter, she had to step up and live her dreams. So she made a decision to get a divorce and go after her dream of empowering others to discover and live their best life ever. It was what she'd always wanted to do. She chose to combine that dream with her passion for yoga. This was the place that she felt totally safe and at peace with herself and others.

It was at that point that I first met Sally. After a number of years in marketing and as a yoga teacher she was now ready to jump in with both feet and open her dream business—a thriving yoga studio that helped men and woman open up and live their best lives ever. She had her dream, yet she just didn't know how she was going to do it.

Sally captured her dreams by using the following powerful yet simple steps. These steps have helped hundreds of people to live their most rocking lives. If you relate to Sally's story, then here's what you can do:

10 Steps to live your most rocking life:

Step 1: Plan a trip away from your normal surroundings. This is important so you can see beyond your everyday life. **Where do you find peace?**

Step 2: Spend Day 1 of your journey without your cell phone (even if this is your most prized possession). Plan a day of bliss. For example, Sally took a three-hour hike near a river and included a very special session with a walking meditation teacher. She even spent the evening at a spa to totally pamper herself. Sally was in bliss. **How can you find bliss?**

Step 3: On Day 2, dive into what really inspires you. As Sally went through her life she realized that all along she had wanted to move and motivate others. That letting go of her past with respect and love was important for her to move forward. **What can you let go that no longer serves you?**

Step 4: On Day 3, dive into how to finally make it all happen. Sally and I went through many of the skills she already knew and she soon realized how these skills she already had could help her in her new life. **What skills do you have that can be used in different areas?**

Step 5: When you're ready, move into living your dream with specific steps and actions you can use in your new life and your new business. Today, Sally is using her tools to thrive and live with new vigor. **What actions do you need to do to live in your dream life?**

Once you have your new life and business in place, here are the next five tips you can use to help your new business thrive:

Step 6: Create and write a clear vision statement for your business. I strongly encourage you to keep your vision statement short and precise. Some business owners are even able to keep it to one sentence. Regardless, a paragraph or less is best. Your vision statement can then be used to help guide you in your business plan and in the direction of your company.

Step 7: Be the best you can be. Constantly hone and strengthen your skills. Attend classes and workshops that apply to what you do. Buy and read books that give you insight. Hire a coach or mentor that will help you develop yourself and your business. You may have incredible talent, but unless you practice your skills, the talent is wasted.

Step 8: Develop clear systems and procedure manuals. This will help streamline your business and keep it running smoother. I have found that the more detailed you are, the better. As silly as it seems, detail everything your business does and everything you do. At first it will take a little bit of time, but it will be well worth it, particularly if you own your own business. It is likely that with procedure manuals your business will be more valuable when you are ready to sell.

Step 9: Keep your surroundings fresh and clean. There are so many reasons to do this. It helps keep you organized. It helps keep your mind clear. It helps your computers and other equipment stay in good working order. If you have customers that come to you, it impresses them. Having a dirty working environment will drive your customers away—and they won't even tell you why they no longer do business with you.

Step 10: Celebrate your customers and clients. Send thank you notes. Mention them in social media. Profile a customer in your newsletters. Do a short customer video testimonial and post to your website. Make an offer they can't refuse. Provide special discounts. Take them to lunch. Do anything in your business that will acknowledge your customers in a thoughtful and meaningful way. When you do this they will keep coming back and give you referrals too.

Let's get back to Sally. Through her process of re-discovering her dreams, Sally truly understands how every struggle in her life shaped her into the person she is today.

This state of vitality can be re-awakened in all of us, just like it has in her. What is it that you really want to do in your life? If you are not doing it, why not?

Executive coach Donald Burns[21] says, *"It just might be time to re-package yourself."* Are your skills much greater than you realize?

Not realizing we already have the skills to lead the live we want happens to all of us. In fact, not long ago I was talking to a friend of mine, Thomas Bahler. Thomas is a well-respected and accomplished music producer that has worked with many of the top entertainers in the music business. I mentioned to him that if I were to do it all over again I would be a singer and entertainer. He gave me a funny look, tilted his head forward, and asked, "Can you talk?" I said "Of course." He replied, "Then you can sing." Immediately I knew that I always had the skills I needed to sing. I just needed to do it. The realization also came through that I needed to help others find their skills, before it was too late for them.

What skills do you have to create your innovative reinvention?

MICHAEL HARRIS is an expert in personal and professional transitions and helps people live their lives beyond any pre-conceived limitations and boundaries. For more information, see Michael's bio in *Meet The Experts*.

---

21   See Chapter 6

8

LIVE A LIFE THAT'S FREE, FUN AND FABULOUS——AT ANY AGE!

Babs Kangas, PhD

Brrrr... Cindy shuddered. There it was again, that dreaded feeling in the pit of her stomach as she reluctantly pressed the "Up" button on the elevator. She forced a limp smile as she headed back to her tiny cubicle. At least she had experienced some relief during her brief lunchtime walk. How long could she continue to endure this tortuous job?

"*Be positive,*" she mumbled, "*At least I still get that paycheck.*"

Ever since her husband had left her, she'd been supporting her twin daughters on her own. She was proud of that. And now, the twins were getting ready to leave for college. The house would be so quiet. And while she was sad about the prospect of being alone in the house, it also got her thinking.

Cindy felt a flicker deep inside—a stirring of discontent mixed with possibility. Over the years, she'd dreamed of creating her own business. She used every opportunity to draw on napkins, envelopes— any scrap she could find. Was it too late? She was almost fifty-three. Could she possibly make a living doing something she truly loved?

Settling into her small chair, Cindy closed her eyes and again fantasized the GREAT ESCAPE that had kept her going for the past three years…She pictured herself stuffing that adorable photo of the girls into her purse, leaping over the wall of her cubicle, high heels clicking down the stairs (not even stopping to push that dreaded elevator button) and racing out of the building. Finally, free at last!

Cindy's story is one I hear every day. Her life was filled with signs that it was time to reinvent her life:

- A boring job that didn't utilize her full talents,
- A divorce that left her managing life without a partner and
- A pending empty nest that would leave her all alone.

Of course, these are only some of the signs that indicate it's time for reinvention. People facing mandatory retirement or lay offs begin to wonder,

"Now what?"

"What will I do all day?"[22]

No matter where you are in your life, here are six steps you can use to make sure your life is free, fun and fabulous:

Step 1: Become aware of the need for reinvention so you can create a life that is free, fun and fabulous!

This awareness comes from paying closer attention to your thoughts and emotions. Unpleasant feelings arising deep inside you may indicate the need to reinvent your life. If you experience vague sinking sensations of discontentment, tune in and monitor these

---

22   See Chapter 9 for Suzanne Nault's information on retirement strategies

feelings. Also, listen carefully to your thoughts and notice how what you're thinking is telling you it's time for a change.[23]

Step 2: Give yourself permission to have a free, fun and fabulous life.

Vow not to worry about what others will think. You will often hear chatter inside your head trying to discourage you. Acknowledging where the noisy voices come from helps to shut them down. Are your parents saying you need to have a "real" job? Is a friend saying you should play it safe? Is your subconscious whispering, *"Don't achieve more than your parents did?"* Are you feeling guilty that if you follow your dream you will not have time for your grown up children [24].

Step 3: Make a choice to take a fifteen-minute daily quiet time-out——a short pause to help you gain clarity about what you really want in your life.

Try to schedule your quiet time at the same time each day. Start by closing your eyes and taking several deep breaths. Visualize each breath traveling through your heart all the way down to your feet.

Practice focusing without distractions. Turn off your phone and close the door. You will probably find that most distractions will come from your own thoughts. When you become aware of a distracting thought, notice and label it. Then, consciously push it over to the side of your mind. For example, if a thought about what to have for dinner floats in, you can simply notice and identify the thought, *"I'm thinking about dinner,"* and then consciously push it over and continue. Other distractions come in the form of emotions, but feelings can be dealt with much the same as intrusive thoughts.

During your quiet time, if you feel anger begin to surface, acknowledge and label the feeling, and then push it to the side

---

23 For a clear explanation of managing your thoughts see chapter 12 by Jennifer Rosenwald.
24 See BJ Rosenfeld's Chapter 17 for communications between parents and adult children

of your mind. You might say, *"I'm feeling angry, but I'll deal with that later."*

Step 4: Decide the area of your life you want to reinvent.

When you feel comfortable and quiet, read and answer the following questions:

Think of a period of time in your life when everything was going well: What was going on? What were you doing? What strengths did you see in yourself? Who was with you at that time? What emotions did you feel?

Another helpful question to ask is: What did you love to do as a child?

Your answers are important because they help you get in touch with your true inner-self—your interests, strengths, values and passion—all key to your personal reinvention. Write down your answers to these questions in a notebook or journal.

While you are quiet, simply allow images to enter your mind that represent successful and happy times in your life. Write down the images that appear and note any common themes or patterns. Emerging patterns may begin to suggest a starting point for your personal reinvention. Do you need to think about a new career, make changes in your relationships or start exercising more?

Step 5: Write down one simple action step you can do immediately that will lead you closer to your fabulous new life.

Make sure that the action step is something you are willing to do right away to begin your proactive reinvention. Will you take a vigorous walk[25]? Write a list of possible careers to research? Make a phone call to a loved one?

Creating an action step and completing it immediately gives you a feeling of accomplishment and builds momentum for future progress.

---

25 See Chapter 19 to learn how to stay agile after 45.

Step 6: After each idea in your journal, write the reason it is important to you.

Figuring out your "WHY" propels you forward and gives you motivation to continue reinventing your life. Your WHY is all powerful—it emerges from deep within you generating the energy you need daily to create your best life.

My client, Gena[26] began incorporating quiet times into her life. She felt stuck in a boring job. She wanted to write a novel but was paralyzed with writer's block. She realized she had lost touch with her creative side and began thinking of ways she could reintroduce imagination and fun into her life. She explored some ways to make her job more bearable. She made some of the boring tasks into games and promised herself small rewards when she completed them. She began taking creative writing classes, started keeping a notebook of writing ideas, and brainstormed ideas to put more fun back in her life.

Are you waiting to give yourself permission to reinvent your life? This is your time! Listen to your intuition, and decide what YOU want. When you decide to reinvent yourself, it is important to focus on your self-care[27]. Nurture yourself gently and enjoy the process.

Remember, reinvention is not totally changing who you are. It is about taking what is already inside you and bringing it together with a new focus. It is a personal growth process, where you find the "true" you—your core essence—and freely express and share your uniqueness with the world.

Right now take some time to clear your mind and discover the important authentic you. Let the images of your future life roll! It is never too late! Creating a life you love will be an ongoing reinvention process. Take mini-steps every day toward creating your best life.

Imagine how free you will feel when you finally figure out what you really want to do. How much fun you will have! Moving purposefully through each day guided by your passion, you will

---

26 Not her real name.
27 See Chapter 15 for excellent tips on how to live your life right now.

be flourishing and living a life of joy and peace, doing work that is much more like play. You will thrive, help others and live your unique FREE, FUN and FABULOUS life.

Discover how to create the best life for you and enjoy it, because every moment is precious!

BABS KANGAS, PhD, Doctor of Psychology, is founder of Free, Fun and Fabulous, a program designed to help men and women over fifty create the life they love. For more information about Babs, see her bio in *Meet The Experts*.

)9(

THREE STYLES OF RETIREMENT: WHICH IS BEST FOR YOU?

Suzanne Nault, MPs PCC

Arriving early at a recent workshop, I was approached by a distinguished gentleman in his 60s.

"May I ask you a question?" he asked.

"Of course" I replied.

"I could retire anytime but I just don't know what to do with my time. I don't want to be sitting on the couch all day. Will you be covering that?"

I smiled and said, *"You have asked the most important question about retirement! Work takes a lot of space in our lives. An extra 50 to 60 hours of free time a week can be scary — especially if you don't know what to do."*

Retirement is being redefined by baby boomers. First, baby boomers live longer and are healthier than previous generations. In fact, boomers often have another 25 to 30 years to design the next chapter of their lives.

Second, poor financial planning and the global economic crises have changed the way we think of retirement. The Centre for Retirement Research at Boston College found that 51 per cent of today's working households are "at risk" of being unable to maintain their pre-retirement standard of living in retirement[28].

In their latest global survey, Ledbury Research and Barclays Wealth found that 60% of people who could easily afford retirement instead continue to work. They found that retirees divided their time between family, traveling, pursuing hobbies, socializing as well as working part-time—40% of retirees over the age of 65 work more than five hours each week[29].

Imagine your ideal day in retirement. What does it include? Are you sipping your morning coffee with those you love? Are you stretching your muscles in your favorite yoga class? Are you painting a magnificent sunrise as it peaks over the horizon? Are you working part-time at the library? Have you started your own business? Are you mentoring younger people? Are you writing your first book? Are you volunteering for your favorite charity?

Three years into his retirement, Wayne, an expert in contract negotiations, was invited to come back to work.

"I seriously considered the offer, but the more I thought about the commitment, the less interested I became. I like my newfound freedom. There is no amount of money that can buy the quality of life I have in retirement. You know what retirement gives me Suzanne. I listen to the news and when the announcer says, 'this week we'll see perfect conditions

---

28   Centre for Retirement Research at Boston College, National Retirement Risk Index, June 2012

29   Barclays Wealth Insights in collaboration with Ledbury Research, September 2010, Volume 12: The Age Illusion: How the Wealthy are Redefining Retirement

for skiing,' I can pack the skis and go. I no longer have to wait for the weekend; I can go when the hills are empty.

"In the summer, both my wife and I enjoy golf. Gone are the days when we rushed after work to play nine holes. I have never been in such good shape. When I am not on the hills or golf course, I am at the gym. My wife and I have been on several trips at a fraction of the cost because we can take advantage of amazing deals. Retirement even allows me to spend more time with my family.

"Tomorrow, my grandchild is coming to spend March break with us. Spending time with my grandchildren is priceless. Retirement even gave me the time to help my brother when he decided to start his home renovation company. I had the time to help him get started, and now whenever he needs extra labor, I'm able to help out."

On the other hand, Judy, his wife who retired a year ago is back at work on a part-time basis.

"Before I retired, my employer asked me if I would consider coming back when they were short staffed. I told them I would as long as I always had the choice to say no if I had other commitments."

This arrangement works really well for her. It allows her to catch up with her colleagues and provides extra money.

"Did you ever regret not going back to work?" I asked Wayne.

"Absolutely not. As a retiree, I spend time on what I like and do not feel the pressure to have things done immediately. I can't describe to you the difference in my quality of life. I certainly do not miss the stress I used to have when working."

When Anne, an executive with the federal government, retired a year ago she decided not to rush into anything. *"I explore my new life with curiosity. I am gradually establishing a new routine. There is a different rhythm to my life."*

Always passionate about helping her employees grow, Anne pursued a professional coaching certification while still working. Eight months into retirement, Anne started working with a few clients.

"If biking and hiking keep me in shape, work stimulates my intellectual capacities. All these activities allow for stimulating and

nourishing relationships as well as the opportunity to contribute. Keeping a balance between my heart, head and body as well as staying active in my community are what is important to me."

Anne took advantage of the space that retirement created in her life. It is an amazing opportunity to reflect, explore and see what else can emerge. Retirement is a powerful time to reconnect with those you love. What would you like people to know about you?[30]

From these examples and others like them, I have identified three main styles of retirement: Total, Partial or Re-Invention. Wayne chose a total retirement while Judy went for partial, and lastly, Anne decided to re-invent herself in retirement.

What style of retirement is right for you? Do the following 3 steps and discover how to fill your time in retirement in a meaningful and purposeful manner.

STEP 1——What Type of Retirement Do You Want?

The first step is for you to decide if you are considering work in your retirement. Some of my clients are very clear that they do not want to work; some are open to opportunities but will not go out of their way to find work; some want to continue to work in their own field of expertise but under their own conditions while some want to do something totally different. If you opt to work in retirement, decide how many hours you want to work and whether flexibility is important to you. Be clear about why you want to work[31].

STEP 2——Build the Foundation Upon Which You Want to Retire

Take stock of your life. Wayne, Judy and Anne invested in different areas of their lives prior to retirement which contributed to an easier transition to retirement. Look at the Life Domains listed below. Write what you do in each domain. For example, how are you contributing to your retirement goals? What do you do to

---

30   I invite you to read Kris Landry's Chapter 22 on the power of stories.
31   If you are interested in reinventing your work, check out Donald Burns' Chapter 6.

stay healthy? What do you do for fun? What hobbies do you have? What expertise are you gaining at work?

Domains in Life	Activities	Where I need to focus
Finance [32]		
Health [33]		
Work		
Family		
Social		
Community/ Volunteer		
Hobbies		
Intellectual Stimulation		
Spiritual		
Self-Development		
Fun		

Which domains require your attention? Choose one domain and identify one activity you can start in the next few months.

STEP 3——What Brings You Joy?

Start taking note of what you pay attention to in your life. Have you ever noticed that when you buy a new car, suddenly you see them all over the place? As you go through your day, notice when you lose track of time. When we are passionate about something the last

---

32　For tips on how to keep your finances healthy, see Dr. Lorie Nicholas' Chapter 21.
33　Read Elizabeth Phinney's Chapter 19 if you want to create a healthy life.

thing we do is look at our watch. Remember the last time you were so engrossed in a book that you didn't realize hours had gone by?

Notice those activities that energize you. When we are passionate about something, we feel alive. Notice when friends describe their latest adventures. If you feel excited about them, write them down. The same goes when you watch television or a movie. If you hear yourself say, *"I would love to do this?"* then take note.

For example, at the end of the workshop, Greg came up to me with a big smile on his face.

"Suzanne, after doing these exercises, I decided that I can continue to work part-time in my field, spend time with my family and pursue my passion—photography." [34]

Perhaps the hardest thing to do is to give yourself the time needed to discover which style of retirement best suits you. With these proven techniques, you can begin the process of designing your ideal retirement. You, too, can have the most exciting and rewarding time of your life. After all, you are not retiring from life!

SUZANNE NAULT, MPs PCC, licensed psychologist and professional coach, is a sought after speaker on psychological and lifestyle issues related to retirement. For more information, see Suzanne's bio in *Meet The Experts*.

---

34   I invite you to read Bonnie Goldstone's Chapter 15 if you want to learn how to let go of limiting beliefs to move toward the life of your dreams.

10

BIG BOLD AMBITIONS

Randy Stanbury

A s a young boy I remember wanting to become an NHL Hockey Player and I believed this would happen as sure as the day follows night. For me it was a matter of time, not a question whether I could. Then I made the mistake of telling my family and friends about my plans.

It amazes me how quickly people are willing to squash our ambitions.

"Do you know what the odds are of making the NHL? You will never make it."

I would hear this from everyone. Can you relate?

For some people, ridicule of their ambitions only fuels their desire to achieve even more. But the sad fact is for most, this shuts them down and forces them to play small.

Playing small becomes a nasty thief in our lives, stealing what should be a life of happiness, greatness and fulfillment. It's time to take your life back and start the journey of playing big with Big Bold Ambitions!

What happened to your dreams and ambitions? Are you living them or did you decide they were silly and unrealistic? Who determines what's realistic? When you were a child anything was possible. What happened to that kid in you that loved to dream and dream Big?

For most of the world's population dreaming big with Big Bold Ambitions is craziness. Remember this:

"The day before something is a breakthrough it's a crazy idea," Peter Diamandis.[35]

My friend Peter Diamandis is a perfect and inspirational example of someone who never let anyone take away his Big Bold Ambitions. As a kid growing up in the Bronx he dreamed of space flight. His dream was relentless and powerful. Peter possessed a deep desire, an obsession. He knew with absolute conviction that somehow, some day his *"crazy idea"* of space flight would become a reality.

Yet becoming an astronaut was not on his radar so how would this be possible? The question never left Peter's consciousness. He knew if he asked himself the question enough times the answer would present itself.

Years passed when in 1994 after reading Charles Lindbergh's *The Spirit of St. Louis*, his illusive answer seemed to appear. He created The X PRIZE to fund and operate a $10,000,000 incentive competition intended to inspire a new generation of private passenger-carrying spaceships. His competition inspired 26 teams from around the world to build such a spaceship. The winning team was 'SpaceShipOne' with its first journey to space on September 29, 2004. Peter had accomplished the so-called impossible.

---

35 Peter Diamandis #22 of Peter's Laws—The creed of the persistent and passionate mind.

Peter is just a regular guy. He was not born with super human powers to accomplish great things. The difference between Peter and most everyone else is his ability to turn a deep desire into achievement. This ability is not something sacred for only the gifted, most talented or 'well off' people in the world[36]. Peter was none of the above. In fact talent played no part and when his XPrize was announced he did not even have the prize money. He was Bold enough to announce his plan to the world believing that if he made such an announcement somehow the massive funding would become available for such a Big Bold Ambition. And of course it did some 6 years later.

So how can you achieve Big Bold Ambitions? Start Here:

7 Steps to Achieving Your Big Bold Ambition

Step 1: Deep Desire

Ambitions will be fleeting at best if you don't have a deep desire. You must know 'why' achievement of your ambition is so important to you, to others and to the world. Your why will be your power to continue striving towards achievement when times get tough. Your why will be the only thing that gives you the courage and the strength to bust through any road block without hesitation. Your why has to have a very deep and powerful meaning.

Wanting to lose 100 lbs. is not enough to do whatever it takes to make it happen. What will the loss of weight give you? Better health, more adventure, perhaps that man or women you desire or the ability to play with your kids and be around long enough to play with their kids. Your why has to be powerful enough to create a deep desire, an obsession.

---

36 If financial health is one of your Big Bold Ambitions, see Dr. Lorie Nicholas' Chapter 21.

Step 2: Thoughts, Words and Actions

Thoughts will either be empowering or disempowering.[37] Your thoughts become your words—which are also empowering or disempowering. Your words then dictate the actions you take. The words you choose have a massive influence on the actions you choose to take.

Begin a daily log of your thoughts words and actions. Get a notebook and split the book into three sections: one each for your thoughts, words and actions. Make two columns per page in each of the sections. Title one of the columns empowering and the other disempowering.

List your daily empowering and disempowering thoughts, words and actions in the appropriate section and column. Discipline and consistency of your logging on a twice daily or even hourly basis is crucial. The little gremlin in your head will be playing tricks to stop you from believing in your thoughts of Big Bold Ambitions. Strengthen your beliefs by taking small consistent actions towards your Ambition. By doing so you will begin to see progress, strengthening your belief muscle and silencing that gremlin. Of course family and friends will begin to tell you how crazy your ideas are. Your job is to control your thoughts and the words you use for empowerment only.

Step 3: Visualize

You must practice and be able to visualize exactly what your Big Bold Ambition will look like, feel like, smell like and be like when it is achieved. You must be able to do this as if this achievement of your Ambition has already happened. The more detail in your visualization the better the results. See yourself living life after your achievement. See the people you have impacted and how their lives have changed as a result of your Ambition. Make it as real as possible.

Breathe in your success and sense how good it feels. Your mind does not know the difference between a visualization state and reality. Your mind is an incredibly powerful tool and as you visualize

---

37   For more on powerful thinking refer to Dr. Cheryl Lentz's Chapter 5.

your brain will begin searching for creative solutions to problems that can only be found in this state.

Step 4: Play "Follow the Leader"

Make it easier and shorten the time to achieving your Ambitions by playing "Follow the Leader." In other words, model after those that have already been there done that. Your job is not to just find anyone but those that are masters. Masters know the best, shortest, quickest path to achieving your Ambitions. Get to know as much as you can about them, call and meet them if possible, study them and do exactly what they have done. Results are closer than they seem if you simply follow the leader.

Step 5: S.I.P. and R.A.W.L.

Great knowledge and expertise is required to achieve Big Bold Ambitions. To simplify what you will need to do in order to improve your knowledge and create a plan in any area of your life, simply SIP and RAWL:

- **S.I.P.**—Study, Implement and Practice
- **R.A.W.L.**—Read great books, Attend great seminars and events, Watch powerful DVD's of masters and Listen to great audio from experts.

Step 6: Create your Plan

A plan is like a map. Without a well-designed plan how is it possible to know how to get where you want to go and how you're going to get there?[38]

Your plan should include well-defined goals with timelines of achieving them. Plans are wonderful things but rarely perfect from the get-go. Plans must be adjusted along the way as you find your first plan not producing your desired results or failures hitting you

---

38 If a career change is your Big Bold Ambition refer to Donald Burn's Chapter 6 on career change for your best plan.

through your process of achievement. Do not be discouraged! Every great achievement had initial failures requiring adjustments to their plans along the way.

Step 7: Who you Hang With

Over time you become like who you hang with. People with no Ambitions will only hold you back from achieving what you desire. If you're playing follow the leader than follow leaders and understand that may not include your current group of friends.

Look at the results of the people you hang with. If their results are anything less than what you desire for yourself start thinking about how much time you spend with them and find people that have the results you desire. The level we live our lives is a direct result of the people we spend time with. If you want to raise your standards and expectations then raise the quality of your friends [39].

Find and hire a success coach. A coach will keep you and track and focused towards your Ambitions. Join or create mastermind groups. Become part of a community focusing on Ambitions whether online or in person.

The fact is the ability to turn a deep desire into achievement is not something sacred for only the gifted most talented or 'well off' people in the world. You have been given this ability too. Begin with the 7 Steps for Achievement of your Big Bold Ambitions. And then ask yourself these questions:

- What if anything was possible?
- What if you were able to do and become exactly what and who you always wanted to be?
- How much fun would you be having?
- How would you be making a difference in the world?
- What if no matter where you are today, you could change anything, become and do anything you truly desire?

---

39   To improve the quality of your love relationships, see Chapter 18 by Dianne Flemington.

You have one life to live so don't settle for anything less than a li of happiness, greatness and fulfillment. Whatever that is for you, it's time to fuel your passion with a deep desire and develop an obsession powerful enough to turn your Big Bold Ambitions into reality.

RANDY STANBURY, entrepreneur, author, speaker, life and business coach and founder of 'Big Bold Ambitions' has created a well-defined and easy to follow program to achieve big dreams, bold goals and deep desires. For more information, see Randy's bio in *Meet The Experts*.

)11(

ESS——FEEL LIKE A KID AGAIN

Jeffrey Kurtz

When I was a kid, I played all the time. My best friend and I would play the latest Nintendo video games, do cannonballs into his backyard pool and dive head first into piles of leaves in the front yard. At home, I'd build entire cities out of Lego's in my basement and I'd draw floor plans for massive city buildings. As an actor in high school, I played great roles like Tevya in *Fiddler on the Roof* and Henry Higgins in *My Fair Lady*.

But something terrible happened during school: I learned to think.

Now, thinking is great, and it's given me a thriving career, effective decision-making skills, and many rewarding conversations. The problem is when I started thinking, I stopped playing. And when I stopped playing, I stopped truly living. As a result, in my

20s, I found myself bored, unhappy, unfulfilled, anxious, and stuck in jobs and relationships that I hated. I was barely having any fun in my life and I knew something had to change.

Everyone has had moments in their lives when they've felt bored or stuck, stymied by a lack of money or fulfilling relationships, feeling like there's something missing. It's human to experience these things once and a while, at least for a short period of time. But when these feelings last for months at a time—even years, we begin to feel depressed.

I'm not talking about clinical depression—though that can happen. I'm talking about a lack of fun, pleasure, joy and true meaning in one's life. I'm talking about feeling stressed, overworked, not having enough time for yourself, and living out an endless, exhausting daily routine.

Does this sound like something you've experienced? If so, you're not alone. Most people want to enjoy the work they do every day, feel good in their bodies, and have loving relationships—both platonic and romantic. They want to feel happy—maybe not all the time, but at least some or most of the time.

The problem is by the time most people leave college they've stopped playing. And without play, we can't experience the fullness of excitement, spontaneity, or joy [40].

It doesn't have to be this way. After years of feeling depressed and unhappy, I finally said, "*enough is enough.*" I knew a better life was possible and I was determined to live it.

I started doing research, reading every self-help book I could get my hands on. I talked to experts in psychology and neuroscience and went over every period in my life, looking for those moments when I felt most joyful and alive.

Finally, it hit me: when I learned to think like an "adult," I learned to play like an adult, which is to say, not play at all.

---

40   You can read more about how happiness and play are interconnected in Chapter 12 by Jennifer Rosenwald and more about relationships and play in Chapter 18 by Dianne Flemington.

The one thing that was a consistent feature of my childhood was gone. No wonder why I felt so depressed. So I made a choice: whatever it took, I was going to give myself permission to play again.

I started slowly, but pretty soon I had brought play back into my life. I joined a theater company, I took trips to places I had never been, I took flying lessons, I found new activities to do with friends, I read new books and articles, I attended seminars and workshops, I became a Certified Health Counselor and Certified Emotional Freedom Technique Practitioner, and I let myself imagine fun and fulfilling activities, events, and relationships that I wanted to have in my future. And guess what? Slowly but surely, I started feeling better.

Over time, I felt lighter, more joyful, and happier. I was more in touch with what I wanted in and for my life. Even my health improved—I had more energy, better concentration and focus, and I was more productive at work and at home.

So how did this happen? Why was play the catalyst for so much of my improved mood, health and relationships? Good question.

Most people recognize play in children and animals as normal, productive, and even essential. But it turns out that it's also all of those things for adults. Skeptics believe that play in adulthood is frivolous, childish or immature, but it's actually the exact opposite:

Play is critical to normal functioning and affects everything from social and emotional intelligence, to our capacities for sympathy, empathy, and love, to complex brain functioning, including sensory and information processing, motor function, emotional wellbeing, decision-making, sex, attention, and language-processing.[41]

According to Dr. Stuart Brown, M.D., *"Play is correlated to the development of the brain's frontal cortex, which is the important brain region responsible for much of what we call cognition: discriminating*

---

41 Stuart Brown, M.D., with Christopher Vaughan, *Play: How It Shapes the Brain, Opens the Imagination, and Invigorates the Soul* (New York: Avery, 2009).

relevant from irrelevant information, monitoring and organizing our own thoughts and feelings, and planning for the future."[42]

Some researchers believe play may have a vital role in slowing the progress of age-related cognitive decline, as well as Alzheimer's and dementia. Additionally, and perhaps most importantly, play increases one's chance of survival. In observing animals, researchers have discovered animals that play more have better survival rates than animals that play less.

Want to live a long and healthy life? If so, one thing is clear: you must play.

Just for a moment, I want you to imagine waking up in the morning and feeling excited about the day ahead. What would it be like to feel more alive? What would it feel like to have an unlimited source of creativity that you could tap into at any moment? What would it feel like to have a greater sense of meaning in your life?

Now, you might be thinking, "*OK, that all sounds great, but I don't have time to play.*" Or, "*What if I look ridiculous?*" Or, "*But I don't know what to do!*"

Well, I've got some good news for you:

First, playing doesn't have to involve a lot of time—in fact, you can do it while driving to work, on your lunch break, or even lying in bed.

Second, you don't have to put on a clown costume and a red fluffy nose to play (though it wouldn't hurt). You can play without anyone else even knowing—and if they find out, they just might want to join you.

Third, you're in luck, because I'm going to teach you exactly what you need to do to bring more play into your life! Even if you haven't played since you were a kid—even if you *never* played as a kid (and that's highly unlikely), the step-by-step formula that I describe below is easy and most importantly, it works.

---

42 *Ibid*, 34.

The Magic Secret Play Formula revealed:

Step 1: Take a few minutes to think about a moment in your life when you felt most alive or joyful. It might be something from your childhood, or something more recent. It might be an activity you were doing, an event you were attending, an interaction with a friend or loved one, or just a moment in time.

Try not to think too hard on this—there's no right or wrong moment to choose. Once you have one, take one sheet of blank paper and "free-write" about the experience. Here are some questions to get you started:

- What were you doing/what was happening in this moment?
- Were you alone or with someone else?
- What was the environment around you like?
- What were you feeling?
- Why do you think you were feeling this way?
- What other moments in your life, past or present, have made you feel similarly?

As you write, you may hear your internal critic—you know, that nagging voice that lives inside you—say, "*this is terrible*," or "*I can't/ don't want to answer these questions*," or "*why are we doing this?*" If you hear any of those, just tell that voice that it's OK, it doesn't have to be perfect and there's a purpose to this exercise. When you've finished, go on to Step 2.

Step 2: Draw the scene you wrote about in Step 1. "*Wait*," you're saying to yourself, "*did he just tell me to draw?*" Yes, I did. But here's the thing: it doesn't matter whether you're an expert sketch artist or have never drawn in your life. We're not going for a work of art we're just going for something that feels truthful.

First, get a box of crayons, colored pencils, or markers (you could even use paint if you want)—but no pens or regular pencils.

Next, get a blank sheet of paper, at least as big as a regular letter-sized sheet, but bigger if you'd like.

When you draw the scene, make sure to draw yourself and anyone else who was with you (they can be stick figures), the environment around you (buildings, nature, furniture, etc.), and any other details you can remember. If you can't remember where you were or what it looked like, make it up—what would you have wanted it to look like? Fill up as much of the paper as you can, and when you're done, go on to Step 3.

Step 3: Choose an activity that elicits the same feelings you wrote about in Step 1. It could be anything: singing, dancing, taking a walk, gardening, drawing, skipping, playing pretend, taking a trip, building something, watching theater or a movie, spending time with children or animals, or doing something you've never done before. Choose something simple and preferably, something you can actually do within the next 7 days.

Then, do it! Play! Let yourself be free and experience the feelings you had while playing earlier in your life. Hopefully, after playing once, you'll want to do it again and again.

That's the formula—not so complicated, is it?

So, now you have a choice: you can continue living your life just the way it is, or you can make a conscious decision to create more joy and fulfillment in your life through play.

Whatever you choose is OK. Only you can make this choice and only you will be accountable to it. But one thing I know is this:

The very moment you start to play is the very moment you become fully alive, living the deepest expression of your true, authentic self. As Dr. Charles Schaefer, a world-renowned psychologist and the father of Play Therapy has said,

"*We are never more fully alive, more completely ourselves, or more deeply engrossed in anything, than when we are at play.*"

Who wouldn't want that?

Jeffrey Kurtz is an author, speaker, actor, director, Certified Health Coach and Certified Emotional Freedom Technique (EFT) Practitioner and founder of A Better Perfect. For more information, see Jeffrey's bio in *Meet The Experts*.

›12‹

DO THIS, DON'T DO THAT: SIMPLE STEPS FOR YOUR QUALITY OF LIFE

Jennifer Rosenwald

David[43] drove home from the job he'd worked so hard to earn in the car he coveted. As he pulled into his driveway he thought, *"Man, I hope all those lights were green, 'cause I didn't notice one of them."*

Here he was at the house he and his lovely wife had aspired to own, so their kids could have a big yard and go to the best schools. But he couldn't get out of the car. He unclenched his fists from the steering wheel, slumped back into the fine leather seats, and sighed.

"I thought getting to this point, achieving all this, would feel better. But everyone's working my last nerve, and I'm sweating through my shirt."

---

43   Not his real name

He was tangled: irritable, annoyed at people just not getting it, not doing everything they should. He was worried about everyone he cared about and every to-do on his list. He had set up his life to be busy, to spin many plates–but was weighed by the niggling notion that it wasn't making him happy.

"I have GOT to get my head straight, 'cause I'm missing the boat. Life is short. And I bet my bad back, headaches, and drinking have something to do with this."

Laurie[44] was in the same boat: doing well but not feeling well. She was ready to figure it out, the way she had figured out so much of her life.

"I want all the hard work to be worth it—to feel like it's worth it. I want to feel, in the end, that it was a good ride, that I was the best everything I could be, for everyone. But I want it NOW, too."

Laurie had already mastered the first step in getting her head in shape: noticing the disconnect between the thoughts in her head and those she wanted to have, between how she felt and how she wanted to feel. She learned it's simple, *"like flipping a switch,"* and as important to health as exercise is for the body. Instead of "gain" coming from "pain" as it does at the gym, Laurie learned getting in mind-shape involves learning to release pain, which brings instant rewards.

Laurie decided to invest in herself, like she did in so many other people and projects, using skills already mastered to achieve other successes. She realized she'd be no good to anyone, especially herself, if she didn't.

Today she feels lighter, with her *"head matching [her] heart,"* as she says. She sleeps better and feels better. She laughs all the time now, *"Finding the humor in things was key to shaking off the negatives, and that, as you taught me, is key to getting untangled."*

Feeling tangled comes from focusing, often unconsciously, on what's worrying or aggravating you, rather than on what's going on around you. Chewing on past or future concerns is like a hamster

---

44   Not her real name

wheel of worry—or what I call it the *snark loop*. It actually *feels* like a tangle: You're ill at ease because your thoughts don't match the way you see yourself. Your body is in knots, discomfort or literal disease evidencing the discord.

Scientific research supports the mandate to manage your thoughts, even pursuing happiness *first, in order* to achieve success.

- **HEALTH:** We've heard it before: The body believes what the mind tells it. The World Health Organization (WHO) predicts that by 2020, depression will be the second leading cause of morbidity in the world, affecting 30% of adults. Studies conducted at major research universities reveal that stress, anger, anxiety, depression and sadness are linked to increased incidence of heart disease, strokes, elevated blood pressure and cortisol levels, gastrointestinal problems, headaches, shorter life expectancy, substance abuse and failed relationships (at home and work). A Harvard study concluded people who report high or improved levels of happiness/life satisfaction have a 23% drop in fatigue and 31% less depression than their less happy counterparts.

- **HAPPINESS FIRST, SUCCESS FOLLOWS**: Shawn Achor, former Harvard professor and author of *The Happiness Advantage*, teaches when we attain what we think of as success, we often do not experience lasting satisfaction: the goalpost moves. Studies suggest happiness leads to behaviors that lead to further success in work, relationships and health and success thus stems from positive feelings. *"...happiness, in many cases, leads to successful outcomes, rather than merely following from them,"* says Sonja Lyubomirsky, PhD, University of California at Riverside.

Now, imagine you're in your car after a rough day. You remind yourself to notice, look around and take in the sky or someone singing or laughing in a car near you. You decide to play. You make an adventure out of the mundane! Then *you* laugh and give yourself permission to dance in your seat to a great beat. [45]

You notice what is good and right and beautiful around you. You're here, now, versus living in the "*wish it was different*" past or "*OMG, what if!*" future. You pull into your driveway and look with appreciation at your house, your children, spouse, parents, pets, all of it, thinking you are lucky. You sigh deeply before getting out of your car, not feeling defeated, but feeling satisfied. It *IS* ok.

The steps that follow will help you get what you really want.

Step 1: DESIRE. If you want success and satisfaction with that success, get successful at being satisfied.

No expectations. The philosopher Epictetus wrote, "*People are not disturbed by things, but by the view they take of things.*" What bothers us, sets our teeth on edge, is the expectation that people and events *won't* set our teeth on edge. What works to make a happy life is to not *expect* happy—especially to not expect easy or control. I'm not suggesting you have low or cynical expectations; those are still expectations. I'm suggesting you try not to have expectations at all.

Give yourself permission. Allow yourself to feel satisfaction and joy. Hard work and self-sacrifice do not mean no pleasure or smelling of roses.

Step 2: DECIDE. Use the skills you already have and develop new ones using new tools.

Take responsibility. Own It. You get the cake you bake. Everything with your name on it is your responsibility. No blame. No victims allowed. It may not be your fault, but it is your responsibility.

Think about thinking. Of course you know how to think or you wouldn't have accomplished so much. This is about right-thinking, wrangling and managing your thoughts so they don't

---

45   Read about strategic and targeted benefits of *play* in Jeffrey Kurt's Chapter 11.

manage, or worse, hijack you. Once we become aware of our thoughts, we can use tools to change them. Think about thinking the way you would think about anything you want to be good at.

Step 3: DO. Doing makes the difference between wishing you had something and getting it. For some this formula is easy. Others spend real time and effort to put these lessons into practice.

Notice. Step outside yourself and objectively observe what you're thinking. Notice what you're feeling: mental or physical pain, clenching, sweating, fatigue, anger, anxiety. Next, notice what's going on around you (like whether the traffic lights are red or green!).

Replace. Positive observations and thoughts replace negative ones. Think about what *is* good. This requires:

- **Assessing and prioritizing:** In five years, heck, in five days, will this *really* matter? If you are thrown by hurt or grief or shock, assign a value and a time limit so you don't get stuck; then continue with this process.

- **Letting it go:** Don't hold on to whatever has you in the *snark loop*. Put your dukes down. Shake it off. "*Get over it*", as the saying goes; there will always be "it" to get over. Learn to forgive. Holding on to resentments "*...is like drinking poison and expecting it to kill them*" (attributed to many). Change your perspective: give people the benefit of the doubt, understanding that others' actions are most often not intended to upset or hurt us. Remember this: "*What you resist persists*" (attributed to Carl Jung).[46]

This is important: Notice when you notice! You'll do it more often. And give yourself a *huge* pat on the back for doing so, especially for replacing thoughts and feelings about what's wrong with ones about what's right.

---

46 I encourage you to get to the bottom of whatever sabotages your efforts to right your thinking and perspective. For more information, see Dr. Babs Kangas' Chapter 8 on reinvention, Patty Soffer's Chapter 3 on partnership and Dianne Flemington's Chapter 18 on romantic relationships.

Sure, there will always be *those days*. You have three choices in a tough situation: Accept, change, or walk away. The past is the wake behind the boat, and the future is yours to steer toward. *"The happiness of your life depends upon the quality of your thoughts."* —Marcus Aurelius

Turn your troubling thoughts into a virtual hot stove, making them dangerous to your peace of mind and your health to touch. Putting the Desire/Decide/Do formula into practice will make you recognize and more quickly release the thoughts that keep you tangled in the *snark loop*, the hamster wheel.

What's in it for you to change how you think? You will have command over your perspective and therefore your mood. Your mind and body will feel better, lighter, more agile and strong. All your relationships will improve. You will be present for and appreciate the people you've chosen to be in your life and the mastery of your plate spinning.

You will love your life, not endure it. And you will laugh so much more, delighted by what you notice all around you, realizing that you have made it all more than *worth it*—that you are getting—for *you*, along the way and not in the end—what you want from your one shot at *your* life.

JENNIFER ROSENWALD is dedicated to your having The Good Life: the experience, not just the stuff. She has helped hundreds of busy, productive people have better quality of life while they achieve their goals. For more information, see Jennifer's bio in *Meet The Experts*.

13

LIFE-AUDITING FOR THE OVERWHELMED

Lupe-Rebeka Samaniego, PhD

It is Tuesday and I am soon to see John[47], a 43 year-old individual, who was recently promoted to a leadership position at his company. John struggles with some of his employees, especially those who are *below* him.

As he enters the room, his overwhelmed look strikes me as he speaks of feeling like "*an imposter*" at work. When he mentions his 60-hour or more workweek, I notice his load is similar to mine where most days evolve into long evenings.

"*John,*" I ask, "*and how are you loving?*"

---

47 Confidentiality Note: John is a hypothetical case based on the author's 30 years of clinical experience. Any reference or resemblance to any person or organization, whether living or dead, existing or defunct, is purely coincidental.

"How?" he remarks as he slouches in his chair. *"Well doc, I am not certain. You see, 'my soul' was murdered in childhood. And I am searching for 'my soul'...so to answer your question, I don't have real love to give."*

He adds that he fears losing his family and has neither patience nor time for his two young children. At the core of his existence, he carries *"a secret known only to a few."*

I sense a deep shame and quietly wonder if he is aware of it.

With a voice filled with tension, he continues, *"That's why I am here. I am not sure about anything these days...I feel tired all the time and my wife doesn't notice me anymore and that makes me really, really angry. I am angry at everything...I despise company meetings. I like being in charge but I strike out when others challenge me. I hate it. When employees ask questions, I dread it."*

I ask, *"What do you dread?"*

He averts his eyes as he responds, *"Making a fool of myself, not knowing what to say. I feel out of control most of the time and I want to yell, 'shut up'!"*

He sits up suddenly and looks me straight in the eyes. I feel drawn in emotionally as he enunciates, *"Do you think there is something about me that may be getting in the way?"*

John has asked a crucial question needed for growth to occur. He has a beginning awareness of the role he plays and seems to be telling me that he desires to do the work 'now' so that he does not end up 'in the end' with regrets[48].

In both his business and private worlds, John is experiencing a common and resolvable problem: OVERWHELM.

Overwhelm hurts an individual's personal and professional life and physical health. Functioning with overwhelm can have serious consequences.

Individuals in positions of leadership are especially vulnerable to challenges in these arenas. In severe cases, the overwhelmed individual develops chronic health conditions because constant exposure to

---

48   See Chapter 22 by Kris Landry

stress interferes with the immune system. Severe stress also affects your brain functioning, and in turn, your decision-making and interpersonal relationships.

A state of overwhelm makes the brain more aroused or less able to remain calm, and less likely to see the larger picture. As long as your brain is over-stimulated, it can become disorganized, develop depression, and interfere with clear thinking and decisions, relating well, and managing emotions [49].

At a professional level, without a calm leader, even the most motivated organization will lose direction. In chronic cases, businesses and organizations fail, partnerships are severed and individuals hurt for years to come [50].

The Solution to Overwhelm begins by reflecting daily on these 3 questions:

1. HOW AM I LOVING? … am I loving with compassion or do I blame the stress on those closest to me? Do I have passion for my job or do I fear it?
2. HOW AM I LIVING? … am I living a secret life that exhausts me and makes me feel 'broken' and 'flawed'? Do I find it difficult to re-charge after a disappointing experience? At a deeper dive, do I live with sadness, hurt, and/or shame?
3. HOW AM I MAKING A DIFFERENCE? … am I leading departmental meetings with vitality, or do I withdraw with anger or react impulsively when others disagree or challenge me? In my state of overwhelm, am I having a negative impact on my employees?

Next, remember one of the most important characteristics of highly successful professionals is their ability to establish

---

49   See *Use Your Brain to Change Your Age*. Amen, Daniel (2012) and "The Four Components of Trauma and Effective Treatment" by Van der Kolk, Bessesl (2013) in *The National Institute for the Clinical Application of Behavioral Medicine* www. nicabm.com.
50   See Chapter 3 on business partnerships by Patty Soffer.

inner calm in the face of being overwhelmed. An action that is immediately effective and has powerful results is a researched process that I call the **PAUSE—RESET—REFLECT** model. The action involves an immediate action that is inner-directed while simultaneously sustaining an outer-directed action.

You can actively engage in this experience quietly and unobtrusively at any moment and at any place without anyone knowing. This model becomes very useful in moments of stress such as during executive meetings and encounters with family members. It is also useful in anticipation of a meeting.

Step 1: PAUSE (Internal action)

Become aware of your internal sensations. Notice the muscles in your neck, your shoulders, your back, your face, your hands, your feet; notice, explore, observe and accept any sensations that are present such as any tenseness in your body.

Step 2: RESET (External action)

You are resetting your internal thermostat, your aroused nervous system, by engaging in the external action of rhythmic breathing. Inhale through your nose, and take several deep, deep breaths, exhaling oh so slowly and continuing this slow rhythm, throughout an entire activity, for example, throughout a meeting. Allow the air to flow throughout your entire body as if you are expanding your body with air, and slowly, oh so slowly breathe the air out, as if you are blowing the air through an open window at the tip of your toes.

Step 3: REFLECT

As you engage in the above, ask yourself, "*What is important to me, at this very moment in time?*" If you feel distress, take additional deep breaths, squeeze your hands and let go, breathing in and out simultaneously, and tell yourself, "*I am present now, I am safe now. What do I want/need to happen right now?*"

When you follow these 3 steps, **PAUSE...RESET... REFLECT...** you will feel calm internally and begin to re-engage with more presence. You will be better able to read what others are saying and respond accordingly.

More calmness ultimately leads to more meaningful connections at work, at home, and in life in general. Feelings of despair, anger and hurt experienced as a result of betrayal and unfairness move into a space of less importance.[51]

The strength in acknowledging one's role in what has gone wrong and the freedom in accepting the flaws in others and in one's self becomes liberating. A past experience of being overwhelmed moves into a place of living and leading with vitality and calmness in the present.

To become a true and vital leader in one's profession or in one's business or one's home depends on your ability to become a whole person free from stress and overwhelm. You need to be able to sense, hold and contain within you powerful emotions and internal sensations.

We all need to *feel within us* so that we may *feel felt*. Yet, we also need to observe these emotions and sensations and reflect upon them at the same time. We can now move towards choice, action and change.

When we engage our mind and our body in this manner, we are able to contain the overwhelm and the emotions and the sensations do not seem overpowering. And with time, these internal experiences become less debilitating.

We are in essence utilizing different parts of our brain that allow us to feel alive and aware. We ultimately feel compassion for others and for ourselves. The unifying experience—of our brain and mind with our body—becomes the power of a team or of an orchestra performing in concert. When a team, like an orchestra, combines strengths, the benefits of the whole resonate with everyone while the individual weaknesses fade.

---

51 A process of life-auditing that leads to personal/professional change includes viewing the struggles through different and integrated lenses. For 'resolution of conflict and forgiving' please Lisa Gibson's Chapter 4, for more on balanced medical health Dr. Irina Koles' Chapter 20 and for solving adult-offspring relational problems, see BJ Rosenfeld's Chapter 17.

So it will be for you when you reflect on the 3 questions daily and use the 3 steps to reduce overwhelm. It will keep you on the path to success.

Lupe-Rebeka Samaniego, PhD, licensed Clinical Psychologist and Certified High Performance Coach, inspires professionals daily to transform their lives. For more information, see Lupe's bio in *Meet The Experts.*

14

FLIP YOUR SWITCH—— IT'S TIME TO SHINE AGAIN

Janet Swift

She went to boarding school at the age of just seven and was placed in a class with students who were two years older than she, the usual entry age being nine. Sitting in her first geometry lesson, she heard the teacher give verbal instructions to construct a diagram.

The teacher asked everyone except her for their answers and each gave the wrong one. Up went the hand of this open and happy new girl and she answered correctly. The cold accusatory stares pierced her from every angle as the teacher smiled warmly, saying *"Excellent, very well done."* The lesson ended and this innocent child was confused and frightened as the group united in their hatred towards her.

That night in the dormitory, desperately gasping for air through the blankets pressed against her face, she stopped responding and lay still. Acceptance brought relief as the weight of several bodies lifted from her and hot life-giving air brought her back from the edge of unconsciousness. This bright young child knew she had to protect herself from further attack, instinctively dumbing down to avoid the physical and emotional torture that would surely follow any expression of her true ability.

A few weeks later, the Headmistress sent for her father. Nothing was said but she knew it was serious. As he finally emerged from the oak-paneled room, she crumpled with relief as the Dad she adored smiled and winked at her. Apparently, his daughter was a *compulsive liar in need of psychiatric intervention*. She'd said she'd been up Mount Kilimanjaro in Kenya and was the 'Under-Fives' Shark Fishing Champion' in Bahrain. Her father's response to all this? A simple: "*She has and she was.*"

A very unique early life was this child's truth and yet, as with her exceptional ability, expressing it brought pain and punishment. For the next five decades, she dimmed her light, afraid to stand out.

Perhaps you know a child like her? Perhaps you *were* a child like her? The sad truth is far too many grow up like her, most never finding their way out of that place. They live their lives as underachievers, denying their potential and avoiding the opportunities they see but are afraid to embrace—until someone encourages them out of the shadows and they allow their lights to shine.

I first learned about this pattern on September 18, 1963 when I witnessed first-hand how a child's light is dimmed. You see, I was that child at boarding school and grew up hiding my potential. Now I devote my life to helping others live in integrity with their purpose and to express their true essence. As Patty Soffer so accurately says, "*If you're not in partnership with yourself, how can you ever be in partnership with human relationships, either personally or in business?*"[52]

Perhaps you know people who have hidden their light believing that the 'big dream' just isn't going to happen? Their habits keep them anchored, enjoying the familiarity of feeling safe and yet in danger of

---

52 See Chapter 3.

never becoming who they truly are. Perhaps they're successful in their field but were forced to live someone else's dream, not their own? Is that you?

Maybe your relationship with your grown-up family is in crippling crisis or conflict with parents is inhibiting you as an adult? Either way, BJ Rosenfeld has shown you can heal adult-to-adult relationships, freeing you to move forward[53].

Stepping up and shining your light changes dreams to reality. Elizabeth's story perfectly illustrates this point:

Moving forward from ill health, failed marriages and a draining low-level corporate job, Elizabeth turned her life around in just 18 months. Now she is running her own flourishing hotel and a thriving business. And to think she almost denied herself this success! Instead, she chose to shine her light on full beam and now she's happier and more fulfilled than she's ever been.

Maybe it's time for a change for you too or, as Dr. Cheryl Lentz says, *"To think in a different way to identify problems and find solutions, just like Einstein would."*[54] After all, Einstein's definition of madness was to carry on doing the same things but expecting a different outcome!

Life's so busy and it's easy to feel overwhelmed and off balance when challenges strike. Someone always needs something –the kids, the boss, someone you care for—and time's limited, right? Remember, the highest achievers have the same number of hours in the day as everyone else! Far too often we look after the car but not our bodies, water the plants but leave our spiritual garden in drought and feed our social media accounts but not our minds.

Do you still feel that child-like thrill when you see a rainbow? Can you remember joy and happiness, sheer pleasure and exhilaration, curiosity and excitement all fresh and unimpaired by responsibility, routine and revenue? Do you want to?

---

53   See Chapter 17
54   See Chapter 5

Tina Sacchi, a holistic and spiritual author says: *"Permission to express your spirituality comes from within, allowing you to nurture your own growth with self-love and self-acceptance."*[55]

Imagine a brand-new you filled with positive energy and vitality, living your dream lifestyle and expressing your true passion. Perhaps you'd love to be an artist, musician, chef, dancer, write the book you know lies within, or gain the qualification you've always wanted? You could say goodbye to plowing through each working day, frustrated and longing for the clock to free you—instead, see yourself as you never have before.

When every day is filled with things we love doing, when we're following our passion and shining our light, we feel alive and energized as we're 'on purpose.'

Right now, is your light shining on full beam or has it dimmed to a flicker? Perhaps you're very successful in your field but have a dream, a passion inside that still yearns for expression? Or perhaps you consciously choose to hide your light. Wherever you are, it's time to give voice to your dream.

3 Steps to Give Voice to Your Dream

Take some time to sit quietly where you won't be disturbed. Work through the following three-part exercise and write down your first answer to each of these questions:

1. **What Would I Really LOVE To Do? Not Sure? Ask Yourself:**
    - What excited me as a child?
    - What did I want to be when I grew up?
    - What would entice me out of bed at 5:00 a.m. because I can't wait to start my day?
    - What do my life experiences and intuition say about me?

---

55 See Chapter 16

2. **What's Been Holding Me Back? Is It:**
   - FEAR—are thoughts of failure, success, ridicule or the unknown overwhelming?
   - PROCRASTINATION—takes away life potential. Do my dreams exist only in my sleep?
   - COMFORT ZONE COZINESS—the adult equivalent of a comfort blanket; has mine become a fire blanket extinguishing my spark?
   - LACK OF SELF-BELIEF—why do I think my offering/ life experience is any less worthy than anyone else's?
   - LACK OF FOCUS—do I have a scattergun approach and can I change it to laser-sharp focus and really see results quickly?

3. **What Are My Goals? For Each Goal Consider:**
   - What do I already have to equip me for success?
   - What do I still require/need to do?
   - What action can I take to satisfy these requirements?
   - What will it cost me in time, money and work?
   - What sacrifices will I have to make?
   - Am I prepared to compromise?

For me, the key to unblocking and unlocking lay in mentors who supported, encouraged and stretched me when limiting beliefs kicked in. Did you know some of the most influential people in history had mentors? Homer started it. No, not Homer Simpson but Homer's Odyssey. The Goddess of Wisdom used Mentor, a debilitated old man, to guide Odysseus' son through a difficult time. Socrates was the mentor of Plato and Plato mentored Aristotle who went on to mentor Alexander the Great. You'll be in great company because our very own 21st Century Bill Gates was mentored by Warren Buffet who was guided in the way of the markets by Ben Graham, an influential economist.

Bonnie Goldstone[56] has been on her own emotional journey believing her experiences, both good and bad, have taught her

---

56 See Chapter 15

valuable life lessons. Bonnie says, *"The good news is you don't need to win the lottery to start living your dream life right now."*

I invite you to imagine what your life would sound like if it were a piece of music. What notes would you hear—dark and melancholic, energetic or tinkling, fun and sweet to the ear? It's time to give yourself the freedom to write your own score, making it as challenging, exciting, invigorating and satisfying as you choose.

Living life with your full orchestra playing, shining your light and sharing your gifts will attract the success you deserve. One thing's for sure—we entered this life with nothing but a divine purpose to fulfill. Now is your time to step into yours and enjoy the journey to success.

Through careers in nursing, the police, the corporate world and as a successful business owner, JANET SWIFT hid her potential until life's hobnail boot startled her awake. Today, she helps clients shine by living in integrity with their values and aspirations. For more information, see Janet's bio in *Meet The Experts*.

▶15◀

I LOVE MY JOURNEY

Bonnie Goldstone, CHT, NLP

A t one time or another, most people dream of living in a tropical hideaway—or at least enjoying an extended vacation there. They imagine being surrounded by the lush green of a dense jungle, watching monkeys swing from tree to tree while brightly colored birds glide across the blue skies. They visualize the sweet fragrance of a multitude of exotic flowers as they mix with the deep aroma of the musky jungle floor. They imagine a gentle tropical breeze whistling through a treetop canopy caressing and cooling their warm bodies.

Sounds wonderful, doesn't it?

Many of us have dreams and desires of our perfect lives however few actually make their dreams come true. Fear, money, limiting beliefs and busy lives seem to stand in the way of turning their dreams into achievable goals.

Whether you dream of living in a tropical paradise or on top of snow covered mountain… whether you long to help those less fortunate or to make your business a total success… no matter what your dream, the secret is to discover how to turn it from fantasy to reality.

Most of us lose track of the dreams we once had as life's challenges and daily grind get in our way. Now is the time to pick yourself up, straighten out, dust off and decide on a life journey destination.

You can do it! It is not too late! You deserve to live your own exciting and wonderful life![57]

Where it all begins

We are all born perfect little human beings arriving here as innocent, amazing little people. Immediately we began to absorb and learn from our environment. Our parents, our aunts and uncles, our grandparents and our siblings all became our teachers.

As we absorb new information, we use our innocent perspective to create *files* that become limiting beliefs and emotional baggage. Those files are stored in our subconscious minds for the rest of our lives—unless we do something to clean them out.

As children, we watched and observed everything and we determined how life should be through our innocent perspective. The adults around us were like gods in our eyes. What they did and what they said was TRUTH! So when we heard statements like, *"You cannot do that," "You are not capable," "You are a brat,"* and *"You don't deserve X,"* we filed the statements as if they were factual.

Were these statements true? No, of course not! Consciously we know that now, but our subconscious mind has all these statements imbedded within us. These perceived truths become our beliefs!

As an adult you may wonder why you stand in the way of your own success and happiness. You might not even realize the limiting beliefs contained in your subconscious mind are the biggest obstacles to living your amazing and extraordinary life![58]

So what can you do about it?

The first step is to start noticing how much these limiting beliefs are holding you back and determine how you can release them so you can reach your goals and dreams.

Every day I see my clients release unwanted emotional baggage and limiting beliefs. There's nothing more exciting than seeing them allowing themselves to become empowered and create the life they truly desire and deserve.

What would you create if you had no obstacles or limiting beliefs? Where would you be today?

Start Here

When you were very young (under the age of 6) you probably lived in your imagination. As you began school you were probably told to stop daydreaming and pay attention! Life became real, imagination and fantasy were discouraged.

I want you to know using your imagination is an important tool in the overall creation of your amazing life. Maybe you have heard the expression, *"What you think about, you bring about?"* It is absolutely true! If you constantly think of how difficult your life is and you revisit thoughts of doom and gloom that is exactly what you will be experiencing. On the other hand, the optimist views life's ups and downs as learning experiences and personal growth. This person's life is exciting and extraordinary.

You might be wondering, *"How can I decide what is it that I want to create in my life? What does my perfect life look like? Am I on the right path?"* [59]

---

58 Do you have Big Bold Ambitions? Randy Stanbury shares proven steps to bring your ambitions to reality in Chapter 10!

59 If you are nearing retirement, check out Suzanne Nault's Chapter 9 on retiring from work and not from life.

The secret is to listen to your all-knowing, wise inner voice. Take time each day to quiet your mind and connect with your inner guidance system. Here's how:

3 Quick and Easy Steps to Find Your Inner Voice

STEP 1: Bring yourself into the present moment.

We do not have personal power in past or future events. The goal is to open yourself to listening to your inner voice NOW. To do this you simply become aware of your breathing, your own heartbeat, your own body. As busy thoughts pop into your mind, acknowledge them and let them go.

STEP 2: Allow yourself to experience deep relaxation.

When we allow our eyes to relax, our body begins to let go. Simply close your eyes and notice all the tiny muscles and nerves in and around your eyes. Allow all these muscles and nerves to let go, to become loose and limp. Notice how you are in complete control of the depth of relaxation you choose. With practice you can experience complete relaxation in the eye area, so your eyelids become very, very heavy and relaxed.

STEP 3: Send a wave of relaxation down through your body from the top of your head to the tip of your toes.

Simply count backwards on each exhale from 5 to 1 as you send a wave of relaxation down your body relaxing every muscle and every nerve.

As you practice these steps daily you will find it easier and easier to create the deep state of relaxation you choose to experience. The deeper level of quietness you create within your mind the more open you will be to listening to your own inner voice.

Your inner voice will guide you to create your dream. The possibilities are endless. This vision will create a fire and excitement within and start you on the process of turning your life into the dream you have always wanted. Whatever your dream life is, it can be yours. Live your life now so you can wake up each morning and say, "I love my journey!"

BONNIE GOLDSTONE, CHT, NLP, founder of the online community, "I Love My Journey" is a sought-after, leading-edge therapist. A Board Certified Hypnotherapist, NLP Master Practitioner, Reiki Master and intuitive healer, Bonnie empowers her clients to live fuller and happier lives. For more information, see Bonnie's bio in *Meet The Experts.*

›16‹

MY SPIRIT DOES NOT LIVE IN A BOX

Tina Sacchi

OPEN to Expressing Spirituality YOUR Way

O n the way to religious service, a mother asked her young son, "Why is it important to be very quiet in church?" Her son replied, "We need to be quiet because people are sleeping. Mommy they're bored!"

The crowd roared with Angela's tone and delivery of her comedic act. She was feeling the deepest joy to be able to express her beliefs in a way which people related to and accepted.

According to the Daily Local newspaper, Angela was considered the "funniest, most popular local comedian and entertainer."

She loved being a comedian because it enabled her to express her true feelings, beliefs and highlight her religion's idiosyncrasies that affected her and obviously her audience. Not only was Angela funny, she was also in pain!

Angela dreaded Sundays. The many rules that existed before, during and after church service didn't make sense to her and they combined to make Sunday her least favorite day of the week.

"*Just get through it!*" she thought. "*Too many man-made rules, ugh!*"

On one particular Sunday, Angela woke up feeling hungry—physically, emotionally, mentally and most of all spiritually. Physically she was ravenous however she was not allowed to eat breakfast since she was going to church, an ancient rule that one must fast in order to receive the sacrament of communion. She could still hear her grandparents, now deceased, hound her with this rule:

"*It's a mortal sin to eat before church. No food until you get back from church or God will punish you!*"

She was mentally exhausted with her recurring thoughts of punishment, sin and ancestors dictating her life. She felt like she was living a double life: who she felt inside was the opposite of who she portrayed to the world.

"*There must be a better way!*" she thought.

Angela began thinking about no longer attending Sunday services. The thought led to many sleepless nights and daily headaches. She was gaining weight by stuffing her feelings and escaping her pain with food. Her body was reacting to her unhappiness.

She was tired of acting as if everything was perfect.

"*There is one way to heaven,*" many would recite.

"*Really?!*" she wondered.

In her heart, Angela felt that God always knows our true intention and is not a punishing being but rather a being with compassion who loves us unconditionally.

"*Religion is boxing me in, too confining with too many rules, too constricting—and forget about laughter and fun!*" she exclaimed.

She spoke freely to her audiences, "*Confession is amazing to me. It didn't matter if we lie, curse, steal, or create an unkind act, as soon as you say a few prayers, as directed by the priest, you are cleared for another week. Wow! How could a priest—a mere human being—have so much power, yet we are not able to do this for ourselves?"*

The crowd cheered and gave a standing ovation. *"My audience shares the same beliefs and feelings. I need to shift this guilt out of me since it's immobilizing me and making me sick.*

As Angela recounted her situation during her appointment with me, she added,

"I want to live my life free and openly without all these rules. My spirit feels caged in. I am an adult for goodness sake! Why do I allow everyone and their beliefs to rule my life? I feel sad and angry with myself for not living my authentic life openly. All sorts of physical issues arise especially when it's time to go to church or socialize with certain people."

Angela went on and on.

She didn't realize it at the time, but Angela's challenge was extremely common. What she was experiencing is known as SBNR: Spiritual But Not Religious. This is a popular lifestyle where people explore other ways to connect with their faith without following rules that don't make sense to them.

At the time of this publication and according to the Huffington Post, it's estimated that 1 in 5 Americans have no religion and most of them consider themselves SBNRs. Thirty percent of this group are under the age of 30 and SBNRs are on the rise especially with the younger generations. In addition, a recent Gallup poll concluded that 77% of Americans say that religion is losing its influence on American life.

If this describes you, or someone you know, below are 4 steps you can use to express your spirituality freely.

4 Steps to Authentically Express Your Spirituality

In order to be OPEN to authentically expressing your spirituality your way:

Overcome obstacles and optimize your life to new ideas and other ways to be spiritual. When others don't agree with your ways of connecting, bless them and move on. We are not here to convince anyone of our way of thinking and believing. We are here to enlighten and encourage others. So bless the others who don't agree with you, change conversation and move on, even if you must move on physically.

Permission comes from oneself. Remember you must give yourself permission to connect to the Great Spirit, God or whatever you call the Creator, the way you want to connect. It's your life that you are living and no one else's. At your deathbed, I believe you will have to answer to only one being and that is YOU.

These are the questions you will ask yourself whenever that day comes when you drop your physical body and move to your next place of existence:

- Did I do what I came here to do?
- Did I allow myself to be happy and love myself unconditionally?
- Did I live and love openly, spiritually and authentically?

If you can't answer "yes" to each question above, there are some changes that need to be made.

Enlightenment tools for connection and moving forward. There are so many tools to connect with your spirituality deeply and lovingly. These include prayer, meditation, affirmations, energy healing, mantra chanting, retreating, hypnotherapy, nature walks, etc. Utilize tools that are enjoyable so that you can raise your vibration to a happier and loving vibration. When you feel the joy in your life, this is an excellent indication that you are going in the right direction.

Nurture spiritual growth with self-love and self-acceptance and surround yourself with like-minded people. Assemble your Divine support team here on earth, which includes spiritual mentors and guides. You want people to raise your vibration, not diminish nor judge you. Find your place, your tribe, and a like-minded community to promote love, peace, and growth. And when those places and people start feeling heavy or incongruent to your spirit and journey, move on with love, and gratitude for experiences and lessons you have gained. Bless them with your heart and move on.

There are so many ways and tools that one can transform, transmute, and transcend limiting beliefs. One tool we already have innately in our being is laughter. Laughter shifts our mental thoughts and emotional feelings that are not congruent with our core. Laughter is not only good for the mental and emotional bodies, it's also healing for the physical body and the soul[60].

By using various tools, you will connect with your spirit, your purpose and your passion. Your spirit wants to blossom, live and not wither and die. Allow your light to shine[61].

Create a big and bold ambition and live the life the way YOU want[62] so at your deathbed, you'll know you've lived the life you want and can die without regrets[63].

And when you are stuck and have a difficult time moving forward on your own, it's time to consult with a spiritual mentor to help and guide you through it. Sometimes we just need a push and other times a little nudge. It's all about expressing YOUR spirit your way!

When people can't give you what you need, you need to move on. They can only give you what they have. Furthermore, people who want the best for you will want you to be joyful, free, and OPEN!

When you use the OPEN formula, you will truly be the spiritual peace and love you seek, one spiritual step at a time. Love yourself unconditionally. Only you know what it takes and how to love yourself deeply. Live YOUR authentic life openly now!

TINA SACCHI is the best-selling author of *My Spirit Is Not Religious: A Guide to Living YOUR Authentic Life*. She helps people self-heal by guiding them to release limiting beliefs and patterns so they live a spiritually open and authentic life. For more information, see Tina's bio in *Meet The Experts*.

60　Read Irene Tymczyszyn's chapter for how healing laughter is for everyone – coming soon in *The Expert Success Solution, Volume 2*.
61　See Janet Swift's Chapter 14 for more on letting your light shine.
62　See Randy Stanbury's Chapter 10.
63　See Kris Landry's Chapter 22 for more on how to die without regrets.

)17(

JOIN THE PAC (PARENTS OF ADULT CHILDREN) AND NEVER LOSE YOUR CONNECTION!

BJ Rosenfeld, MA, MS, COGS

As a mother I think one of the most wonderful experiences we'll ever have is to be close to our kids. What could be better than knowing your children are safe, that they'll tell you their secrets, come to you for advice and stay connected to you forever? Of course that closeness can go away if you say something your kids don't want to hear. And that happens more and more often as our kids get older.

Even if you aren't at a place in your life where you are a parent of adult children, read on. The information here will help you make sure you avoid some huge problems and enjoy your relationship with your kids for as long as you live.

The Problem

As a parent of an adult child, you have many opportunities to question the choices your kid makes. You know your adult children would be a lot better if they would just do what you tell them to do. Of course, if you actually TELL them that, they'll probably stop listening—or worse- they'll stop communicating with you at all.

So what do you do if that happens? What do you do if your adult children are making decisions you don't like? How do you keep the closeness when your kids don't do what you want them to do? How can you get your adult kids to change?[64]

Been There Done That

For years I shared a special relationship with my older son. I'll never forget how cute he was when he was a baby. I loved to hold him in my arms. The first time he smiled at me, I was so excited I called everyone I knew. And I didn't stop smiling for the rest of the day.

I still have his first pair of shoes. They're so tiny. He could never fit into them now but they were perfect when he was learning to walk. He used to take one step, fall down and then stand up to try again. Whenever he held my hand, I felt so special. Pretty soon he was walking on his own. Then he learned to run and wanted me to chase him. Before long, I couldn't catch up with him but I still felt that strong emotional connection. I loved my son and my son loved me. We were close. I wanted things to stay that way forever. Maybe you can relate to this.

Years later my son got married and had a child, my grandchild. I was so, so happy the day she was born that my fingers tingled.

Everything was perfect until my son decided to move his family half way around the world, thousands of miles away from me. When he told me he was going, I couldn't believe it. What an insult! How dare he do that to me? I wanted to be able to spend time with my beautiful grandchildren whenever I wanted. Why was he taking them

---

64   For more information about problem solving through effective questioning, see Dr. Cheryl Lentz' Chapter 5.

away from me? I was so scared I might never see them again. My stomach hurt every time I thought about it. Didn't he love me any more? Wasn't I good enough? Did I do something wrong? Didn't he care about my feelings? Why was he doing this to me? I started crying whenever I walked past his old room.

So I did what every self-respecting parent would do. I told him I thought moving was a really stupid idea. I told him he was making a huge mistake. I tried to get him to change his mind. But he wouldn't listen. Didn't he respect me anymore? I was scared we were becoming strangers.

The Reality

Why is it some parents have perfect kids who grow up to be perfect adults? Why do some parents seem to always have all the answers? How come some parents have no problem staying close with their adult children even if their children move away? How come some parents feel they don't know their children any more? And most important, how come some parents never feel like their adult children don't have room for them in their busy lives?

As Dianne Flemington says, "*Sometimes people don't know how to communicate their needs to gain more understanding.*"[65] Too bad we can't just plop our kids into a gelatin mold and have them turn out exactly the way we want. The truth is there is no way to guarantee that our kids will grow up to be the adults we want them to be.

Lesson Learned

It took a long time for me to realize I was treating my son like a little kid instead of a married man who has a family. It was up to him and his wife to decide where they want to live.

I remembered back to when I got married and my parents expected us to live near them. Boy were they surprised when we didn't. There was nothing wrong with the town where they lived but it wasn't where my husband and I wanted to live.

---

65 See Dianne Flemington's Chapter 18 on creating relationships that thrive.

I finally reminded myself that I wanted my son to be independent and make his own decisions. And that's what he was doing. I had to remind myself that respect goes both ways and that part of being a parent is letting your kids be who they are. When I realized all of this, I told my son. And everything went back to normal. We were close again even though we lived so far apart.

The other day my granddaughter called me from half way around the world.

"*Hi,*" she said. "*I just learned how to dial the phone. I don't want to talk any more. Goodbye.*" And she promptly hung up the phone.

That made it all worth it.

You're Not Alone

In a 2013 survey, 93% of parents reported there is something missing in their relationship with their adult children. That's 93%! I speak at conferences around the world and the question parents ask most often is,

"*What can we do to feel we're still important in our kids' lives especially after they grow up?*"

All parents have two experiences in common. The times when we say exactly the right thing and our children are ready to run into our arms. And the times when we say exactly the right thing and our children don't want anything to do with us.

It's perfectly normal for our children to grow up and pull away from us. But it's not easy to let them do that. We were once the most important people in our children's lives. Many parents find it hard to give that up. It's hard to stop treating our adult children as little children in adult bodies.

The good news is there are proven and easy strategies you can use:

Imagine how wonderful your life would be if you could get and sustain the relationship you want with your adult children![66] Would

---

66 See Janet Swift's Chapter 14 for more on how to live your dreams.

you have less stress?[67] More fun?[68] More happiness? Whatever it is for you, the important thing is to know you have the power to make it happen.[69] It all begins by asking yourself three critical questions:

- **Question #1. What are your adult children doing that you don't like and what are they doing that you do like?**
- **Question #2. What are you doing that your adult children don't like and what are you doing that they do like?**
- **Question #3. How can you come together?**

Take some time now to write out your answers to these questions. You might be surprised by what you discover.

The Proof

George wasn't sure how to get the relationship he wanted with his son. He and his wife had divorced years ago and George hadn't seen or heard from his son for a really long time. When his son suddenly started sending him emails, George wasn't sure what to do. He was happy to hear from his son but was afraid of losing him again. He answered the emails but felt awkward because he was never quite sure what to say.

I asked George the 3 critical questions and he turned around and emailed the questions to his son! He got a huge surprise when he read his son's response:

"I like that you're giving me advice and I want you to keep doing that for me. I don't like that you're not taking care of yourself. I want you to be healthy and live a long time. I want you to go to the doctor. I want you to learn to Skype with me so I can see you and you can see me. And I want you to visit me and go to Comic Con."

George was so excited. It took him a few minutes to catch his breath. He then picked up the phone, made an appointment with his doctor, decided he was going to Skype with his son that very afternoon and made plans to meet his son at the next Comic Con.

---

67 Have a lot of stress in your life? See Dr. Lupe-Rebeka Samaniego's Chapter 13.
68 See Dr. Babs Kangas' Chapter 8 for how to more fun in your life.
69 See Bonnie Goldstone's Chapter 15 for more on living your life now.

George discovered a crucial piece to the parenting puzzle:

If you want your adult kids to behave differently, you might have to do some things differently too.

Begin by answering the three critical questions and then share them with your children. This will be a huge step to getting the relationship that will carry you into the future together.

Remember…

As parents, we need to understand that no matter what they do and no matter how old they get, our children still need to know we love them. After we're gone, that's what they will remember most. So remember to do whatever it takes to get your children to love and include you no matter what—because no one should die alone.

BJ ROSENFELD, MA, MS, COGS, is founder of No Matter What Parenting, the simple solution for parents of adult children. Through speaking, coaching and writing, BJ helps parents relieve stress and get the relationship they want with their adult children. For more information, see BJ's bio in *Meet The Experts*.

)18(

A LASTING, EXCITING LOVE RELATIONSHIP

Dianne Flemington

No one dreams of becoming a divorce statistic. Yet in the United States, 50% of marriages end in divorce. That means approximately 1 million Americans end their marriage each year. [70]

All of these statistics make for a clear message; we aren't learning the skills necessary to keep our relationships lasting, loving and exciting.

What is the cost of all this? Financially, it's extraordinary.

Matrimonial law is now a 28 billion dollar industry in the United States annually[71] and the number of couples choosing to marry

---

70   National Health Statistics Report, March, 2012
71   Lean Hoffman for Forbes.com

decreases every year[72]. Of course, these statistics do not include partners that separate or couples that remain in sad and unfulfilling relationships.

Add to these numbers the fact that the average wedding cost in the United States is just over $27,000[73] and you see the tremendous financial cost of relationships gone wrong.

What if you invested in your relationship what the average couple spends on a wedding? What if people learned how to create and sustain great relationships? What if couples actually focused on making their relationships thrive, rather than waiting for crises to occur? The answer is simple:

We would see an increase in success of marriages last as they were meant to last—forever. More men and women would be happier at home and work and their children would be raised in stable environments that would teach them how to grow up and have great relationships of their own.

Let's start with you! Have you ever asked yourself *"Is this the right person for me?"* or *"Is this the best it's going to get?"*

Perhaps you've spent time with other couples wondering how they manage to be so happy all the time or maybe you believe the myth, *"The honeymoon always ends."*

If you can relate to that, then know you're not alone. How does this happen? Here's an example:

When I first met Jack, he was a young executive at a pharmaceuticals company. He had been married only a couple of years and his wife Lisa was a full time nurse in the Emergency Room at their city hospital.

Jack's ambition and extra long work hours combined with Lisa's ever-changing work schedules created a situation where they rarely saw each other. When they did get home, they took care of the basic household responsibilities, leaving them too exhausted for each other. Their relationship had lost the excitement they once enjoyed.

---

72   National Health Statistics Report, March, 2012
73   Reuters, 2011

Sound familiar? This happens far too often. So what can you do about it?

Start by following these 4 steps

4 Steps to a Lasting, Exciting Love Relationship

Step #1: KNOW YOURSELF

You've probably heard this and it's worth repeating here. *"You must love yourself first before others can begin to truly love you."*

What makes this so important? If you don't know and love yourself, you can't possibly communicate your needs and wants with sincerity and truth. You need a clear vision of yourself you can honour, then you need to set boundaries to assure your vision is sustained.

Not having a clear self-identity is an extremely common phenomenon and one of the primary reasons people can feel so misunderstood or lost in relationships. As it turns out, they are just lost in themselves!

You can solve this by taking the time to be curious about yourself. Start here:

Uncover who you are by listing your values, passions, personality traits and everything you can think of that describes you. Get clear on the person you want to become (your ideal self or best self) and then set up a plan to Grow in the Gap™ by listing specifically what would need to change for you to become the person you want to be.

Step #2: DESIGNING THE ALLIANCE

Designing the Alliance is about being purposeful about your direction and appreciating the differences between you and your partner. It allows you to stand in your individuality and still move together through challenges, events and projects of life with a strong sense of support and safety.

Designing The Alliance consists of:

- Asking each other powerful, information-gathering questions

- Creating desired atmospheres that reflect what you both will want for certain events, projects
- Getting clear on what you can count on from each other when challenging moments arrive
- Sharing responsibility for the work of creating and sustaining your relationship
- Being clear about your feelings, boundaries and desired outcomes
- Taking steps to understand and value your partner
- Making time to design the alliances necessary for both partners to feel safe and secure in the relationship[74]

Step #3: LEARN & PRACTICE

Successful relationships flourish when you integrate consistent learning and growing—as an individual and a couple. As with all things in nature, if your relationship is not nurtured and growing, it's fading and dying. If you want to build and encourage a powerful connection with your partner, learn and practice the following critical skills.

SKILLS	
Effective Communication	Vulnerability
Handling Adversity & Learning Resiliency	Uncovering Your Creativity
Creating Lifelong Intimacy	Use of Playfulness
Honouring Yourself in Relationship	Presence
Building Trust & Respect	Gratitude & Contribution
Understanding Masculine & Feminine Roles	Honesty & Integrity

---

74 Handling conflict is an important skill to learn. See Lisa Gibson's Chapter 4.

STEP #4: REGULAR RELATIONSHIP CHECK-UPS / CHECK-INS

One of the greatest invisible risks to relationship well-being, is when couples let themselves go into 'Default Mode.' Over time, your life becomes set to autopilot and all your behaviours and daily routines happen without any purposeful connections in your relationship. You're simply 'managing' or 'coping' with daily demands.

You'll know when this is happening to you because you'll start to hear common statements such as:

- *"We don't do anything together anymore."*
- *"We don't have any fun."*
- *"I hardly see you."*

Once that begins, it's common for one or both members of the relationship to feel alone, to perceive a gap between you and your partner and to get angry for no apparent reason.

Just like our health, our relationships need consistent check-ups to help make the hard times more manageable and to ensure there is more of what we desire in the relationship[75].

How to Check-In or Check-Up

Schedule "talk times" where it's only the two of you with NO distractions.

When you talk, consider these topics:

- Where will you go for your next vacation?
- What are your visions for the relationship?
- What are some unresolved arguments or disappointments that need to be discussed further?
- What has happened that is positive and needs celebrating in your lives?

---

75 Feel like this may be too ambitious for you? Read Randy Stanbury's Chapter 10 on Big Bold Ambitions.

Discuss with each other whether you're spending enough time together and make sure your relationship is getting enough fun. Does your relationship need you both more?

Does all this work? Well, lets go back to Jack and Lisa…

Jack was worried about his relationship with Lisa and decided to get purposeful.

They went through all the steps above, talked about the importance of having a lasting, exciting marriage and ways they could bring fun back and find more time and energy for each other. They both agreed to do whatever it took to stay deeply connected and have a lot of fun along the way.

Today, Jack and his wife are excited about their lives and balance two very high level careers. Jack is now a Senior Account Executive at the same pharmaceutical company and Lisa built a successful online dog accessories business[76].

So can you do what they did? Absolutely. Being proactive and learning the skills to have lasting, exciting relationships, you can begin to feel the connection with your partner, with unconditional and non-judgemental support.

Develop the tools you need to plan, build and live your desired lives together. Couples who take the time to make that happen actually look forward to going home every day and experiencing easier connections and more intimacy.

Whatever you do, DO NOT WAIT for things to go wrong in your relationship. Be proactive, NOT reactive! Be clear on the relationship you desire, be intentional about getting it and DONT BE AFRAID to get help!

Everyone deserves lasting, exciting love! Especially YOU!

DIANNE FLEMINGTON is a relationship trainer and coach for men and women who desire to create lasting, exciting, love! She combines her wealth of relationship experience and

---

76   If considering a major career transition, read Michael Harris's dynamic Chapter 7 on transferring skills to create a new future.

two decades of research into powerful speaking, workshops and online courses. For more information, see Dianne's bio in *Meet The Experts.*

)19(

STOP GETTING OLD: 3 SIMPLE STEPS TO GET YOU STARTED

Elizabeth Phinney

What on earth happens to our bodies when we hit our mid 40s? It might start with menopausal symptoms (male or female), or a little soreness in the shoulder. You have to hit the snooze button more than once. Maybe it's that high school knee injury that seems to be haunting you or the actress in the television episode you watched last night, what was her name? Are you with me?

You might joke and say, *"I'm just getting old!!"* And, guess what? That's exactly what's happening. Your body and mind are aging. And although time marches unfailingly along, there is a way to take control over your body's reaction to aging.

During the last 12 years, I have worked with hundreds of men and women over the age of 45 with virtually every aging issue that could possibly arise. Without exception, every client exhibited some symptom of aging. Many were able to banish their particular issue with help and dedication and many did not. The difference between their success and failure was based on one factor and one factor alone.

Throughout the first four decades of our lives, we have a tendency to simply go along our merry way, expecting our bodies to be there and able to respond to whatever we ask of it. It always has…so why should we expect anything different? We take and take from our ever-ready body and eat what we choose to and don't take time to exercise.

Others are very active and have taken on the responsibility of not just taking from, but giving back to their bodies by eating the right foods, exercising regularly and paying attention to how their bodies react to activity and nutrition. These are the fit and active people—the thriving men and women most people envy.

For the majority of the population, the problem arises when we enter our fifth decade and the body starts to break down. Once this process starts, what we do thereafter determines our quality of life in the decades to come. Fortunately for most of us, when this deterioration begins there is something we can do to enhance our future and even erase some of the past. It truly is not too late!

As each decade passes, it gets a little more difficult, but it still is not too late. Recognize the time it has taken for you to get where you are now, and consider a 20-year plan: it's the habits of fitness we develop now that will determine the quality of our lives 20 years from now. The longer you wait to begin, the higher the risk and *the less control you have*.

You may be aware of the double-edged sword needed to defeat this aging dragon: diet and exercise. And, very possibly you have heard it all before. But it's not so much about what you have heard it's about *implementing what you have learned*. That means practicing a healthy lifestyle and recognizing the #1 responsibility you hold in your hands: giving back to your body and to yourself.

Have you ever really thought about the life you want in your 60s and 70s, even 80s? I had my youngest child at 40. When I was 45, I realized if she waited until 40 to have a child, I would be 80! That truly motivated me to get started as I want to be able to play with that baby and beyond. I want to be around when that child graduates from high school—heck, college!! And I don't want to be the old, dependent granny sitting in a wheelchair that everyone pushes around and feels like they have to include. I want to be an active participant in all of it.

So I began to research and read and learn and change. And at 60, I am in the best shape of my life. It hasn't been easy, and certainly, at times, I have been far from perfect. But is it worth it? You bet it is! I can literally do any activity I want to do, whether it's rock climbing, a 25-mile bike ride or raking out the leaves in the garden for spring-cleaning WITHOUT hurting my back! My body now gives back to me because of all the attention and respect I have been giving to it.

So what is your vision for life after 60 or 70? How active do you expect to be? Is your partner younger (or older) than you and in better shape? Are there active grandchildren in your present or future with whom you want to play and for whom you want to babysit? Do you envision some travel? Do you see yourself working into your 70s? Or, can you honestly say to yourself that you will be happy if you retire and are simply too run down to live it up?

You do have the ability to choose the quality of your life. You simply need to make the decision to **give back to your body after all these years of taking from it.**

Understanding this simple reflection on a daily basis will help to ensure your success in aging. But you also need a plan. So here are the three simple things you can do to get you started and virtually guarantee your success:

STEP 1: WRITE DOWN YOUR GOALS

Sit down and write out your vision of your life over the next 20-40 years. How will you fill your days? Will you still be driving?

Will you be able to travel? Will you be caring for your own home? Caring for yourself? BE SPECIFIC!! What do you want to be able to do ten years from now? Twenty years from now? Thirty years from now? People often laugh and think that goal-setting into their 90s is a bit over the top, but why not? If your plan works and your activity level is high, why not continue into your 90s?

My mom is my inspiration. At 90 years old, she has a multitude of friends, is on the phone every evening catching up with someone, does all her own cooking, does her exercises faithfully every day, tries to drink enough water and still enjoys shopping and lunch out with the girls. People are flabbergasted to learn how old she is because her spirit and determination are so much a part of who she is. So much of your aging is in your mind, so *go there* and create your dreams of what your life will be like in the decades to come.

STEP 2: GET HELP

Find yourself a personal trainer or wellness coach as well as a food expert. These professionals can guide you and help you set up your physical and dietary goals.[77] In order to get the proper care, it is critical the experts you choose understand aging and have experience with older adults.

Make sure the people you choose to help you are certified and insured. The most important trait trainers need to have is astute listening skills so they really hear what your goals are and what your aging issues are. They need to customize every exercise for you and your body.

Stretching is an integral part of strength training and needs to be interspersed throughout your workout. Balance and synchronized breathing are also key in enhancing your strength and flexibility. Remember that at this stage of life, flexibility is as important as strengthening.

---

77   Dr. Irina Koles has some wonderful guidelines for learning and maintaining healthy eating habits. See Chapter 20.

If personal training isn't financially viable, do your own research and create your own program. As daunting as it may sound, simply keep in mind that anything in a forward direction is better than where you are now. There are other kinds of coaches who also can help.[78, 79]

Remember, **when you give to your body, your body will respond to you in kind.** It's about giving back to your body, so whether it is food or exercise, ask yourself, *"What choice would my body want?"* I guarantee your mind and body will be able to answer you.

STEP 3: MAKE A COMMITMENT TO INVEST IN YOURSELF

It is important to realize that reversing your aging will take time, dedication and a lot of hard work on your part. The steps you need to take in creating your own anti-aging program begins with some serious self-examination. It is a personal journey where **you** are the main focus. Taking some time to enhance your health isn't selfish; it will make you even more available and productive for those you love.

Being healthy is life's greatest gift. It allows us the freedom to do whatever we choose to do each and every day. Don't forget, this is the rest of your life. So you have plenty of time! Do the best you can, but be true to that commitment—it **is** the best that you can.

When you learn to simply give back to your body and yourself, life can be yours even as you get older. Getting old doesn't have to be scary when **you** have the control. Remember, you aren't getting old, you are simply getting older. So, write your goals down, commit to them and get some help to support you along the way. You will soon find that nothing is more important than your good health and its maintenance. Because, when you have your health, you truly do have everything!

---

78   See Dr. Babs Kangas' Chapter 8 on reinvention.
79   See Suzanne Nault's Chapter 9 on retirement.

ELIZABETH PHINNEY is a Certified Personal Trainer with the American Council on Exercise. Her passion is fitness after forty-five and her mission is to inspire and teach people to take control of their aging by getting stronger and more flexible along with stopping and reversing aging issues. For more information, see Elizabeth's bio in *Meet The Experts.*

)20(

BREAK THROUGH TO YOUR HEALTHIER AND HAPPIER LIFE

Irina Koles, MD

Imagine the following email appeared in your inbox:

> *"Hi dear,*
>
> *How have you been? I haven't heard from you in a while, so I decided to drop you a line. Can't wait to share some exciting news with you.*
>
> *You know how I struggled with my weight for decades? Do you remember how we practiced one diet after another? Oh, I remember how horrible I felt at parties, where I was literally starving. I never told you then, but the truth is as soon as I'd leave the party, I'd run home and eat whatever I could find in the refrigerator. Do you think I felt better after that? If only!*

The worst part was ahead. Physical discomfort sure, but that was nothing compared to what it did to me emotionally. Huge feelings of guilt and unworthiness stressed me out. I did it AGAIN…Why? Why am I so weak? I was mad at myself and scared, because I felt hopeless. I couldn't escape from that cycle and didn't see any solution…"

Let's stop here for a moment. If you got that email today, what would you think? Would you be surprised? Would you relate?

Statistics say over 60% of adults and 17% of adolescent Americans are overweight or obese. Dieting has become an epidemic, but only 10% of people can keep their weight for at least one year. Isn't it scary? After all that struggling and deprivation, only one person out of ten is able to keep his/her weight off for more than a year.

What's wrong with us? What are we doing wrong and where do we fail?

I recently conducted a survey of people who want to lose weight. In that survey, respondents were asked to list their reasons for dieting and what kind of results they would like to achieve. The top four results people reported wanting to achieve were:

- Improve my health (71.9%),
- Feel lighter (59.4%)
- Be better looking (59.4%)
- Develop new, healthier eating habits (53.1%)

Being healthier, feeling lighter and living longer—isn't that what we all want?

The survey also showed that 87.5% of people are willing to make a commitment to eating healthy. The rest are not sure, or thinking about doing it someday, but not now.

Yep, we are good at finding excuses and procrastinating the important things in our life.

Let's face it—we like to eat and are not willing to put any effort into something we find too hard to do. So many people try dieting and, if they fail, they give up. They simply don't want to fail again. The good news is—there is a solution!

The secret is to stop paying attention to calories. In fact, don't even look carefully at the amount of ingredients on the label. Just the opposite—

Focus on things that should NOT be there.

The main thing you need to worry about is the Glycemic Index (GI) of the foods you eat—and that applies only to foods that contain carbohydrates. In simple words, the GI is the potential of each carbohydrate to increase blood sugar levels.

The higher the Glycemic Index of food, the bigger elevation in the blood sugar after consuming that food.

Since lipids and proteins do not contain carbohydrates, they do not have a Glycemic Index. To make it simple, divide all carbohydrates into two big groups:

- Carbohydrates with a low GI, or GOOD carbohydrates
- Carbohydrates with a high GI, or BAD carbohydrates

Bad carbohydrates, those that have high GI, lead to a significant increase in blood sugar and, as a result, to a significant secretion of the hormone insulin. Insulin plays the major role in regulating carbohydrate and fat metabolism. It stimulates uptake of glucose (sugar) from the blood to the cells in the body. The glucose may then be used for our energy needs, or stored as a body fat.

A high blood level of insulin is the main determinant of whether or not we accumulate fat.

In other words, we gain weight—not because we eat too much, but because we eat the wrong carbohydrates.

Basically, each of the bad carbohydrates can be assigned to one of the following:

- Sugar
- White flour
- Starch

These are the "three elephants" responsible for weight gain. Isn't it simple? We have only three ingredients to avoid or to replace with healthier ones.

However, it is not the whole picture. The majority of people fail in the long term because they focus on the nutritional part only. The missing link here is in developing the ABILITY to adjust and the WILLINGNESS to implement a new way of eating, so you LOVE it and become passionate about your new lifestyle.

I always liked inspiring messages from fortune cookies. They are so touching and wise. Many years ago, one of my messages said: *"Learn from the past, live in the present, dream of the future."* Since then it has become my motto. Ignore any piece of that puzzle and you'll restrict your way to a happier and more successful life.

It can be easily applied to each area of our life, including health and weight control.

Learn from the past:
- Evaluate your hereditary conditions, family traditions, eating habits, knowledge and beliefs;
- Analyze previous failures and achievements;
- Be open-minded and ready to relearn.

Live in the present:
- Get familiar with the Glycemic Index principals as a new way of life;
- Realize that your biggest asset is YOU; invest in yourself— your health, body, mind and spirit.

Dream of the future:
- Use the power of imagination to picture a better you;
- Trust your intuition;
- Unleash your desires to live your life fully;
- Express your feelings freely;
- Engage your subconscious mind to attract your desired life.

So now let's continue the email and see where the writer ended up...

> "It has been a year since I went through this transformation and believe me, I am literally a different person now with much better values and a fuller life. It is not about losing those 42 pounds I'd always dreamed of. It's about FEELING great!
>
> I am light and energized, people find me sexy and attractive! Isn't it cool? Between us, my intimate relationship and pleasure skyrocketed J I feel so fulfilled physically, emotionally and spiritually.
>
> I also started yoga classes, got a personal trainer and spiritual teacher[80].
>
> I finally understood where I was going wrong. I was a prisoner of my bad eating habits, unhealthy thoughts and wrong beliefs. Can you imagine that? We both believed food was the real problem, but it wasn't. The food is secondary. Our THOUGHTS are primary. I am so lucky I've got it right now!"

So, a happy ending for the writer of the email. And now it's your turn...

Every process of transformation takes time and requires a commitment. You need to reevaluate your approach to dieting, be ready to relearn and to change your Eating Blueprint, and (oh, you bet!) you need to take action.

Now, I have great news for you:

You only need to do it ONCE!

When you do it correctly and passionately, you'll achieve great results and will never have to go through the process again. You will never be starving or deprived, feeling guilty about having each extra meal, feeling unworthy and hopeless. You'll be able to savor your

---

80 For more information on the physical and spiritual pathways to wellness, read Chapter 7 by Michael Harris, Chapter 19 by Elizabeth Phinney and Chapter 16 by Tina Sacchi.

meals, to enjoy foods you declined for years and then watch your pounds drop away.

Recall the *"Learn from the past, live in the present, dream of the future"* message. Are you happy today? What lessons did you learn from your past? What kind of future you are seeing for yourself?

It is never too late. Dream BIG. The bigger you dream, the more you achieve.

Remember, it is NOT about your weight, it's about your whole LIFE!

DR. IRINA KOLES, M.D. is the author of the bestselling book, *Taste of Thoughts*™ *Improve Your Health and Whole Life,* **and the founder of** *Journey to YOUR Destiny.* **She holds a medical degree and a master's degree in Healthcare Management and is committed to helping people live happy, healthy lives. For more information, see Irina's bio in** *Meet The Experts.*

▶21◀

SURVIVIN' TO THRIVIN' THROUGH FINANCIAL DISTRESS

Lorie A. L. Nicholas, PhD

Sitting on the floor of my one bedroom apartment, surrounded by my loan documents and mortgage contract, I waited with fingers crossed hoping this time someone would help me.

I had already been through several disappointing phone calls. My heart beat with anticipation that this time the response would be positive and they would help me.

Representative: *Ms. Nicholas based on my calculations, your debt to income ratio is too high and your credit scores are very low. The only thing you qualify for are food stamps. If you go to this website, you can find a location near you for a soup kitchen so you can get a hot meal and apply for food stamps.*

Me: *But, all I want is assistance with reducing my mortgage interest rate. If I get my interest rate fixed and reduced, I will be able to pay my bills and can buy my own food. All I am asking is for assistance with lowering my interest rate.*

Representative: *Sorry Ms. Nicholas. We are unable to help you reduce your interest rate at this present time. Perhaps you can try calling back in 6 months.*

Me: *6 months? I may be in foreclosure by then or might have had to file bankruptcy or walk away from my apartment.*

Representative: *When you get to that point, maybe we might be able to help you.*

Me: *"Maybe?"*

Representative: *Yes, maybe. It is not a guarantee. I'm sorry Ms. Nicholas but we are unable to help you at this present time.*

Every call to a mortgage company, bank or credit card company ended the same way.

"I'm sorry but we are unable to help you."

Each rejection took another emotional toll on me. While the interest rates on my mortgage and credit cards increased, my self-esteem and self-confidence decreased. I was falling into a deep depression, suffering from financial stress. I felt as if everything was hopeless.

As a counselor, I had always been the one doing the helping. Now, I needed help. I was told to get food stamps, eat at soup kitchens and to stop paying my bills (which would bring my credit scores even lower and further increase my interest rates). I was sure there had to be a better way. And so I found it…

Step 1: TIME FOR A CHANGE

When people are in financial distress, it's easy to feel angry, sad, guilty, embarrassed and scared. I felt all of that and I knew I wasn't alone. I couldn't find anyone who was making an effective effort to help out families who were losing their homes. These families were losing that American Dream they had worked so hard to achieve.

I wanted to make a difference in their lives as well as mine and now it was time for a change. If you, or someone you know is in a similar situation, know you are normal! The first step to dealing with this is to make a decision to make a change. As soon as you've made that decision, move on to Step 2.

Step 2: PLAN TO THRIVE

If you are in financial distress, you can empower yourself to overcome financial hardship and go from Survin' to Thrivin' in your finances. Before reading on, write out what SUCCESS in your finances means to you. For example, when I teach financial education, some of my students view SUCCESS as being debt free, having an emergency savings set aside, being able to take a vacation fully paid, or paying for items with cash instead of a credit card. List what you want your SUCCESS to be and then, re-write your list as financial goals you would like to achieve.

For example, if you would like to have your credit cards paid off, then you would write a goal that says, "*I will have a zero balance on my credit card by December 31.*"

Research has proven that writing your dream as a goal makes it more likely to happen because it engages your mind in the process.

Step 3: HEAD FOR SUCCESS

Next, we are going to go through the 7 strategies to guide you toward achieving your goals. Think of success as an acronym. The acronym will pertain to the following words:

S=Stress
U=Understand
C=Challenge
C=Create
E=Educate
S=Self-Confidence
S=Self Determination

STRESS—According to a study by the American Psychological Association (2010) money has been cited as a significant source of stress. It is important to know when you are under stress and to recognize the physical and psychological symptoms that are connected to it. Some of the physical symptoms may include heart disease, high blood pressure, ulcers and headaches. The psychological symptoms may include: depression, sleep difficulties, anger, fatigue and anxiety.

What types of physical and psychological symptoms do you feel when you are stressed about your finances? Write them down and see how they connect with the types of financial stress you are currently experiencing.

UNDERSTAND—It is important to understand how the values and beliefs about money you may have internalized during childhood have shaped your thoughts and feelings about money today. Messages we receive about money come from a host of sources, such as parents/guardians, other family members, school, peers, television, newspapers and other media sources, music, religious/spiritual values, etc. Perhaps you heard comments like, *"Money doesn't grow on trees,"* or *"I'm just a paycheck away from being broke."*

Think of the messages you received about money and reflect on how these may have affected how you handle money today. For example, someone who was always told: *"No, we can't afford it"* might make up for that later in life by spending their money on anything they want, which may leave them with a significant amount of debt. Through financial education and with implementation of the SUCCESS strategies, that individual can learn how to change thoughts, feelings and actions as to how to handle money and reduce any financial stress.

Now it's your turn. What messages did you receive and how have they affected how you spend money ?

CHALLENGE—In order to change your financial situation, you've got to challenge yourself to change your thoughts, feelings and actions about money. Here's how:

- <u>Think</u> about the significant amount of stress you're dealing with,
- Notice how you <u>feel</u> in response to your financial stressors and
- Review the <u>actions</u> you took that brought you to the point of your financial crisis.

Then change your thoughts, feelings and actions to get you OUT of your crisis. You have the power inside you to pursue and achieve prosperity.

CREATE—To change your thoughts, feelings and actions, create positive affirmations, then recite them daily. An example of a positive affirmation (and you could have many of them) is *"I am the CEO of my finances and I manage my money successfully."*

Make a list of 10 affirmations and keep them where you can review them.

EDUCATE—There are many resources available to help with your finances. Read and attend workshops on getting out of debt and improving your finances. Speak with financial counselors. Use online resources. Do whatever you can to learn, because that is what will show you the path to freedom from debt.

SELF-CONFIDENCE—As you begin to get your finances into place, your self-confidence will improve and you will feel positive about other areas of your life as well. The confidence in yourself will be reflected in your thoughts, feelings and actions.

SELF-DETERMINATION—Your financial goals are critical in creating the future you desire to have for yourself. You can succeed despite the obstacles and barriers from the past, or even despite your current circumstances. Remember to review your financial goals from Step 2 and no matter what, do not give up!

Step 4: THRIVIN' ONWARD AND UPWARD

Now that you have the 7 strategies, it's time to create your plan of action. Imagine what your life would be like if you improved your relationship with your money and achieved financial success. Now, I challenge you to explore outside of your comfort zone as you read all the chapters in this book. Bonnie Goldstone[81] will guide you toward living an amazing life without having to win the lottery and Jennifer Rosenwald[82] will help you untangle your life so you can achieve what you want.

As discussed earlier, financial stress can impact your health. My co-authors Elizabeth Phinney will provide some strengthening and breathing techniques to help stop the physical aspects of aging without drugs, while Dr. Irina Koles will teach you how to eat right to maintain good health[83].

Maintenance of health and wealth can lead to an optimal life. As you learn to free yourself from financial stress and take care of your body, remember to laugh and have fun and let my co-author Jeffrey Kurtz[84] teach you how to put the element of fun back into your life.

I challenge you to make a commitment to change your financial future and develop a healthy relationship with your money by starting today with the 7 quick action strategies for $.U.C.C.E.S.S . Take action and complete a tip of success each day and within 7 days you will have moved from simply Survivin' To Thrivin' Through Financial Stress.

LORIE A. L. NICHOLAS, PHD is known as the Financial Recovery Doctor. She is CEO of Dream Builders United, an organization designed to help individuals and families overcome financial hardship, recover from debt and achieve financial freedom. For more information, see Lorie's bio in *Meet The Experts*.

---

81 See Chapter 15.
82 See Chapter 12.
83 See Chapters 19 and 20.
84 See Chapter 11.

›22‹

DIE WITHOUT REGRETS

M. Kris Landry, MRE

As the hospice chaplain, I visited Ann many times. At first, when I would ask her how she was doing, she would greet me with a big smile and tell me she was doing *just great*. She answered me this way for some time until one day, when I entered her room, I found her crying. Family and friends had just been to see her, but she seemed sad instead of happy after their visit.

"Ann," I asked, "*what seems to be the matter?*"

"*Sometimes it just seems so hard to keep smiling when I'm really crying inside,*" she told me.

I offered that she might want to share her real feelings with her family and friends the next time they came to see her.

With tears streaming down her beautiful face, she told me, "*Oh no Kris, I couldn't do that, because then they would feel sad, too.*"

In the days that followed, I met with Ann's family and friends and asked them how their visits with Ann were going. They were able to tell me that it had become really hard to stay "upbeat" because they'd been visiting her for so long and knew she would not be coming home to them.

Ann was a thirty-eight-year-old breast cancer patient who had been living on the hospice unit for more than six months. They felt it was their obligation to be cheerful, otherwise Ann would feel sad.

It seemed to me no one was able to say how he or she was truly feeling. So during my next visit with Ann, I asked her if she would like to share her story and write to the people she loved in a way that would express how she felt about them. In this way, she could leave them something from her heart, while telling them how much they meant to her. To my surprise, her face lit up!

"*I'd love to do that Kris, but I can't write anymore.*" The solution was simple: I offered to write down the messages she wanted to share.

Anne became excited about this very real act of living. For weeks, during our visits, Ann would give me names of friends and family she wanted to write to. She would dictate to me her thoughts and make revisions along the way. She would tell me,

"*Oh, that's what I've always wanted to tell [her or him].*"

And, she would thank me for the chance to share her feelings.

The day came when her "story" was complete and I told her I would type it up and give it to her family when the time came of her passing. With great authority, she told me,

"*Oh no, Kris. I don't want my family and friends to wait to know how I feel about them, I want to read this to them now!*"

Wow! This really surprised me because Ann had been so afraid to say how she felt just a few short weeks before. Yet now she was saying that she actually wanted to read her feelings out loud. And…she wanted me to invite all of the people on her list to the hospital so she could read her thoughts with everyone she cared about surrounding her. I told her I would see what I could do.

I brought this news to the nursing staff and it was met with amazement and real joy. They told me they felt Ann had been using all of her strength to bolster everyone's feelings and as a result, her own feelings had been neglected. One nurse shared with me,

"This writing project has allowed Ann to be who she really is: a courageous woman on an amazing journey. By telling her story, her spirit seems to have been lifted and she has lifted ours too."

We made arrangements for Ann's family and friends to meet in an unoccupied laundry room. When I told them what Ann wanted to do, many of them seemed scared.

"What does she want to say to me?"

"What am I supposed to do?"

"What will I say to her?"

"I feel like crying already!"

These were just a few of the responses I received.

The nurses were scared, too. For days, they would whisper to me,

"Can Ann really handle this?"

"Is this too much for her family?"

"What are WE supposed to do?"

Their nerves were spilling out everywhere. Even I was a little nervous. None of us had been part of a gathering like this before.

The one who kept smiling with anticipation, however, was Ann.

"Oh Kris, I can hardly wait for everyone to come. Do you think we could have a few treats for people after I speak?"

The day finally arrived. People were streaming down the corridor—each one looking more afraid than the last. We entered the tiny laundry room where all the supplies had been pushed against the walls. I wheeled Ann into the center of the room, and we encircled her.

With the brightest smile you can imagine, she sat there with her written story in her hands and began speaking to the first person on her list. She didn't get very far before we all burst into tears, including the staff.

Ann was magnificent as she went from person to person, sharing her love for each and expressing gratitude for all the time and effort they had given her while she was in the hospital. Anne made it clear how important they each were in her life.

Ann's story of love and courage made a difference to every person who was in the room that day, including me.

The lesson I learned is one we all need to know:

Many people do, indeed, die with their stories inside them, including their secrets and regrets.

Along the way, I've met many people *dying to tell me their stories* before it was too late. This set in motion a mission in me to spread the word that *you don't need to be dying in order to tell your story.*

How does this play out in your life?

Start where you are in telling your story, and then help someone else tell his or her story.

For many, telling one's story happens in retirement—and many authors—who are also coaches and mentors—work to facilitate this development. Dr. Babs Kangas[85] coaches people over fifty on how to reinvent their lives. In order to know what they want to change, she believes they have to know their stories. Janet Swift[86] helps her clients recognize the events that shaped their lives—the stories they hold that inform them about their values and aspirations.

Suzanne Nault[87] helps retirees in transition never to retire from life. One of Suzanne's messages is that the gift of retirement may well be the first time a person can finally stop and reflect. She believes it's a perfect time to share one's story, because doing so brings purpose. *I couldn't agree more.*

3 Steps to Help Someone Tell His or Her Story

If you are helping someone else tell his or her story, you may begin by asking a parent, grandparent, or loved one to share. Here's how:

85 See Chapter 8.
86 See Chapter 14.
87 See Chapter 9.

Step 1: An easy beginning would be to ask about his/her parents.

Step 2: Offer to write or record his/her story—allowing this person to share more freely.

Step 3: Invite him/her to share the story with family and friends. What you end up with is a reminder of a precious life.

Several months after Ann shared her story in that tiny laundry room with all of us surrounding her, she died. At the ceremony of the celebration of her life, I was greeted by Ann's family and friends.

With tears streaming down their smiling faces, they shared that Ann telling her story before she died was deeply meaningful and that the memory of her joy at being able to tell them how she felt had moved them deeply. It was an experience they would never forget.

I invite you to spend time with your loved ones and begin a conversation that allows their stories to be heard. It is never too late to share the untold stories inside of them.

And if the untold story is yours, then get started. What are you waiting for?

M. Kris Landry, MRE, is a speaker, singer/songwriter, counselor, and former hospice chaplain who encourages people to help their loved ones share their stories before it's too late. For more information, see Kris' bio in *Meet The Experts.*

Congratulations! You've finished reading.
So now what?
So much information…
Where do you begin?
First, turn the page and "Meet The Experts."
Get to know the very real people who have
shared their hearts and strategies with you.
Then, go back to the beginning
of this book and start again!
Begin with the Preface and review
the 6 critical questions for your success.
Then, one by one, review each
chapter and gradually incorporate
the Expert Success Solution into your life.
Remember:
success only comes with implementation.
So start now…and don't ever stop
until you have everything you truly
want—in your business and your life.

MEET THE EXPERTS

Wendy Lipton-Dibner, MA

WENDY LIPTON-DIBNER, MA is a two-time bestselling author and internationally recognized authority in the psychosocial factors that move people to action. President of Professional Impact, Inc. and founder of the highly acclaimed *Move People To Action System for Experts, Executives and Entrepreneurs*™, Wendy has built 10 successful businesses serving every industry from healthcare to hair care.

A highly respected keynote speaker, Wendy has addressed the U.S. Senate and delivered thousands of high-impact programs for healthcare, Fortune 500, non-profit and entrepreneurial audiences. She serves as a trusted advisor, trainer and master-level speaking coach for top influencers worldwide.

Wendy is known for pulling back the curtains on her own career to reveal proven success formulas that enable her clients to grow their businesses by focusing on making an impact. More than a teacher, Wendy walks her talk. She's touched millions of lives, helping people get solid results through her bestselling books, live seminars, online training programs, media appearances and speaking engagements.

When Wendy speaks, people change…and that means impact – for your business and your life.

Connect with Wendy and get free weekly tips to increase your impact at

www.MovePeopletoAction.com and www.Pro-Impact.com.

Rick Frishman

RICK FRISHMAN, publisher at Morgan James Publishing in New York and founder of Planned Television Arts (now called Media Connect), has been one of the leading book publicists in America for over 35 years. He's helped bestselling authors such as Mitch Albom, Bill Moyers, Stephen King, Caroline Kennedy, Howard Stern, President Jimmy Carter, Mark Victor Hansen, Nelson DeMille, John Grisham, Hugh Downs, Henry Kissinger, Jack Canfield, Alan Deshowitz, Arnold Palmer, and Harvey Mackay.

Rick has also appeared on hundreds of radio shows and more than a dozen TV shows nationwide, including *Oprah* and Bloomberg TV. He's been featured in the *New York Times, Wall Street Journal, Associated Press, Selling Power Magazine, New York Post,* and scores of other publications and has appeared on stage with notables such as The Dalai Lama, Sir Richard Branson, T. Harv Eker, Jack Canfield, Mark Victor Hansen, Tony Hsieh, David Bach, Brian Tracy, and Brendon Burchard.

Rick has co-authored 13 books, including national bestsellers *Guerrilla Publicity, Networking Magic, Where's Your Wow, Guerrilla Marketing for Writers* and his recent release, *The 250 Rules of Business.*

Rick is a sought-after lecturer on publishing and public relations and a member of PRSA and the National Speakers Association. He and his wife Robbi live in New York with their two Havanese puppies, Cody and Cooper. They have three children: Adam, Rachel, and Stephanie.

Go to www.RickFrishman.com for more information and get Rick's Million Dollar Rolodex.

Patty Soffer

"Business is personal," says seasoned strategist, author and partnership expert **PATTY SOFFER**, *"and companies that don't operate that way have little chance of enduring."*

A 30-year veteran of the strategy, branding and design world, Soffer went from a long career as a New York model to co-creating a successful branding agency recognized by *Entrepreneur Magazine* as one of the nation's Top 500 Small Businesses. Then her business partnership exploded, destroying her self-esteem, health, income, friendships, confidence, support system and, finally, the business itself. After a long break, much soul searching and training with the business world's best minds and hearts, Soffer realized their demise was caused by putting the business before the partnership, which created the deadly-yet-avoidable Partnersh*t.

Soffer's mission is to prevent Partnersh*t from crushing others. A business strategist and partnership expert, she works with new, established, family and stalemated small business co-owners on developing partnership and business strategies for maximum stability, happiness and financial reward. She spreads her mantra of *People, then Business* via speaking, teaching and coaching, and has written two important books on the subject: Partnership or Partnersh*t: You Decide and The Workbook.

For more information, visit Patty at
www.AHumanFoundation.com

Lisa Gibson, JD

LISA GIBSON, JD is an attorney, internationally acclaimed conflict and forgiveness expert, mediator, and certified trainer in managing workplace conflict. She is an award winning and best selling author of "Life In Death: A Journey From Terrorism To Triumph" and "Releasing The Chains: Timeless Wisdom On How To Forgive Anyone For Anything" and the audio series "Learning To Forgive: Your Pathway To Inner Peace."

Lisa lost her brother in the 1988 terrorist bombing of Pan Am flight 103 over Lockerbie, Scotland. Rather than succumbing to bitterness, she met with and forgave former Libyan leader Muammar Gaddafi, the mastermind behind that terrorist attack. Because of Lisa's personal experience, she now specializes in cross-cultural conflict resolution and has trained thousands of government, business, healthcare and nonprofit leaders in conflict-ridden countries in how to forgive and resolve conflicts more effectively. She has been featured in such media outlets as CNN, ABC, NBC, CBS, FOX, BBC, MSNC, Wall Street Journal, USA Today, New York Times, and countless others.

In 2013 Lisa was given the distinguished honor of being chosen as an "Exemplar Of Love And Forgiveness In Governance" by Fetzer Institute and the School For Conflict Analysis And Resolution" and in 2010 was chosen as one of Ten Outstanding Young Americans by the US Junior Chamber of Commerce.

Visit www.ConflictCoach.biz/freetraining/
to download your free audio training.

Dr. Cheryl Lentz, DM, MSIR

DR. CHERYL LENTZ, DM, MSIR, is the multi award winning publisher of the internationally acclaimed series, *The Refractive Thinker*- a collaboration of more than 80 contributing doctoral scholars from around the world. As President of The Lentz Leadership Institute, she is dedicated to publishing exceptional dissertation research.

Cheryl is also a 16-time award winning author known globally for her writings as an authority on leadership, critical and refractive thinking, as well as an educator integrating emerging technology as part of her teachings in her ground breaking book: *Technology That Tutors: 7 Ways to Save Time Using the Blog as a Teaching Tool.*

As an accomplished university professor, speaker, editor, and consultant, she is a highly sought after expert in teaching thousands to apply critical thinking skills to problem solve in record time.

Join Dr. Cheryl as she offers proven strategies to shorten your learning curve to think beyond limits when facing problems in your personal and professional settings.

Learn to fail faster to succeed sooner using proven skills to move you forward more effectively through individual coaching, Tele Seminars, and online classes using *The WRIST Method.*

Invite Dr. Cheryl to make an impact at your next event!

Visit www.ThinkingBeyondLimits.com for more information.

Donald Burns

Since 2008, **DONALD BURNS** has served as an Executive Career Coach, helping hundreds of people transition into better jobs and more fulfilling careers.

Right after high school he joined the Army, served in Asia, and later earned advanced degrees in electrical engineering.

Burns advanced through engineering and sales management at Motorola during the 1980s.

In 1991 he graduated from the School of Journalism at Columbia University and launched his new career—copywriting and technology reporting.

Later in the 1990s he was based in Samsung Corporation's HQ in Seoul, Korea and produced multimedia advertising.

Then in 2008, Burns responded to the call of senior executives who were suddenly displaced by the great crash. He adapted his advertising and copy writing tactics and produced unusually persuasive "leadership briefs" that broke the rules and opened doors for displaced executives and Ivy League MBAs who had never needed to market themselves. By 2011 he had become the sought-after career coach in a wide range of industries.

"*I'm the poster child for job changers,*" Burns says. "*I've enjoyed each of my five careers, but wasted too much time on each transition. I learned by trial-and-error, but you need not do that. Just tell me where you want to go, and I'll show you the shortcuts!*"

Get Donald's free weekly videos to enhance your career at www.CareerDefenseTV.com

Michael Harris

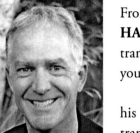

From the moment you meet **MICHAEL HARRIS** you'll know he is unlike any transformation expert or business coach you've ever met.

His insights and experience have helped his clients through personal and professional transitions.

Michael helps his clients realize they have everything they need to live life with complete fulfillment. His unique background includes financing and small business ownership and he is considered an expert in yoga.

Michael has coached thousands of individuals and small business owners to live life without the constraints of pre-conceived limitations. He has the unique ability to zero in on how you can create the life you want to live.

In addition to personal and business coaching, Michael is a #1 bestselling author and radio host. He has been interviewed by a broad range of media, including NBC, NPR, BBC, The Los Angeles and others.

Michael is driven by an incredible enthusiasm for living life to the fullest. In his spare time he loves to hike in the mountains near his home in Central Oregon.

Visit Michael at www.InnovativeReinvention.com

Dr. Babs Kangas, PhD

BABS KANGAS, MS, MA, PhD., Doctor of Psychology, is founder of Free, Fun and Fabulous, a program designed to help men and women over fifty create the life they love. Dr. Babs, an expert in motivation, personal change and positive psychology uses her own experience, professional research, coaching work and interviews with hundreds of individuals to create a highly effective reinvention process. Through coaching, speaking and writing, Dr. Babs helps her clients determine what they want to change, develop an action plan and use proactive strategies to create the life of their dreams.

After a difficult move from Kansas to the New York City area and a challenging mid-life divorce, Dr. Babs began her own reinvention immersing herself in graduate study. These experiences inspired her to create an individualized process to help others short-circuit the challenges she faced and create their own unique free, fun and fabulous life.

She loves to see that spark of insight as her clients gain clarity and motivation to move forward and is committed to helping them realize that positive change is possible at any age. She helps her clients know it's never too late to discover the best life for you and enjoy it, because every moment is precious.

**For more information and to receive
your free quick start e-book,
visit www.FreeFunAndFabulous.com.**

Suzanne Nault, MPs, PCC

Photo by Cpivrette/Ottawa
www.couvrette-photography.on.ca

SUZANNE NAULT, MPs PCC, is a licensed psychologist and certified professional coach with New Ventures West and the International Coach Federation. She is also the co-founder of Profound You, an international training and human development company.

Suzanne is a sought-after speaker and coach on psychological and lifestyle issues related to retirement. When asked why retirement, Suzanne answers "*I love this stage of life where people are more in touch with their being rather than doing—getting in touch with who they are.*"

Suzanne has conducted over 1500 seminars and helped over 10,000 executives and employees design the next chapter in their lives. She is a regular guest speaker with the Canadian Forces where she addresses specific issues military personnel encounters in retirement.

Here's what some participants say about Suzanne:

"*Very dynamic, fun and incredibly thought provoking—the help we need making retirement decisions.*"

"Excellent presenter—really engaging. Her presentation and theory was thorough and well organized. I doubt you would be able to find anyone better! !"

"*Very good in touching an array of topics; the fact that I am now thinking of areas that I previously did not cause me to pause, which reflects the quality of her presentation.*"

Suzanne is fluent in both French and English.

For more information, visit www.ProfoundYou.com.

Randy Stanbury

RANDY STANBURY, entrepreneur, author, speaker, life and business coach and founder of 'Big Bold Ambitions' has created a well-defined and easy to follow program to achieving any big dreams, bold goals and deep desires.

Randy's fascination with achieving the "impossible" has led to a lifelong quest of mastering the principles of achieving any 'Big Bold Ambitions'.

His purpose and passion is sharing with the world what he's discovered, along with his own experiences of achieving the Big, Bold and Ambitious. His 18 years as an entrepreneur, currently running 2 successful businesses, a high level peer group and life long study has given him the expertise and tools required to create such a cool, powerful, exciting, and fun program.

Randy knows and has proven over and over that within us all is the ability to achieve anything we desire. This ability must be tapped and unleashed. Once tapped, you will find yourself heading for fulfillment, desiring more for your life and others.

Join Randy on his mission to change the world through the accomplishment of your own 'Big Bold Ambitions'.

"There is nothing more exciting and fun than accomplishing what others call impossible! :)"

Go to BigBoldAmbitions.com to get tapped in and unleashed.

Jeffrey Kurtz

JEFFREY KURTZ is an author, speaker, Certified Health Coach and Certified Emotional Freedom Technique (EFT) Practitioner. He has been a stage actor for over two decades, and has over 10 years of experience in web and mobile technologies, currently serving as a Product Manager for Google.

In his early 20s, Jeffrey found himself bored, unhappy, unfulfilled, anxious, and stuck in jobs and relationships that he hated. He was barely having any fun in his life, and he knew something had to change. He finally said, *"enough is enough,"* and spent the next few years studying the latest research in the psychology and neuroscience of happiness, creativity and play.

As an actor, and later a director, he learned about the value of play. But it wasn't until he experienced immense challenges in his life that he learned how to turn play into a powerful healing tool.

Jeffrey is now dedicated to helping people feel happier, healthier and more truly alive through the use of structured play. With his company, A Better Perfect, he teaches clients how in just minutes a day, they can re-experience the joy, presence and freedom they had as children, in their every day adult lives. Jeffrey has a BA in Theater Arts from Brown University and currently resides in New York City.

Visit Jeffrey at www.ABetterPerfect.com

Jennifer Rosenwald

JENNIFER ROSENWALD is dedicated to your having The Good Life: the experience, not just the stuff. Her practical tools, tips and tactics have helped hundreds of clients, employees, and even unsuspecting strangers get what they want: less stress, anger, and/or worry and better quality of life while they work to achieve their goals. Better results and a better experience of those results.

A former Fortune 500 Managing Director and award-winning trainer, Jennifer is now a business/life coach, author and speaker. Being appointed to Fortune magazine's "100 Best Companies to Work for" selection committee, and then later researching the science behind those accomplishments, taught her that a healthy, happy, charitable perspective drives success, no matter what you're doing.

Indeed "*Happiness first, success follows*" is now Jennifer's charge. She teaches the how-to of right-thinking and other mood-wrangling perspectives, saving busy, productive men and women time, money, and professional and personal relationships. She uses, as one client called it, an "*uncanny ability to understand people*" to personalize and make the learning enjoyable.

Will Rogers said, "*Just because it's common sense doesn't mean it's common practice*". So as researcher, reporter and results-maker, Jennifer teaches and helps people practice the how-to of managing their minds in order to have success *and* satisfaction.

Visit Jennifer at www.JenniferRosenwald.com.

Dr. Lupe-Rebeka Samaniego PhD

LUPE-REBEKA SAMANIEGO, PhD, licensed Clinical Psychologist, inspires individuals daily to transform their lives. She is an expert in human development and traumatic stress.

For over three decades, Lupe has influenced individuals to create meaningful connections, live with inner calm and vitality, and make a difference in their lives through her clinical practice. Her passion led to the creation of Colorado Center for High Performance Living where she guides professionals, through her workshops on Life-Auditing for High Performance Living™ with skills leading to a life of vitality, inner calm, and meaning.

A sought after psychotherapist/psychoanalyst, speaker and mentor, Lupe integrates brain science within a developmental framework and influences individuals daily to deepen compassion and empathy. In addition, Lupe is a Certified High Performance Coach, has extensive teaching experience, authored articles on topics related to loss and trauma, and received awards for her contributions in teaching and service.

To honor her and continue her legacy, the Graduate School of Professional Psychology at the University of Denver, Denver, Colorado, created the Lupe-Rebeka Samaniego, PhD endowed scholarship fund that benefits future generations of psychologists.

**Visit www.DrSamaniego.com and
www.ColoradoCenterforHighPerformanceLiving.**

Janet Swift

For 50 years, **JANET SWIFT** accumulated every experience life could offer, seeking fulfillment through careers from nursing, police officer, 20+ years in the corporate world and finally, as a successful business owner.

Despite her success, she felt a burning sense of underachievement. Recognizing her latent potential but still believing it wasn't safe to shine her light, she allowed her childhood decision to 'play small' to inform her next five decades, until life's hobnail boot startled her awake.

Janet's unique early life experience set her apart and the bright, intelligent expression of her truth was dimmed to survive as a seven-year-old child at boarding school. Raised in Bahrain, Malta and Germany, she's ensured her children are global citizens, encouraging them to pursue their dreams.

Now a writer and Reiki practitioner, Janet shares her extensive knowledge and experience with her clients. She enables clients from all walks of life to identify the events that have changed and shaped their choices.

Janet offers workshops, talks and books designed to captivate, inspire and encourage everyone to live their life on purpose and express their truth and asks all her audiences:

Are you living your dream or someone else's?

Visit Janet at www.LifeChangingCafe.com.

Bonnie Goldstone, CHT, NLP

 **BONNIE GOLDSTONE, CHT, NLP**, founder of Stingray Hypnosis Consultants International, Extraordinary Hypnotherapy and the online community, "I Love My Journey" is a sought-after, leading-edge therapist. A Board Certified Hypnotherapist, NLP Master Practitioner, Reiki Master and intuitive healer, Bonnie empowers her clients to live fuller and happier lives.

One of Bonnie's greatest joys is helping couples resolve unexplained fertility issues so they can enjoy calm pregnancies, peaceful births and their journey as new parents. Men and women seek Bonnie's expertise to resolve a wide variety of life-disrupting issues, including reduction of anxiety and stress, difficulty losing weight, sleep disturbance, post- surgery healing, phobias and PTSD.

Bonnie believes everyone deserves the chance to love their life journey. So when her husband retired from the Royal Canadian Mounted Police, they stepped outside their comfort zone and moved their family of six to Costa Rica, Grand Cayman and finally the British Virgin Islands. After 15 years abroad and another 5 years sailing the beautiful Caribbean waters aboard Privelege Catamarin, Bonnie is back on the mainland, inspired to touch the lives of others with her message that dreams do come true. She is motivated and committed to help others get out of their own way and live the life they dream of so they can wake up every morning and say, "I love my journey!"

**To learn more about Bonnie and
her programs visit her website at
www.ILoveMyJourney.com**

Tina Sacchi

TINA SACCHI is one of the nation's foremost Holistic & Spiritual leaders. Bestselling author of *My Spirit Is Not Religious: A Guide to Living YOUR Authentic Life*, Tina is the creator of some bestseller series of highly successful meditation and hypnotherapy audio programs and hosted an international radio show: *Living A Spiritual Life with Tina Sacchi*

Tina's passion is helping people recognize and utilize their innate ability to self-heal on all four levels: spiritually, physically, mentally, and emotionally.

In her position as a spiritual leader, Tina uses fun, loving, motivating, and highly effective alternative healing techniques to help her clients release, resolve and heal limiting beliefs, behaviors and patterns that no longer serve them.

Through her loving and caring guidance, Tina shows people how to find their inner truth, live their authentic life and make their transition to their own spiritual calling. As a result, her clients are living a spiritually open and authentic life.

Tina's practice offers intuitively guided private sessions, group workshops, classes, and retreats worldwide.

For free meditation downloads, tools, tips and to implement the OPEN formula and be part of Tina Sacchi's global spiritual community, visit her website at www.TinaSacchi.com.

BJ Rosenfeld, MA, MS, COGS

BJ ROSENFELD, MA, MS, COGS, Certificate of Advanced Graduate Study in Educational Administration is founder of No Matter What Parenting, the simple solution for parents of adult children. Through speaking, coaching and writing, BJ helps parents relieve stress and get the relationship they want with their adult children.

BJ's decision to help parents develop unshakable relationships with their adult children came as the result of a very difficult experience in her own family. Before she discovered the secret to staying connected, she almost lost her adult son. Through trial and error, she found the strategies that worked and then made a commitment to share her tips with parents worldwide. It all begins with three critical questions.

From her early career as a teacher of French, Spanish and reading, BJ has spent her life fostering the communication skills sorely needed in interpersonal relationships.

She has proven over and over that it is possible for parents to get the relationship they want with their adult children.

When children choose a different way of life than their parents, families have to work to stay together. How far should a mother cross the line to save the love of her children?

BJ's memoir *The Chameleon in the Closet* is a humorous yet touching tribute to all parents who support their children's life-changing choices. Her passion and purpose lie in helping parents do whatever it takes to get their adult kids to love and include them no matter what—because life is too short to lose the connection.

Go to www.NoMatterWhatParenting.com for more information.

Dianne Flemington

DIANNE FLEMINGTON is a relationship trainer and coach to men and women who desire to learn the skills to create lasting, exciting, love!

At the age of 16, Dianne found herself in the middle of her parents frustrating and contemptuous relationship. She was their mediator, confidante and untrained counselor.

Later finding herself without the skills and unsuccessful in developing her own adult relationships, Dianne sought help. She researched and studied relationship systems and self-development for two decades and became a trained life coach, organization and relationship systems coach and psychometric tools facilitator.

Dianne is the founder of RemarkableLove.com, a membership-based website that provides an array of relationship building skills, tools, information, psychometric testing and coaching options to empower individuals in relationships. She is also a couples workshop facilitator, speaker and trainer to youths and corporate organizations who recognize the importance of learning the fundamentals of relationship building to create a strong, sustainable and valuable future.

Dianne's ability to keep the education process fun, listen deeply, communicate clearly and ask powerful questions empowers people to move forward building successful relationships of their own.

**To learn more about Dianne and her products, workshops
or to contact her, please visit: www.dianneflemington.com.**

Elizabeth Phinney

ELIZABETH PHINNEY is a Certified Personal Trainer with the American Council on Exercise. She also holds a certificate from the American Senior Fitness Association and is an affiliate of The American College of Sports Medicine. She has been named Top Female Executive with Worldwide Who's Who and VIP of the year in Health and Fitness for 2013.

Elizabeth's passion is fitness after forty-five and her mission is to inspire people to plan their Physical retirement as they plan their Fiscal retirement. Her caring and compassionate fitness advice is customized for each individual and her positive instructive manner motivates her clients to succeed in controlling their own aging.

Over the last 13 years, she has been developing and fine tuning several fitness techniques and theories that are successfully practiced. Not only has she helped hundreds of people get stronger and more flexible, she has helped them slow down, stop and reverse aging issues that they had been plagued with for years.

Her flagship product is BodSpir™, a meditative strength training technique she created and has taught thousands of times in her classes and one-on-one private training. Other programs include the Get F.I.T. Workshop (Fitness Inspiration Transformation) and My Own C.A.R.E. Package (Consultation, Assessment, Recommendation based on an Evaluation.)

Visit www.ElizabethPhinney.com for further information.

Dr. Irina Koles, MD

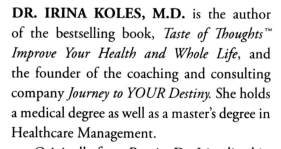

DR. IRINA KOLES, M.D. is the author of the bestselling book, *Taste of Thoughts*™ *Improve Your Health and Whole Life*, and the founder of the coaching and consulting company *Journey to YOUR Destiny*. She holds a medical degree as well as a master's degree in Healthcare Management.

Originally from Russia, Dr. Irina lived in Israel where she practiced as a primary care physician. Today she lives in Boston, MA, where she helps people get healthy by recognizing the secret is to "*count thoughts, not calories*." She helps her clients develop a new eating blueprint so they can enjoy their healthy lifestyle.

Dr. Irina has helped hundreds of people internationally to achieve and maintain their desired weight in a healthy way. Her approach is based on the Glycemic Index of foods, which allows people to normalize blood sugar, cholesterol and triglycerides levels and get slim and stay slim—all the while enjoying delicious foods and culinary adventures.

She is the creator of the weight loss and life coaching programs: *Taste of Thoughts*™ '*Choose Your Weight*' *Workshops* and *Taste of Thoughts*™ *Cooking Classes*.

Dr. Irina is passionate about serving her clients and taking them to a higher level of healthier and happier life. After two immigrations and absorbing new cultures, she is a great example of courage and life wisdom.

Dr. Irina lives with her son Roman and lovely cat Supik. She speaks English, Russian and Hebrew, and loves connecting with people.

Reach out to Dr. Irina at www.WeightDestiny.com

Dr. Lorie A. L. Nicholas, PhD

DR. LORIE A. L. NICHOLAS, PHD is known as the Financial Recovery Doctor. She is CEO of Dream Builders United, an organization designed to help individuals and families overcome financial hardship, recover from debt and achieve financial freedom.

Dr. Nicholas has counseled hundreds of families. The primary factor that always stood out throughout her work was the problem families had as they struggled with managing their finances, often falling into debt.

As a contributing author in *The Law of Business Attraction* and *The Success Secret* with Jack Canfield, Dr. Nicholas' interest in providing financial education came as a result of wanting to help improve the lives of her clients and was compounded by her own personal experience when she fell victim to the subprime economic crisis. She is committed to making a difference in the lives of the people she touches.

As the Financial Recovery Doctor, Dr. Nicholas is on a mission to make a significant difference in people's lives through financial education so as to prevent or reduce financial stress and financial hardship. Her goal is to help people improve their relationship with money so they can overcome debt and develop effective strategies for managing money, while building a legacy of financial freedom for themselves and their families.

Visit Dr. Nicholas at www.TheFinancialRecoveryDoctor.com

M. Kris Landry, MRE

M. KRIS LANDRY, MRE, is an author, speaker, singer/songwriter, counselor, and former hospice chaplain who encourages people to share their stories before it's too late.

Weaving story with song in all her presentations, Kris shares the heart-opening experiences and untold story she found within while working as a hospice chaplain.

Kris's words and music harmonize her invitation to look within one's heart for the sometimes-secret story that creates the tapestry of life and brings meaning and purpose to one's sacred journey. As Kris states, "*Inviting people to share their stories before dying made me realize that people of all ages have stories they are dying to tell.*"

Kris believes there is a silent generation of people waiting to be asked to share their stories—and it's her mission to help their voices be heard.

In addition to conducting speaking engagements, Kris works with young people to help them connect with elders in assisted living centers. She helps youth to invite seniors to share their untold wisdom stories, creating compassion and connection in the communities she serves.

"*When someone shares their story with you, they give you something...a gift to hold in your heart,*" states Kris. "*Therefore, the story never ends.*"

Contact Kris at: www.TheStoryNeverEnds.com

CONNECT WITH THE EXPERTS!

Join us on our Facebook page and get ongoing success tips from our experts!

👍 Like

**The
Expert Success
Solution**

We look forward to meeting you in our Facebook Community!

GET HELP FROM THE EXPERTS!

Bring *The Expert Success Solution* Right to Your Door!

Wendy Lipton-Dibner, MA .... MovePeopleToAction.com
Rick Frishman .... RickFrishman.com
Patty Soffer .... AHumanFoundation.com
Lisa Gibson, JD .... ConflictCoach.biz
Cheryl Lentz, DM .... ThinkingBeyondLimits.com
Donald Burns .... CareerDefenseTV.com
Michael Harris .... InnovativeReinvention.com
Babs Kangas, PhD .... FreeFunAndFabulous.com
Suzanne Nault, MPs, PCC .... ProfoundYou.com
Randy Stanbury .... BigBoldAmbitions.com
Jeffrey Kurtz .... ABetterPerfect.com
Jennifer Rosenwald ....JenniferRosenwald.com

Continued

Lupe-Rebeka Samaniego, PhD........................... DrSamaniego.com

Janet Swift... LifeChangingCafe.com

Bonnie Goldstone, CHT, NLP ....ILoveMyJourney.com

Tina Sacchi.. TinaSacchi.com

BJ Rosenfeld....................................NoMatterWhatParenting.com

Dianne Flemington .... DianneFlemington.com

Elizabeth Phinney..ElizabethPhinney.com

Irina Koles, MD ....WeightDestiny.com

Lorie A. L. Nicholas, PhD ....TheFinancialRecoveryDoctor.com

M. Kris Landry, MRE ....TheStoryNeverEnds.com

Woman
to
Woman

Woman
to
Woman

1,000 Conversation Starters for
Talking about Anything

Kim Chamberlain

Skyhorse Publishing

CONTENTS

Introduction vii

Using the book 1

- How the book is organized 1
- A note on choosing conversation starters 2
- Suggestions for using the conversation starters 3

Speaking skills 5

- Understanding conversation levels 6
- Communication behaviors 10
- It's not *just* what you say; it's how you say it 12
- Deeper meanings 15
- How to avoid rambling 17
- Using a framework to structure your speaking 18

1,000 Questions and Conversation Starters 21

INTRODUCTION

Why a conversation starters book specifically for women?

Within a short space of time women's conversation can cover many and varied topics and may include much laughter, intelligent observations on life, and a sharing of innermost thoughts.

While conversation in mixed company isn't always different, there are certainly times when the conversation's tone, the topics covered, and the depth of sharing is different in all-female company. Some topics are those that women would feel comfortable only discussing with other women in an empathetic, supportive, and non-threatening environment.

Although many conversation starters in the book can be used with both males and females, there are also many that are intended specifically for women, such as talking about your body, puberty, pregnancy, women and work, beauty, and other women.

This book is aimed primarily at situations where women are together having a conversation with other women, and builds on this situation by providing a wide range of questions and conversation starters that offer a great way to stimulate many types of discussion. Some topics may be ones that you regularly talk about, some may offer a new slant on a familiar topic, some may be ones you have wanted to talk about but have been uncomfortable about broaching, and others may be ones you hadn't thought about. All will most likely lead you into other conversation topics.

The book also touches on situations where you would use general conversation starters when you are out meeting people, say at a party or network event. A number of conversation starters, tips and techniques cover these issues.

A very easy book to dip into, *Woman to Woman* is suitable for adults and contains conversation starter topics that are thought-provoking, entertaining, controversial, factual, amusing, ridiculous, risqué, intellectual, and intimate. They provide the opportunity for fun, laughter, a way to learn new things, new ways of looking at issues, a chance to be listened to, a chance to work out what your thoughts are on a topic, a way to air issues you'd like to talk about, and an opportunity to discuss serious topics. They may allow you to open up new areas of discussion; perhaps discuss a subject you haven't been able to talk about before. You may be able to talk about issues you can't talk about with your partner or members of the opposite sex, along with the opportunity to develop your communication and thinking skills, and especially the chance to build a deeper level of connection and intimacy with others.

Speaking skills

Along with the hundreds of conversation starters, this book also offers insights into speaking skills, along with many tips and techniques incorporated throughout.

One of the ways to increase your speaking skills is first to become aware of speaking techniques. You may not, for example, have given any thought to issues concerning supportive feedback, interrupting, swearing, paraphrasing, how to avoid rambling, or different types of listening. Once you become aware of them and the factors involved, you then have a choice as to if and how you would like to develop your skills. The techniques will give you suggestions for ways to work on these skills.

USING THE BOOK

A benefit of this book is that you can use it for as long or short a period as you like, either in one-on-one situaitions or in a group. You can simply dip into it when you are with other females and want a bit of light-hearted conversation; you can use it for more in-depth conversations; you can use it for icebreakers; and you can create the right environment and use it as a way to build deeper connections with other women. You can even use the starters on your own to learn how to formulate responses, get to know your own thinking style, and work on your conversation skills.

1. How the book is organized

Speaking skills

The beginning of the book contains awareness-raising information on a range of speaking skills. This can help provide an understanding of some of the issues that are present in speaking and conversation. It also contains suggestions for developing skills in these areas.

Conversation starters

The starters are grouped into one hundred different topic sections, each containing ten questions and conversation starters.

The first topic section covers Easy Conversation Starters, simple starters that can be used in general situations. The others are in alphabetical order starting with "About You," weaving their way through many and wide-ranging topics, and ending with "Your Call!"

The starters fall into different types of categories, including ones that ask about you, "What was your favorite book as a child?"; ones that ask about your views or thoughts on issues, "Is social media helping or hindering *real* communication?"; ones that ask you to use your imagination, "In my wildest dreams this is what I would look like ..."; and ones where people have to make guesses about you, "What types of pictures or posters did I have on my bedroom wall I was a teenager?"

At the end of the book is a page for you to make a note of any of your favorite starters or to compile some of your own.

Conversation tips and techniques

These are practical techniques you can use that will help improve conversation skills. They are included amongst the conversation starters.

There are three types of tips and techniques: Suggestions for asking good questions (Q); suggestions for answering questions (A); and general tips and techniques for conversation skills (G). They will have the letter (Q), (A) or (G) in front of each technique. Some give specific examples related to a particular conversation starter, though the techniques can be used in many circumstances.

2. A note on choosing conversation starters

Please note that some of the starters are not suited to beginning a "cold" conversation. Some starters cover, for example, personal matters, sensitive, controversial, or in-depth issues and are more suited to beginning a new topic during a conversation once things have warmed up, or with people you know well. Choosing these too early in a conversation may make others feel ill at ease, and may work against relationship-building. Choose starters that suit the people, the circumstances, and the flow of the conversation.

As a generalization, the type of starters that are more suited to opening a conversation, especially with someone you don't know, are ones of a general nature that don't delve too deeply into personal matters. This is explained later in "Understanding conversation levels," page 6.

In addition, be aware that some of the topics can produce an emotional response so you may need to check if others are happy to talk about them.

3. Suggestions for using the conversation starters

There are many ways to use the starters. Here are a few suggestions:

- You could have a themed conversation based on a topic area, for example "Beliefs," and work through all ten starters.
- You could have each person choose a different topic area and then choose a conversation starter from this area.
- You can use conversation starters more than once, for example with different people, or by asking another member of the group to start the conversation; this will probably make it go in a different direction.
- You could expand your way of communicating by speaking in the style of a different person, such as a person who has the opposite personality style to you (for example, someone who speaks fast, or uses a lot of pauses, or includes humorous anecdotes, or speaks

succinctly); someone from a different culture; some-one from a different generation. This way you may find other ways of speaking that suit you, as well as gaining an understanding of how other people think and why they speak as they do.

- You might like to practice improving your skills by using role play where one person plays devil's advocate or an angry person or an unwilling conversationalist, for example, to help you practice the skill of dealing with challenging conversations.
- You could specifically choose topics you are keen to discuss and make time to have a conversation with your daughter, sister, mother, grandmother, colleague, or close friend, for example.
- You could arrange to have a conversation with people from other backgrounds so that you can have a differ-ent conversation from your usual ones, or in order to learn about the world they grew up (or are growing up) in, and how their society and life experiences have helped shaped their views and behavior. You could choose people of different ages or from different cul-tures or different social settings.
- On a practical level, you could keep the book in your bag or purse, in the glove compartment of your vehi-cle or in your desk at work. Or you could keep a note of a number of topics, for example, by writing a few of them out or by taking a photo of them with your phone, and keeping them with you to use when you are with other women.

And so, here we go. Ready to get talking?

Happy conversations!

SPEAKING SKILLS

Many years ago I found myself in the office lunchroom with Todd, a man who worked in one of our other branches. Although I recognized him, I hadn't actually spoken to him before. He was the only person in the lunchroom, and as I sat down he looked up at me and uttered—in all seriousness—a conversation starter I will never forget: "So, what do you think of the debacle over the Icelandic fishing limit then?"

Some people are great conversationalists who make starting a conversation easy and effortless, and it's a pleasure talking to them. Others, like Todd, may like to learn a few simple ways to make starting a conversation easier for the other person.

Are great conversationalists born with an innate skill? Probably some people are more disposed to be good conversationalists than others, while there are also many people who have worked at polishing their skills. Don't worry if you think your skills aren't as good they could be; it's always possible to improve.

One of the main ways to improve is to practice—but make sure you are practicing the right things! Practicing the wrong thing will simply make you very skilled at whatever is not right.

Listed below, and included in the Conversation Starters, is a wide range of tips and techniques to help you work on your conversation skills.

1.   Understanding conversation levels

Conversation generally operates on an agreed and unspoken set of rules. Often we don't realize that there *are* rules until we come across someone who operates outside of the accepted norm. One such person was Harry.

A former colleague of mine, Lucy, aged about 20, was a very chatty person who could talk about anything and everything. She was friends with Julie, also aged about 20, who was extremely quiet.

One day Lucy and Julie went for a drink, and as usual Lucy was happy to do the talking while Julie listened. After a while one of Lucy's friends, a young man named Harry, came and joined them. Harry hadn't met Julie before, and was also extremely quiet. Everything was going well, with Lucy chatting, and the other two listening, until Lucy decided to go to the bathroom. Realizing she was leaving her friends in a potentially uncomfortable situation, she leaned over to Harry and whispered "Don't sit there in silence, make some small talk," and off she went.

At this point Harry turned to Julie and asked, seriously, "So, are you a virgin then?"

Julie was appalled!

We know that what Harry did wouldn't be classed as "small talk." We also know from Julie's reaction that she deemed it "wrong." But why is it wrong? It's because Harry started off at the inappropriate level of conversation for the situation he was in.

The accepted norm is that conversation falls roughly into four levels, where people start off at Level One on meeting someone new and over a period of time—the length of which varies greatly from person to person—work through the levels. Harry, unfortunately, didn't start at Level One.

Level One: Small Talk

There are two main functions of small talk. Firstly, it's used as a "finding out" phase when we meet someone new. In small talk we chat about general issues, ones that anyone could easily talk about, such as the weather, in order to check out the other person. We use a somewhat bland conversation topic as a tool to see if there is any synergy with them, and then decide if we want to make a deeper connection.

When someone says "Isn't the weather great today?" or some such phrase, they are not asking about the weather, they are attempting to get a conversation under way and are using the ensuing exchange as a way to make a first impression of you. This impression is based on issues such as your general appearance, and how confident, trustworthy, friendly, reliable and intelligent you appear. The topic area "Easy Conversation Starters" in the Questions and Conversation Starters section on page 25 gives suggestions for small talk topics.

Secondly, it's a way to show acknowledgement of a friend or acquaintance without getting into deeper levels of conversation. For example, saying to a colleague on Monday morning as you are walking through the office "Hi, good weekend?" to which you expect a reply along the lines of "Yes, great, thanks," is using small talk as a politeness tool, a way to make a connection at a fairly surface level without the need for a longer conversation at that particular time.

People have different abilities when it comes to conversation skills, and different needs when it comes to conversing with others. This means that some people may stay at small talk level with others for a long time, possibly forever, while others may skip through the levels quite quickly.

Level Two: Factual Information

If we feel happy to progress further than small talk, the next level of conversation is where we share non-emotional factual information about ourselves. These are facts that will not cause either the speaker or the listener to feel uncomfortable. For example, we may talk about the work we do or the town where we live.

An example of a conversation at this level could be "I see you're new here." "Yes, we moved from New Orleans last month. My husband was transferred here with his job." Here, the second speaker has given away several pieces of non-emotional factual information regarding where she used to live, that she is married, and that her husband has been relocated with his work.

Level Three: Views and Opinions

At this level we start to open up, and may potentially go into "emotional" territory. Some people need to feel fairly comfortable with another person to converse at this level. They feel that if they share their views and opinions on an issue and the other person doesn't agree then there may be some element of rejection.

There are, of course, some people who don't care what others think of their views and opinions and will share them openly, regardless!

An example of Level Three could be a conversation regarding your thoughts about another person or a situation, your views on an item of news, or a sharing of your political or religious views.

Level Four: Personal Feelings

At this level we share our feelings; we share more of ourselves, and of who we really are. We may talk about our thoughts, dreams, fears, shortcomings. It's where we show a level of vulnerability, but it is where the deepest level of connection occurs.

An example could be a conversation between parents of school-age children: "I'm very worried about my son; he seems to be falling behind in his studies," or one between friends "I had some upsetting news from the doctor yesterday." If the other person is happy to converse at this level, they will not only talk through the stated concerns, but may also share some of their own issues.

People work their way through the levels at different rates, and sometimes in a different order. This may depend on a number of factors such as personality type, level of friendship, level of confidence, culture, or the circumstances they are in. Some people may like to stay at Small Talk level for the entire duration of their involvement with someone else, while others may be happy to get to Level Four within a couple of sentences. There is no right or wrong way, per se.

Poor Harry's problem was that he started a conversation in the depths of Level Four with someone he didn't know, who was extremely quiet and who was likely to take some time to open up to someone else. If Harry had been a confident, cheeky, fun-loving person and Julie had been similar, then she might have found his opening comment highly amusing and they might have launched into a great conversation. The issue was that Harry started off at the inappropriate level of conversation for the situation he was in.

The aim isn't to get to Level Four as soon as possible, nor is the aim to get to Level Four with everyone. The aim is to get to the level that both or all parties feel comfortable with at the time. Depending on the people and the circumstances, this may happen quickly, it may take some time, or it may not happen at all. A skilled conversationalist will aim to have a rewarding conversation at the level where all parties feel at ease.

The conversation starters in this book offer the opportunity to talk at any or all the four levels of conversation, so that you can move to whichever level(s) people feel comfortable with.

2. Communication behaviors

There are four main ways we communicate with others. These are sometimes called Communication Behaviors and include aggressive, passive, assertive, and indirect or passive aggressive.

Let's use an analogy and imagine how four people, each displaying a different type of communication behavior, would enter someone else's house. The aggressive person would kick down the door and barge in, whether they were invited or not. The passive person would stay outside hiding behind the nearest bush, hoping someone would notice them and invite them in. The assertive person would simply go up to the front door, knock and wait to be invited in, while the indirect person would go round the back and climb in through the window.

How might this play out in a communication situation? Imagine that you have a manager at work who announces an open door policy. You go into the manager's office to have a word, but the manager doesn't look up. An aggressive person may respond by saying angrily, "You said you had an open door policy but you can't even be bothered to look up when people come in!" A passive person would wait, and wait, and wait. An indirect person would say nothing to the manager, but go back to their office and complain to others about the rudeness the manager had displayed, while an assertive person may say to the manager, "I see you're busy, when is a better time to have a talk with you?"

Taken to the extreme, these are ways that the four behavior types may operate:

Aggressive communicators express their needs and desires in a way that doesn't take into account the needs, desires or well-being of other people. They usually railroad others, talk over them, refuse to let them finish, criticize, and pay little attention to what they are saying.

Passive communicators are generally afraid of confrontation and don't feel they have the right to express their own views. They give in to other people's wishes and opinions even though they may not agree. They may also avoid saying what they want for fear of offending.

Indirect or passive aggressive communicators have difficulty expressing annoyance or disagreement in a healthy manner. They may appear kind and considerate on the surface but may harbor hurtful thoughts. They may make excuses, tell white lies, find underhanded means to get their own way, or agree with someone to their face and then be derisive or aggressive about them to others.

Assertive communicators express their thoughts, feelings, needs, and desires in an open and up-front way. They have the confidence to say what they want or mean, while considering and respecting the needs and desires of others.

Behaving assertively is generally the best way to communicate with others. When people adopt the other forms of communication behavior, it is usually due to a lack of self-esteem or because it's a learned behavior. The good news is that assertiveness is a learned skill. This means it's a behavior you can acquire, and can choose to use. When you choose assertive communication it will help you get to the point, communicate clearly as an equal, and express your views and feelings in a direct and appropriate way. Being assertive means you won't offend others and will have a healthy and respectful sense of control over situations.

One of the ways to develop assertive behavior is to "Act as if." Think of someone you know and respect who tends to communicate assertively. When you are in a situation where your natural inclination is to adopt one of the other three communication behaviors, ask yourself, "How would X behave in this situation?" Work out what he or she would do and "act as if" you were them. A benefit of doing this is that it may give you the sense that you are not tackling the situation on your own, but that X is there with you.

It will take some time "acting as if" until it becomes an ingrained behavior, however it is a very effective way to develop the skills. It's a case of fake it till you make it!

3.   It's not *just* what you say; it's how you say it

Conversation comprises two aspects, verbal communication and non-verbal communication.

The verbal aspect encompasses the words that are said while the non-verbal aspect covers the way people look, what people see them do (visual), along with how they sound (vocal), when they speak. Overall this means there are many factors going on that have the potential to lead to misunderstandings in conversation.

Recently my husband and I went to a café. On the counter was a sign saying FLAPJACKS with a plate of flapjacks next to it. There was also a sign saying BLUEBERRY MUFFINS, but with no muffins next to it.

"Do you have any blueberry muffins?" he asked.

"No, we haven't baked any yet," replied the woman.

"Then I think you might want this," he said, instantly picking up the BLUEBERRY MUFFINS sign and handing it to her.

After we sat down, I said that what he'd done had come across as a bit rude. My assumption was that he was feeling a bit irritated that there was a sign advertising something that wasn't available. He was surprised I saw it that way, as his intention was to save the woman the hassle of having other people ask the same question before the muffins were ready.

So often it's easy to make assumptions that aren't correct and not realize that we have misunderstood.

Meaning is contextual; we get the meaning from the context. Often, the context is wider than just the words that are said. It may be the physical or environmental context, or a context that is "invisible" such as someone's culture, experiences they have had in the past, or their thought processes. Unfortunately not everyone's context is the same. My context and my husband's were different in this instance. It wasn't significant this time, but in other situations it could be. You may be trying to be polite, and be seen as rude or aloof; you may be trying to be friendly and supportive, and be seen as interfering; you may be trying to give someone space, and be seen as uncaring. So many ways to be misunderstood!

While it's common for us to think about the words we say, and to sometimes choose them very carefully, it's less common to focus on our speaking style. Speaking style includes many visual and vocal issues such as eye contact, facial expressions, body language, intonation, use of pauses, how loud we speak, how much we speak, how fast we speak, how long we take to answer a question, whether we use social niceties, and subconscious use of regular phrases, for example apologetic or deferential expressions, along with interjections such as "um" and "er."

What can we do if we don't understand?

Being aware that there are many factors involved in communication and that we may have misunderstood will go a long way towards having good conversations and building strong connections with people. It's not uncommon, for example, for people to communicate in a roundabout way or not quite tell the truth because their main aim is to avoid upsetting the other person or causing damage to the relationship.

If something doesn't sound "right," bear in mind that the average person isn't aiming to offend and that our understanding of what they said, did, or how they looked, may not be what they meant.

A good place to start in these situations is to give people the benefit of the doubt. If it's not too serious we can let it go, making the assumption that they didn't mean any harm. Alternatively we could gently probe into what they meant. Ask questions for clarification, remembering to place the responsibility for understanding on yourself. This means saying something along the lines of "I'm not sure I understood; did you mean . . . ?" and not something like "You didn't express that very well."

What can we do if we aren't understood?

It usually seems obvious to us what we mean, and we may be confused as to why others don't see things as we do. A factor to bear in mind is that it may not have been the verbal or non-verbal factors that caused the misunderstanding, it may simply have been that the person wasn't listening properly and only heard part of what was said. However, if you find you are generally being misunderstood, one of the ways to deal with this is to reflect on the verbal and non-verbal aspects you use that could cause confusion, and then work out how to make amendments. For example, are you being too vague or too abrupt? Are you using so many pronouns ("he," "she," "him," "her," "they") without references to specific people that it's difficult to know who you're talking about? Perhaps you are speaking too rapidly or too softly, or you apologize too often. You may point at people too, rather than referring to them by name.

This may take some time to analyze and understand what to change. When you do change, however, people will respond to you differently. Asking a trusted friend to give you some honest feedback will be a help.

Another option is to consider amending your speaking style when you are with certain people; there may be things you do that act as distractors for them. For example, you may need to try enunciating more clearly, avoiding work jargon, changing your level of formality, eliminating swearing, having more eye contact, or speaking more slowly. Do this sensitively, though—you don't want to come across as patronizing.

Another alternative is, when appropriate, to present your message another way. Again, remember to place the responsibility for helping people understand on yourself. This means you may say "I don't think that came across as I intended; what I meant was . . ." rather than "You haven't understood."

4. Deeper meanings

Conversation also comprises another two aspects, information giving and interpersonal relationships.

Clayton Alderfer, American psychologist, developed the ERG theory (Existence, Relatedness, and Growth) to describe the main needs that humans have. "Existence" needs cover our basic material existence requirements; "Relatedness" needs cover our desire for interpersonal relationships; "Growth" needs cover our desire for personal development.

It's not uncommon to find that in many conversations the primary purpose is not the sharing of information but the social aspect, the building of relationships in order to feel connected to others. This means that while the words you say have a surface meaning (information), there may often be a deeper meaning at play, that of emotional connection.

People fall on a continuum when it comes to relatedness needs. For those at one end of the continuum, the need to feel connected to others is of paramount importance, while for those at the other end of the continuum there is little need to connect, and they prefer a more solitary existence. Most people will fall somewhere between the two. Where you are on the continuum will affect how you prefer to converse. If two people, one from each end of the continuum, were to have a conversation, one would see the giving and receiving of information as the only aspect to cover, while the other would see relationship building as the crux of the interaction.

There is no right or wrong to this; it's simply useful to understand the different ways that people communicate, and to take this into account when trying to work out the deeper meaning behind what they are saying.

When my daughter was little, I took her one day to visit our neighbor Kimberley, a very kindly woman. My daughter stood on a little plastic stool in her house, and a bit of it broke off.

"I'm really sorry," I apologized. "Some of the plastic has come off."

"No it hasn't, it's perfectly fine," Kimberley replied.

"But it's broken," I said, surprised that she couldn't see the damaged part.

"I don't see it," she said.

Eventually I realized that her primary concern wasn't the accuracy of the information I was providing, it was about the relationship. The deeper meaning she was conveying was that something as small as a broken part of a plastic stool wasn't worth worrying about, and that we should carry on our interaction, strengthening the relationship.

Understand that there will be times when what people are saying relates more to the deeper meaning of interpersonal relationship than it does to the surface meaning of information sharing.

5. How to avoid rambling

The Canadian humorist Stephen Leacock wrote about a man who "flung himself upon his horse and rode madly off in all directions." Do you speak like this? Do you tend to fling yourself into a topic of conversation without much thought, then ramble and go off on tangents while you are talking? Or do you find that you start on a topic without an idea of where your thoughts are heading and are not sure of the point you are trying to make?

If so, the following 3-step technique will help you avoid this and speak with impact. While a simple technique, it may take a few attempts to become skilled at it:

1) Pause
2) Work out your end point
3) Go in a straight line

To avoid going off on a tangent when you are asked a question, first pause for a few seconds before you start speaking. This pause provides two main benefits. Firstly it gives you a chance to work out the rough outline of what you are going to say. Secondly it gives the impression that you are going to give a considered response. People will then give more weight to what you say.

During the pause, work out the end point of what you are going to say, that is, the overall message you want to give. Perhaps you may also be able to quickly formulate an overview of the ideas you want to present. If you do this, you will avoid starting to talk without a direction to go in. You will be able to speak "in a straight line" which will significantly reduce rambling. Make sure you have a point you are making; it need only be one point, and the stronger the better.

It's also useful to know when to stop. There is no point in speaking for the purpose of making a noise! People favor to-the-point responses and generally prefer not to listen to long, waffling monologues. Make your point, then stop talking and let others contribute.

6. Using a framework to structure your speaking

If there is a topic that requires some thought which you would like to address it in a fairly structured way, one way to organize your thoughts is to use a framework.

For example, a Before & After framework.

Let's say the conversation starter is *"What kinds of problems are you skilled at helping others with?"* One of the ways to answer this could be to use a Before & After framework. Talk about how things were before, what happened, and then how things have been since then. For instance, your response may be along the lines of "Before I split up with my partner I didn't have much understanding of how to live on a very limited budget. Now that I'm separated I've had to learn many strategies for bringing up children on a shoe-string, and I've built up a lot of information I can share with women in a similar situation."

Or a Past Present Future framework.

If the conversation starter were *"Within your society, what level of acceptance is there for gay females?"* you could start by explaining how the situation used to be in the past, how things have changed to the current situation, and what you expect will happen in the future.

Or a Belief Reason Suggestion framework.

This is where you express your views, and then give the reason to support them, followed by advice or suggestions.

For example, with the conversation starter *"Does marriage counseling work?"* you might say you believe that it does help, the reason being that simply taking time out to discuss issues can be of benefit in itself, over and above what the counselor may say, and suggest that anyone interested could book an initial session to see if it may work for them.

There are many types of frameworks you can use, including:

Before & After
Past Present Future
Belief Reason Suggestion
Goals Obstacles Solutions
Problem, Solution
Advantages & Disadvantages
Cause and Effect
Anecdote
Financial Cost and Social Cost
Local National International
The Ideal and the Reality or Likelihood
Civil Law, Moral Law
Cost and Benefit
Personal Experience
Start with an opinion then justify or explain it
Narrow the topic down
Split the topic into components
Low Medium High
How What Where When Who Why
Us Them

1,000 QUESTIONS AND CONVERSATION STARTERS

This section contains one hundred different topic sections, each containing ten conversation starters. It begins with "Easy Conversation Starters," which are simple starters that can be used in general situations, followed by the remaining ninety-nine sections in alphabetical order.

Incorporated throughout the starters are tips and techniques for improved conversation skills. Those covering tips for questions have a (Q) before them; those covering tips for answers have an (A) before them; and those covering general conversation tips have a (G) before them.

At the end is a section where you can list your favorite starters and include any of your own.

Easy conversation starters
About you
Advice
Age
Animals
Anything and everything
Beauty
Beliefs

Books
Business
Business Partnerships
Career
Childhood
Children
Comfort Zone
Communication

Confidence

Conflict

Coping strategies

Creativity

Dating

Do you like ... ?

Dreams and hopes

Education

Either/Or

Emotions

Entertainment

Family and family life

Fashion, clothes and makeup

Fears

Flirting

Food and drink

Friendships

Fun

Health

Hobbies and interests

House and home

In my wildest dreams!

International Issues

Irritations

Is it appropriate ... ?

It's the Little Things

Leaving this World

Let's guess!

Love

Marriage

Meeting with Friends

Men

Mixed bag

Money

Movies

Music

Names and numbers

Other women

Paranormal

Personality

Physical appearance

Pleasure

Politics

Possessions

Pregnancy

Previous relationships

Problems

Quotes about Women

Quotes by Women

Reactions

Relationships

Romance

School

Secrets

Sex

Shopping

Situations

Spiritual

Star Signs

Stay at Home Mom

Stories

Strangers

Stress

Support

Technology

Teenage years

Temptation

The Common Good

The future

Time

Treating yourself

Truth and Lies

Understanding Behavior

Vacations and travel

Weird and wonderful

What would you do if . . . ?

Wisdom

Women Achievers

Women and work

Women Who . . .

Work-life balance

Worrying

Your call!

Plus . . . Your Favorites & Your Starters

Easy Conversation Starters

You may need to amend these starters to fit the situation.

- The weather's great / terrible / unusual at the moment, isn't it?
- Are you from this area?
- Have you got family around here?
- Do you work?
- Are you planning a vacation this year?

(Q) Start a conversation with easy questions

This technique is especially good to use with people you don't know well. Easy questions are the kind of general questions that anyone can answer. They are ones of a general nature that don't require any specific knowledge and are "non-threatening" topics that don't delve into personal details or cover contentious issues. They fall into the "Level One, Small Talk" level of conversation (page 7).

Example

Topic: Easy conversation starters

Starter: *The weather's very unusual for this time of year, isn't it?*

- I like your outfit / necklace / scarf ... where did you get it?
- How was your Christmas / Thanksgiving / Easter break / weekend?
- Did you see the Super Bowl / the news on TV today / the final episode of ... ?
- Have you been here / to this type of meeting / to Poppy's house ... before?
- How do you know Rachel / Carol / name of host or mutual friend ... ?

(Q) Talk about the environment

When beginning a conversation, particularly with someone you don't have much conversation history to call on, talking about an aspect of the environment you're in is a good starting point. You could talk about the type of event you're at, the building you're in, the scenery, the speaker, the people, the food, the music ...

Example

Topic: Easy Conversation Starters

Starter: *Have you been to one of Jackie's parties before?*

About you

- Do you have any brothers and sisters?
- Do you remember people's birthdays?
- How would you finish this sentence: People say I'm good at ...
- Which three adjectives would best describe you?
- Do you tend to avoid letting people know that you're good at something and hide your light under a bushel, or does modesty play no part and you sing about it from the hilltops?

(Q) Many people like to talk about themselves!

People generally find it easy to talk about themselves, so a simple fact-finding question is a good topic to start with. We all like to feel that someone is interested in us. Always follow up with more questions about them, and avoid turning the conversation back to yourself instantly.

Example

Topic: About You

Starter: *Do you have brothers and sisters?*

- Have you ever done something silly that you regretted?
- What couldn't you live without?
- Do you like your name?
- Have you had a traditional or a non-traditional life so far?
- Have you ever faced an obstacle in your life and overcome it?

(Q) Open vs. closed questions (1)

A closed question can lend itself to a one-word or short answer. Closed questions are okay to use some of the time, though don't use them too much.

Example

Topic: About You

Starter: *Do you like your name?*
The other person could answer, for example, *"Yes," "No,"* or *"Sort of."*

If you know that the person is prone to regularly giving short answers, try amending the question to be more open, for example *"What do you think about your name?* Or be ready to follow up a short answer with an open question, such as *"Were you named after someone?"*

Advice

What advice would you give in these scenarios?

- Your mom is sixty-five and wants to do a university degree, purely for interest's sake. It will mean that she has to spend most of her savings to be able to fund it. She's eager, but you're not so sure, as your family has a history of living to a great age.
- Your friend is in her fifties, and her face is starting to show the signs of aging. She isn't happy about getting older and is wondering if she should get a facelift.
- Your sixteen year old son wants to learn to ride a motorcycle. You have the finances to pay for lessons for him, but are worried about the safety issues involved.

(Q) Let people answer. It's okay to have silence for a while

Once you've asked a question, give the other person time to think. Not everyone can give an answer straight away, and you don't need to fill in the silence. People are more likely give a well-thought out answer if they know you are going to give them thinking time and not rush them to respond.

- Your friend's hobby is ballroom dancing, which she loves. However it takes up a large amount of her time and there is a lot of traveling involved. She finds it a struggle to also cope with a full-time, demanding job, and doesn't feel she can handle both for much longer.
- Your friend has always said that she wouldn't marry, but would happily live with someone. The partner she

has been living with for three years has asked her to marry him. She loves him and wants to stay with him but doesn't see the point of getting married. He is feeling hurt about this.

- Your mom has been widowed for five years and is still young at heart. Your sister would like her to consider dating but your mom is a bit shy and unsure if she could do it.
- Your parents have had a huge win on the Lottery and are wondering what to do with the money.

(G) Giving support—agreeing

You can give support to others by showing agreement with their views or thoughts. You can either do this directly *"I completely agree with that"* or indirectly *"I think Heather's views make a lot of sense."*

- Your colleague has been offered a promotion which will mean moving five hundred miles away. She wants the job, but has never lived outside of her home town where all of her family live. She's worried she will miss them, and vice versa. She is single with no children.
- Your friend has a small child, and she and her partner would like to have another. However her sister, to whom she is very close, is unable to have children and would find it distressing if she were to have another child.
- Your husband is unhappy in his job despite being highly regarded by colleagues and management. He would dearly love to do a completely different type of work. This would require two years' re-training, and the job itself would be significantly lower paid.

Age

- What would appeal to you most about being a child again?
- When did you feel you had changed from an adolescent into a woman?
- Do you feel mature?
- How would you finish this off: If I were ten years younger ...
- What are your thoughts about menopause?

(A) Invitation to speak.

Conversation consists of turn-taking. One of the ways to indicate it's someone else's turn when you've finished speaking is to invite them to speak. For example by finishing with *"Don't you think so?" "What would you have done?"* or asking them the question they asked *you "And what about you, how would you respond to 'If I were ten years younger'...?"*

- What physical signs of aging have you noticed?
- Do you try to hide your age in any way?
- At what age were you happiest?
- What are the advantages of getting older?
- What are the disadvantages of getting older?

(Q) Be careful about asking several questions at once

Sometimes it's okay to ask a couple of related questions at the same time. For example, you might ask a closed question that requires a short answer, along with an open one that will allow the other person to expand on what they've said. For example: *Do you procrastinate? And if so, when?*

However, if you ask several open questions, or several questions that require fairly different answers, people won't know which one to answer. Just ask the one question and leave space for them to speak. You can ask the other questions as the conversation continues.

Example

Topic: Age

Starter: *Do you try to hide your age in any way?*

NOT: *Do you try to hide your age in any way? What are your thoughts on plastic surgery when you're older? And what about Betty, do you think she's had a facelift?*

Animals

- Do you like animals?
- What pets have you had during your life?
- Other than pets, have animals been a part of your life?
- Are you familiar with any incidents of cruelty towards animals?
- Are there any creatures that you are afraid of?

(G) Going off on a tangent (1)

If someone starts to go off on a tangent when you haven't finished the topic, one option is to let them know you'll come back to what they are saying in a minute.

- Have you been, or would you like to go, on a wildlife safari?
- Do some people have animals as substitutes for children?
- Is it okay to house animals in a zoo?

- What are your views on vegetarianism?
- What are your views on hunting?

Anything and everything

- If I were ruler of the country for a week I would . . .
- I laughed so much when someone told me . . .
- On a scale of zero to ten, what score would you give yourself for being a risk taker?
- I love the smell of . . .

(Q) Ask the question without rambling

Ask the question and then stop and let the other person answer. You don't need to keep adding to the question.

Example

Topic: Anything and Everything

Starter: *On a scale of zero to ten what score would you give yourself for being a risk taker?*

NOT: *On a scale of zero to ten what score would you give yourself for being a risk taker? Are you maybe a ten . . . or would you put yourself a bit lower at eight? Or perhaps . . .*

- Are you forgetful?
- If you had to marry a famous person, who would you choose?
- If it were possible to eat any type and amount of food as you liked, without it being bad for you in any way, what would your diet consist of?
- Which of these options sounds the most appealing? Spending a year:

- o Working in the Antarctic as a researcher
- o Fostering three teenage children
- o Writing a biography of a living public figure
- o Training to be—and working as—a comedienne
- o Studying yoga and meditation

(G) Bonding: Use the other person's name (1)

When first meeting someone it's good to use the other person's name. Use it when you first hear it, *"Hi Anne, good to meet you"* and use it again early in the conversation. This will help you remember their name and show you are interested in them. It will begin the bonding process.

Example

Topic: Anything and Everything

Starter: *If you had to marry a famous person, who would you choose?*

TRY: *What about you, Anne, if you had to marry a famous person who would you choose?*

- Do you look at clouds and work out what they look like?
- In some cultures, it is the grandparents—not the parents—who raise the children. When the parents become grandparents, they take on the role of bringing up the next generation. Does this sound like a good idea?

(G) Don't drag out a conversation

Sometimes a conversation comes to a natural end. Don't feel you have to drag it out any longer just for the sake of it. You can finish on a positive note and move on, or change the topic, or suggest you go and do something like have a cup of coffee

Beauty

- What's your beauty regimen?
- Do you spend a lot on beauty products?
- If you could have any plastic surgery you wanted for free, what, if anything, would you have done?
- When have you felt at your most beautiful?
- Who would you describe as being physically beautiful?

(G) Bonding: Use the other person's name (2)

Using the other person's name from time to time will help with bonding, but if you overdo it, it makes people feel uneasy, and will probably sound like you are trying to sell them something!

For example if you are talking about beauty regimens, avoid saying something like *"I think, Joy, that your beauty regimen is very impressive, and Joy, have you ever tried making your own coconut face mask? Joy, I tried it once, and it was…"*

- Tell us about someone who has a beautiful personality.
- Do you surround yourself with beautiful things?
- Describe the most beautiful place you've been to.
- Is there too much emphasis on beauty?
- Why does beauty sell?

(G) Bonding: Use the other person's name (3)

Referring to another person in a positive way is a good way to show respect for them. *"I really like the beautiful artifacts that Gillian has in her house. She's very good at surrounding herself with items she loves…"*

Beliefs

- When we are children sometimes we believe or think things that we later realize aren't correct. Did you have any of these childhood beliefs?
- When you were a child, did you believe in Santa and the Tooth Fairy? Anything else?
- Do you have religious beliefs?
- Can you think of a time when you didn't believe someone but it later turned out to be true?
- Were you brought up in a family with particular religious beliefs?

(Q) Keeping the questions general

There are times when you have the choice of narrowing a question down, or making it more general. Sometimes it's useful to keep the questions general as there may be aspects you haven't considered that the other person wants to talk about.

Example

Topic: Beliefs

Starter: *Do you have religious beliefs?* is a more general question than *Are you a Christian?*

- What thoughts have you had about religion as you have gone through life?
- Do you pray, or do something similar?
- Do you believe in reincarnation?
- It's said that we question all of our beliefs, except for the ones we *really* believe. Agree?
- What's the difference between Christianity and Islam?

(Q) Avoid starting a conversation with a criticism

It's generally a good idea to start a conversation with a positive or neutral approach. Starting with a criticism, especially if it's an issue the other person holds dear, can cause ill feeling.

Example

Topic: Beliefs

Starter: *Do you believe in reincarnation?*

NOT: *Don't you think that people who believe in reincarnation are dumb?*

Books

- How big a part do books play in your life?
- What was your favorite book as a child?
- What is your favorite book of all time?
- Do you remember your teacher reading a book out loud to the class at school?

(G) Shy people—speak first!

If you have a tendency to be shy and usually wait until someone else starts speaking, begin training yourself to speak first. Set yourself small goals initially, maybe to start first just once a week. Learn a couple of simple conversation starters and use those. Increase your goals as you achieve your initial ones.

- Have you ever read a book and then seen the movie of it? How did they compare?
- Do you have a fictional counterpart? Which character in a book or a movie is most like you?

- If you were given a contract to write any kind of book at all, what book would you write?
- Tell us about a book that you couldn't put down.

(G) Going off on a tangent (2)

If someone goes off on a tangent, there are times when this is okay as it can lead to an interesting line of discussion.

- Name all the places where you keep books and reading material.
- It's said that a third of high school graduates never read another book for the rest of their lives. Why? And are they missing out?

Business

- If you wanted to set up in business and needed $100,000 to get it off the ground, how would you go about finding a funding source?
- You want to open up a beauty parlor and spa on the main street of the town where you live. Some lovely premises have become available but are neighbored by a fast food outlet often frequented by noisy teenagers, and a tattoo parlor often frequented by bikers. Would you take them?
- Would you be willing to work seven days a week in the early days of setting up a business?
- It is said that, in general, women set up smaller businesses than men. Why is this?
- Is it possible to be feminine and successful in a male dominated business?

(G) Including others

If someone in the group is very quiet and tends not to proffer information, include them by asking questions or asking their opinion from time to time. They may have something very interesting to contribute.

- How big a part is social media playing in business growth at the moment?
- What are the characteristics a woman may need to become CEO of a large organization?
- Why do businesses need to have a unique selling point?
- Is it okay for large businesses to headhunt from smaller businesses?
- Think of a multinational business. What's its competitive advantage?

Business Partnerships

The following people would like to go into business together using their skills, knowledge and experience to do something different to what they are doing at present. What suggestions could you give as to options that might be worth considering?

- Mother and daughter. The mother works as a kindergarten teacher, enjoys helping children learn, loves planning, variety in the workplace and crafts. The daughter works in a garden center, enjoys physical and practical work, likes being in nature and in peaceful environments.
- Husband and wife. The husband is a real estate agent who thrives on working towards business success. He is good at sales and dealing with finances and would like a change from dealing with face-to-face clients. He

wants to be based in an office full time. The wife is an accountant. She enjoys dealing with people, problem solving, logic, order and methods. She wants to move away from working with finance and figures and is interested in a more "caring" work situation.

G) When to say nothing

There is a quote "A wise man once said . . . absolutely nothing because sometimes it's wisest to keep your mouth shut".

Yes, there are times when the best form of communication is to say nothing. You don't always have to say something, and silence may be by far the most suitable option. It may take a lot of self-control to avoid saying those unkind words that are on the verge of coming out, but bite your tongue and say nothing. You will know when those times are. It's good to learn the discipline of saying nothing when appropriate, and you will be forever grateful for having kept quiet.

- Brother and sister, both young and single. The brother works in a camping store. He is keen on most outdoor sports, particularly in skiing, surfing, kayaking and hiking. He hates paperwork and phone work and wants to be outdoors all the time with groups of people. He doesn't care what the working hours are. The sister works as a swimming instructor. She also loves racquet sports, especially tennis, badminton and squash. She likes being with people, teaching and training them and would be keen on having a café as part of whatever business they set up.
- Two work colleagues, female. Colleague One is a manager in a bank who doesn't find the day-to-day tasks stimulating. She is a voluntary mentor for newer bank staff, and finds this the most enjoyable part of the job.

She wants to work in the field of personal development, and have more variety and flexibility in her work. Colleague Two is also a bank manager in a different branch. She likes the rigid structure of the job, enjoying most of the tasks, but wants to be her own boss rather than an employee. She has great organizational skills and likes new challenges. She has a strong interest in acting and dancing but has never considered bringing this into her work.

(G) Repetition

The best type of situation for people to learn in is one where they *want* to learn, and where there is repetition of the message. This means that if you want to specifically get your message across, you may need to repeat it.

Of course this won't always be the case. If you say something dramatic such as *"I've just inherited a lot of money and I want to give you a million dollars,"* it's highly likely you won't need to repeat that. However, in normal conversation where a lot of information of similar "weight" is being exchanged, your message may get lost if you don't repeat it.

- Two university students, male and female. The male student is studying German and Italian and has a natural aptitude for languages, both spoken and written. He likes to travel, is interested in technology and would like a business that allows him to use technology in an innovative way. The female student is studying English and runs a university group that produces a regular magazine. She is happy to be office-based, researching, collecting and collating information. She is particularly interested in overseas aid agencies.

- A family: mother, father and son. The mother is a house-wife, very involved in all local groups, schools and the church in their small home town. She loves baking, gardening and all home crafts. The father works in a barbershop, a very popular figure who is interested in people. He is one of the leading lights in Rotary, the local choir, and the church, and people often come to talk to him when they have problems. The son runs a teenage youth group at church, spends a lot of time playing sports with friends, and ultimately wants to become a missionary teacher.

- Two sisters. Sister One works in a health food store. She spends most of her free time in the gym or running. She loves to keep fit and eat well. She doesn't like to relax and thinks that life is about being active. Sister Two is a clerical assistant who likes clothes, jewelry, shoes, make-up, and hair. She thinks it's important to look good on the outside as it helps people feel good on the inside. She has no formal qualifications but spends a lot of time reading glossy magazines and working out what's current.

(G) Looking relaxed

People tend to pick up on others' emotions. Generally people want to feel at ease, which means that if you present as being ill-at-ease and are playing with your hair, wiggling your foot or changing sitting position regularly, then they will feel ill at ease too.

Unless there is a major reason for feeling unsettled, aim to look as relaxed as you can. Simply being aware that you are not relaxed is the first step towards being able to make a few changes. Take a few low, slow breaths; do a quick check of how relaxed you may or may not look; mentally take the tension out of any tensed parts of your body, and try to "think" yourself into a more relaxed frame of mind.

- Two friends, male. Friend One plays in a band in the evenings and at the weekend. He loves music and has a huge collection of records, CDs and music memorabilia. He would hate a day job, preferring to sleep in the morning, and hang out late at night with other musicians after the band has performed. His other passion is coffee and he has several coffee machines at home. Friend Two is a college music tutor who spends his spare time writing music and going to music gigs in cafes. He would like a structured business where the focus is on making money.

- Two neighbors, female. Neighbor One is a stay at home mom who loves recycling, upcycling, and making do. She dislikes the concept of waste and feels that people could reduce their consumerism in order to make the world a better place. She can turn her hand to most practical tasks, and would like a part-time business to fit in with child care. Neighbor Two is a part time graphic designer, working mainly with charitable organizations. She sees the beauty in most things and would like the world to be a more colorful place. She wants a business that makes her feel she is contributing to the general good of the community, particularly to making the environment more beautiful.

- Father and son. The father is an IT consultant who enjoys project management, electronics, gadgets and all things IT. He is also skilled at practical work and does a lot of DIY, electronic and building projects at home. He is not interested in sales work. The son is an engineering student who is interested in electronics, gadgets, computer gaming, videos, films, podcasts, and anything related to technology. Both are good at communicating with others and are happy to work long and unsocial hours.

Career

- Give a brief overview of your career. Has it panned out how you hoped it would?
- What future career plans do you have?
- Other than qualifications, what else do you need to be, do or have, in order to succeed in your chosen field(s)?
- Which have been your best and worst jobs?
- Who has been your best boss?

(G) Listening skills: Minimal Encouragers

Minimal encouragers are very simple actions that show the other person you are listening; that you are interested in what they are saying; and that you are "encouraging" them to continue.

Minimal encouragers include such things as nodding, saying phrases like *"yes" "sure" "uh-huh" "okay"*, showing interest or surprise *"wow!"*, and slightly leaning forward when something interests you.

People don't tend to notice minimal encouragers when they happen, but you notice when they are missing. In situations where you have been speaking for a while and the other person hasn't offered any minimal encouragers, you may start wondering if there is an issue *"Am I boring her?" "Have I said something incorrect?" "Is she listening?"*

If minimal encouragers aren't yet part of your conversation tool kit, start to bring them in.

- How did you choose your first job?
- Have you earned the income you feel you deserve?
- Which suits you better: business, self-employment or employment?
- Tell us about some interesting or unusual colleagues you've had.
- Do you plan to retire? If so, when?

(Q) Rephrase

If the starter is phrased in a different way to how you would say it, or in a way that isn't appropriate for the other person, it's okay to rephrase it.

Example

Topic: Career

Starter: *Do you plan to retire? If so, when?*

If the person has already retired, you might say, *"When did you retire? And had you planned this?"*

Childhood

- When you were a child, who was your best friend?
- Was your childhood happy?
- Which was your most memorable birthday?
- What happened when you argued with your friends?
- Which were your favorite TV or radio programs?

(Q) Answering a closed question in an open way

Some of the questions in the book are deliberately phrased as closed questions, designed to let you practice closed *or* open responses.

A closed question generally produces a short response, while an open question produces a longer response. Not everyone is skilled at asking open questions, and you may find yourself in a conversation where the other person asks many closed questions. In these cases it's useful to be able to take a closed question and give a full response.

Example

Topic: Childhood

Starter: *Was your childhood happy?*

This is technically a closed question that could produce a one word response, *"Yes," "No,"* or *"Sometimes,"* for example. What would work better in this instance is to give a fuller response to get—or keep—the conversation going. For example, *"I have some lovely memories of my childhood. Like the times we would go to the beach over the summer and spend most of the time in the water ..."*

- What did you want to be when you grew up?
- What was your bedroom like when you were a child?
- Which was your favorite toy?
- When you were a child, what was your most favorite thing in the world to do?
- Did you have any childhood illnesses?

(Q) Start your answer with a story or anecdote

Using a short story or anecdote is an easy way to begin talking about a topic as it's something that doesn't require much thinking. People love to hear stories, especially amusing, heart-warming, intriguing or shocking ones, and ones they can relate to.

Example

Topic: Childhood

Starter: *Which was your favorite toy?*

Instead of replying *"My favorite toy was a jigsaw puzzle"* you could start with a story: *"One day when I was six years old, my dad came home with something hidden inside his jacket ..."*

Children

NOTE: Please be considerate when using this topic; it may be a sensitive area for some women. Check if it's okay to talk about these issues.

- When you were growing up, did you want to have children?
- How has having children changed your life?
- What do you love most about your children?
- What do your children do that drives you mad or disappoints you?
- Given a complete choice, how many children would you have? Why this number?

(Q) If you think it may be a sensitive topic for someone

Be aware that certain topics may be sensitive areas for some people, depending on their situation; for example topics about children, pregnancy, marriage and money. Check if they are happy to talk about this topic. If not, go on to something else.

- How would you finish this off: Children these days …
- What needs to be done to combat childhood obesity?
- Are children of celebrities and royalty spoiled?
- Do parents pander too much to their children?
- What effect does TV advertising have on children?

(G) Giving support—empathy

You can give emotional support by showing empathy with others, for example: *"Oh my goodness, I know exactly how you feel, the same thing happened to me and I can understand what you're going through."*

Sympathy and empathy are not the same. Being sympathetic means offering consolation when someone is dealing with an issue you haven't necessarily experienced. Being empathetic is when you appreciate the challenges someone has had because you have experienced them yourself.

Comfort Zone

You've been asked to step outside of your comfort zone. Which of these would be more challenging for you, and what would you like to have in place to help you to do it?

- Picking up a large spider or giving a presentation to a thousand people?
- Spending twenty-four hours in solitary confinement or hang gliding?
- Going to a party on your own or doing a five minute slot as a warm-up act for a comedian?
- Sleeping in a haunted castle or going down a cat walk modeling underwear?
- Sitting in a bath full of snakes or going on the world's largest roller coaster?

(G) Chunking

People like things when they are packaged in chunks. If you have a lot to say, you don't need to burble it out in one long monologue.

Split it into chunks. Divide what you want to say into manageable and logical segments, such as stages of an issue or problem, of what happened in the past, what's happening now, and what is likely to happen in the future. People will understand it more and will be less likely to lose interest if you break it up.

- Spending an hour in an isolation tank (a lightless, soundproof tank where you float in salt water) or watching an operation?
- Rappelling one hundred feet down the outside of a building or being trapped in the ghost train tunnel for three hours?

- Having your hair shaved off for charity or having a TV crew film every room in your house without giving you a chance to tidy up?
- Having someone post an embarrassing photo of you on Facebook or being an assistant to a knife-throwing magician?
- Spending a week wearing baggy, scruffy, unflattering clothes without makeup or jewelry, or eating a meal of sheep's eyeballs, boiled grasshoppers, and fried caterpillars?

Communication

- Do you use snail mail?
- If you are on Facebook, how do you use it?
- If you want to ask a friend a non-urgent question, would you call them, go to see them, email them, text them, or contact them in another way?
- Imagine you had to speak at an event in front of an audience of five hundred people for thirty minutes. How would you feel?

(Q) Open vs. closed questions (2)

Open questions tend to lead to longer answers, and are good to keep the conversation flowing. You can change a closed question to an open one if you prefer.

Example

Topic: Communication

Starter: Compare *"Do you use snail mail?"* which can lead to a *"Yes"* or *"No"* answer, with *"When did you last write a letter to someone and mail it to them?"* which is likely to lead to a longer answer.

- Do you think you can generally tell when people are telling the truth?
- If a friend asked what you thought of her new outfit, and you thought it didn't suit her at all, would you tell her?
- If you are having coffee with someone and a friend calls you on your cell phone, is it okay to answer the phone and have a conversation with them?

(G) Actively listen

There is a difference between hearing and listening. Hearing is passive, while listening is active. This means that you need to be actively paying attention to what others are saying.

If you have had the experience of being in a conversation and unable to answer a question as you have let your mind wander, you have probably heard the sound of conversation in the background, though were not actively listening.

A good way to stop your mind wandering is to ask questions from time to time, or use minimal encouragers (page 43).

- Have you ever been too shy to say what you really wanted to say?
- Is social media helping or hindering real communication?
- Large organizations regularly cite "communication" as one of the problems that impedes efficiency. Why is this?

Confidence

- Which aspect of your life are you the most confident about?
- Do you find confidence an attractive trait in a potential partner?

- One of the ways to increase confidence is to "borrow" it from someone who is confident, by acting as if you were them. Have you ever done this?
- Think about all the members of your family. Who is the most confident and who is the least?
- Some women link their level of confidence to how they feel about their body and some women don't. Do you?

(G) Don't aim to impress

When having a conversation, the aim isn't to impress others, be able to ask "clever" questions, or show how wonderful you are! To have a great conversation one of the most important aspects is to simply be friendly.

If you are friendly people will usually respond accordingly and you will be able to start forming a bond. Good bonds lead to good conversations, and vice versa.

- Why do some teenage girls lose the confidence they had when they were children?
- What's the difference between a pleasant level of confidence and over-confidence?
- What is the main cause of lack of confidence?
- What are some of the strategies people use to try to mask their lack of confidence?
- What's the earliest age a child could become aware of confidence?

Conflict

- Are you comfortable with some level of conflict, or do you prefer to avoid it completely?
- Have you had any conflict situations at work?

- Over what kinds of issues did you fall out with your parents when you were a teenager?
- Imagine you had bought a small electrical appliance that didn't work when you got it home. When you took it back you weren't given a refund as the store staff said it looked like you had dropped it. You haven't dropped it. What would you do?

(G) Disagreeing (1)

It's not uncommon to disagree with people's views, and there are several ways to deal with this depending on the level of disagreement, and how you want to tackle it.

One way is to do nothing. You may decide it is not a major issue and that it's more useful to let the conversation flow. That's okay.

- Is there much conflict between you and your partner?
- Does marriage counseling work?
- What would you do if you had a husband who got annoyed with you if you didn't have the evening meal ready for him when he got home, even though you both worked full time.
- If a child thinks one of their parents hasn't behaved well (and is justified in this) should the parent go into "time out" or have some similar consequence?

(G) Disagreeing (2)

If you disagree with what someone has said and decide to say something, the responses can range from humorous, light-hearted, and polite to rude and aggressive.

For example: *"Hey, that's not right, nitwit!"; "I hope you don't mind, but I've found the opposite to be true"; "Let me clarify something as I don't think that's right"; "There's no logic to what you're saying"; "That's a really stupid thing to do."*

The type of response you choose will usually determine the type of reaction you'll get.

- When small children bicker, what's the best way to deal with it?
- Can we learn any helpful strategies from how politicians handle conflict in debates?

Coping strategies

- Do you have a coping strategy for times when something unexpected happens and you know you will be late for an appointment?
- Do you have a coping strategy for when you go to a funeral?
- Do you have a coping strategy for times when you have to say goodbye to people you like and will miss, when *you* are leaving or moving away?
- Do you have a coping strategy for times when you have to say goodbye to people you like and will miss, when *they* are leaving or moving away?
- Do you have a coping strategy for times when you lock yourself out of the car or house?

(G) Giving support

You can give support to someone by staying with the topic the other person is talking about, rather than moving onto something different. Letting them

> talk further on the issue shows your concern. For example: *"It's really hard when things like that happen. What are you thinking of doing now?"* or *"It was frustrating wasn't it?"*

- Do you have a coping strategy for times when you are ill and need to spend time in bed and there are people or pets to look after or commitments you can't fulfill?
- Do you have a coping strategy for times when someone makes disparaging remarks about you that aren't true?
- Do you have a coping strategy for times when you lose something such as your cell phone or purse?
- Do you have a coping strategy for times when you suffer from lack of sleep?
- Do you have a coping strategy for times when someone around you is very angry?

Creativity

- Would you describe yourself as a creative person?
- In which creative field are you most talented? Music, art, writing, dance, food, crafts, etc.
- Give an example of your most creative problem solving!
- What kinds of creative people do you have a respect for?

(G) Starting a conversation—fast or slow?

Some people like to take time at the beginning of a conversation to get to know people and connect with them, while others are happy to get started without the "social niceties." The slower starters may see others as a bit brusque, while the faster starters may want to hurry the others along. Neither is right or wrong, it's simply a matter of personal style, and one that's useful to be aware of.

- Think of someone you would like to organize a surprise celebration for. Devise a fantastic event.
- Your friends are getting married. He is an architect who likes music, and she is a history teacher who likes animals. You have been asked to design a suitable, fun, wedding cake. What would you design?
- You've been offered a free place on a weekend creative course of your choice. What would you choose?

(A) Succinct, full or rambling answers (1)

How you answer a question depends on a number of factors— the type of question, the type of answer the person expects, the situation, your personality and so on. Sometimes a succinct answer is all that's needed.

If the question is a closed question, you may only need to simply answer *"Yes"* or *"No"* or give a short reply, and then let the other person speak again.

- You have to raise enough money to buy kitchen equipment for a local charity. Think of an innovative way to do this.
- Choose a room in your house. If you had to decorate it in a completely different, but recognizable,

style, what style would you choose and how would it look?

- Imagine you are writing a children's fiction book. Create a new type of character.

Dating

- Dating—love it or loathe it?
- What was your worst date ever?
- Who were the people you shouldn't have dated?

(Q) Open vs. closed questions (3)

Open questions often start with "Who," "What," "How," "Why," "When," "Tell me about," "Describe," or "What do you think of." They tend to lead to longer answers.

Example

Topic: Dating

Starter: Compare *"What do you think of online dating?"* which requires a longer answer, with *"Would you try online dating?"* which could be answered with a *"Yes"* or *"No"* response.

- It was your first date, you had a good time, but they didn't call you back. Have you had this experience, and if so what did you do?
- How do you, or did you, choose clothes to wear on a date?
- Did you treat any of your dates badly?

(Q) Impolite questions (1)

Most people want approval, and it's possible to ask a question in a way that works against this and is in fact a put down.

For example if a person answered the question *"How do you, or did you, choose clothes to wear on a date?"* with *"Actually I'm going on a date at the weekend and I've just bought a new red dress."* If you respond with *"You're not going to wear red are you?"* this is likely to be seen as a put-down.

- What was it like falling in love?
- What do you think of online dating?
- Have you ever been stood up?
- What are the best and worst pick-up lines you've heard?

Do you like . . .?

- Do you like having midnight snacks?
- Do you like looking in the mirror?
- Do you like relaxing in the bath with a glass of wine?
- Do you like going to the gym?
- Do you like classical music?

(Q) Open vs. closed questions (4)

Sometimes it's good to ask a closed question first so you can clarify, and then go on to ask a more open question to get the other person thinking. A rough guide is to use one to three closed questions per open question.

Example

Topic: Do You Like . . .?

Starter: *Do you like going to the gym?*

This is a closed question and may produce a *"Yes"* or *"No"* response, which means you can then ask another closed question or two and/or an open question based on their answer.

For example, if *"Yes"* you may ask *"Which one?" "How often do you go?" "What have been the main benefits?"*

If *"No"* you may ask *"Don't fancy it then?" "What kinds of activities do you do to keep fit?"*

- Do you like keeping a diary?
- Do you like entertaining people at your home?
- Do you like eavesdropping?
- Do you like being out in the sun?
- Do you like yourself?

(A) Succinct, full or rambling answers (2)

Don't give succinct answers all the time as it makes it hard work for the other person and the conversation will become very stilted. If you have a tendency to do this, try to fill out some of your answers, even when people ask you closed questions. An expanded answer gives the other person a hook they can latch onto so they can carry on the conversation.

For example if they ask *"Do you like being out in the sun?"* instead of simply saying *"No"*, pad it out a bit. *"Not really. I usually avoid being out in the sun as I'm very fair skinned and I burn easily."* This will give them a hook (skin types) so they can bring this topic into the conversation.

Dreams and hopes

- Describe your dream job or career.
- What were or are your parents' hopes for you?

- What would be your vacation of a lifetime?
- Who has been the person who has most believed in you, and what did they want for you?

(Q) Succinct, full or rambling answers (3)

Sometimes full answers are the best way to go. These are answers that are not too short nor too long or rambling, but give a satisfactory, on-topic answer.

Example

Topic: Dreams and Hopes

Starter: *What were or are your parents' hopes for you?*
A succinct answer could be, for example, *"They wanted me to become a doctor,"* while a full answer would make more of a story of it—what they wanted, why they wanted this, what you wanted, how you resolved it ...

- What dreams and hopes do you have for someone close to you?
- Describe someone you know who is living their dream.
- How would you finish this off: I hope that by next year ...
- Are your partner's hopes and dreams compatible with yours?
- Dream big! What would you really love to do, be or have but haven't dared to dream that big?
- My hope for the next generation is ...

Education

- What do you think of the education system today?
- What has been the most useless subject you've ever studied?

- What are the main skills you have learned in the "school of life" that you didn't learn at school?
- Looking back, what were the best things about your school?

(Q) Subjective and objective questions (1)

A subjective question asks for your opinion, an objective question asks for specific information. There's generally no right or wrong answer to a subjective question, simply what your opinion is.

Example

Topic: Education

Starter: *What do you think of the education system today?* If it were an objective version of this question, it may ask you to describe the current education system.

- If you could be paid to study anything you wanted, what would you study?
- In which subjects did you get your best grades at school?
- Who was the best teacher you've ever had?
- I don't think there's a single teenager leaving college these days who can read and write properly. Don't you think so?

(Q) Winding people up

Only do this if you can say it tongue in cheek, knowing that the people there will see the funny side of it, otherwise you may start an argument!

For example, if you were with a group of teachers:

Topic: Education

Starter: *I don't think there's a single teenager leaving college these days who can read and write properly. Don't you think so?*

- How would you finish this off: If I were Secretary of Education I would . . .
- How do you think we could improve the education system to make students more prepared for the world of work?

(Q) Subjective and objective questions (2)

An objective question asks for specific information, whereas a subjective question asks for your opinion. It's expected that the information you give is correct.

Example

Topic: Education

Starter: *In which subjects did you get your best grades at school?* If it were a subjective version of this question, it would ask what you thought you were best at.

Either / Or

Which of these choices appeals to you more? Explain your thought process and what you think the choice will give you:

- Either a weekend in a chalet in the mountains or a weekend with a good book on the beach.
- Either a free subscription to a healthy lifestyle magazine or a free subscription to an alternative lifestyle magazine.

- Either an hour with a current political leader of your choice or an hour with an historical figure of your choice.
- Either a free membership for the gym or a free course of dance lessons.
- Either a night out at the opera or a night out at the filming of your favorite TV program.

(G) Giving support—sympathy

You can give emotional support by showing sympathy for others, for example, *"Oh you poor dear, that must have been terrible for you."*

Sympathy is different to empathy. Empathy is when you can understand what the other person is feeling because you have has a similar experience or can put yourself in their shoes. Sympathy is acknowledging the other person's emotional challenges and providing comfort.

- Either a tour of a prison or a chance to share lunch with children in an orphanage.
- Either a working vacation in a vineyard overseas or a working vacation at a refugee camp.
- Either a chance to foster a child for a weekend or the opportunity to donate $10,000 to a worthy cause of your choice.
- Either a chance to influence the country's prison system or a chance to influence the country's spending on the military.
- Either a chance to go back in time and amend something you wish you hadn't said or a chance to go back in time and find something you have lost.

Emotions

- What never fails to make you laugh?
- What never fails to make you irritated or angry?
- Do you generally have a tendency to keep your emotions under wraps, or do you wear your heart on your sleeve?
- When choosing a movie, would you prefer one that's emotionally charged or a humorous one?

(A) Succinct, full or rambling answers (4)

Do you tend to give very long answers, speak much more than others, and regularly go off on tangents? What do you think others may think of this?

Full answers are okay, though rambling ones are harder for people to keep interested in.

- Describe a situation that makes you feel very nervous.
- If you were going to be part of a very large crowd, say at a concert or sports event, how would you feel?
- When you think of the main festival of your year, for example Thanksgiving or Christmas, what emotions does this bring up for you?

(G) Avoid excluding others (1)

If you are in a group, be aware of not spending too much time talking about a topic one of the people can't contribute to. It may be that all the people work for the same organization except one, and you are talking about work issues; or that a person has recently moved into the area and you are talking about something familiar to people in the neighborhood; or that you are talking about something that happened a while ago and they are too young to know about it.

While the topic is being discussed, it's polite to explain to the person the background to it.

- Tell us about an emotional time you had at an airport or train station.
- What makes you feel really, really happy and contented?
- Talk about something or someone that is very, very cute.

Entertainment

- Tell us about the most recent live show or concert you went to.
- What are your favorite kinds of TV or radio programs?
- Would you generally prefer to go to the cinema or to the theater?
- Does the cost of a night out put you off going out?
- What's the most unusual or interesting entertainment event you've been to?

(G) Being considerate

Mentally check from time to time that the words, tone of voice, expressions and body language you use are not likely to cause offense.

Offense can be caused in a number of ways, sometimes without realizing it. For example dismissing an interest that someone has *"You don't watch that TV program do you?"*, or the beliefs they have, or the culture they belong to.

Offense can arise from such actions as pointing at people in an accusing way, looking bored, turning away or raising an eyebrow.

- Do you use the internet as a form of entertainment?
- What do you think of events such as the Oscars?
- Do you have a favorite celebrity?
- Why are so many people fascinated by every aspect of a celebrity's life?
- Is there a certain kind of person who goes to the opera or the ballet?

(Q) Are you fishing for the answer you want?

Fishing for an answer is where you have an opinion and are looking for confirmation of it, rather than asking a question to seek the other person's views.

Example

Topic: Entertainment

Starter: *What do you think of events such as the Oscars?*

NOT: *What do you think of those appalling events like the Oscars? Isn't it just a group of overpaid celebrities strutting around in expensive designer gear?*

Family and Family Life

- Tell us about growing up with your parents.
- How is your relationship with your parents now, or while they were still here?
- When I was a child I wish my parents had ...
- How do you get on with your siblings?
- Tell us about your grandparents.

(Q) Avoid being judgmental

Keeping a question open, with ideally a positive or at least a neutral slant on it, will allow for more rapport and a more positive answer.

Example

Topic: Family and Family Life

Starter: *How do you get on with your siblings?*

NOT: *You've got three sisters; I'm guessing you must have a lot of sibling rivalry?*

- Is there a distant relative you'd like to have more contact with?
- What do you wish you'd said to a family member before they died?
- Which member of your close or extended family is most like you?
- Who is the most unusual member of your family?
- Tell us about your favorite family photos.

Family Finances

- What are your main priorities regarding the family finances?
- Has your financial situation had an impact on your decision to have children?
- What advice would you give to a young couple with a baby regarding managing the family finances?
- Do you argue with your partner about how money is spent?
- Between you and your partner which one of you is most prone to impulse buying?

(G) Enthusiasm (1)

People are drawn to enthusiastic people, so the more enthusiastic you can be while you're talking the more people will be drawn into the conversation. Even a topic that others aren't initially interested in can become fascinating if you speak with passion and enthusiasm. Enthusiasm is contagious!

- Between you and your partner which one of you is more bothered about social image?
- If you and your partner had to agree on which expenses to cut, which areas would you decide on?
- Are you saving for anything at the moment?
- Money is a very emotional issue. Do you know what your partner's feelings about money are?
- If you had a child with dyslexia and had enough money to either send them on a special course or have a family vacation, which would you choose?

Fashion, Clothes, and Makeup

- How would you describe your clothing style?
- What kind of clothes would you never wear?
- Does being fashionable have to cost a lot of money?
- Shoes!
- How much of the clothing you possess do you actually wear?

(Q) Play devil's advocate to get a lively conversation going

Playing devil's advocate is when you take a stance you don't necessarily agree with for the sake of debate, humorous or otherwise.

Example

Topic: Fashion, Clothes, and Makeup

Starter: *Does being fashionable have to cost a lot of money?*
You could answer with a reply such as *"Of course it does! No one can be fashionable without wearing the latest designer clothes. There is no other way".*

- How many places do you have to store your clothes, and what have you got in there?
- When it comes to makeup, do you tend towards the minimal look or do you go the whole nine yards?
- Do you shop at thrift shops?
- Do you keep up with fashion trends?
- People will think you're a bimbo if you have high fashion clothes and wear lots of makeup. Agree?

(Q) Starting with a contentious topic (1)

It's okay to use a contentious starter if you want to begin a lively conversation. If you want to create an impact, you can be as contentious as you like! However, always remember to be sensitive to people's needs.

Example

Topic: Fashion, Clothes, and Makeup

Starter: *People will think you're a bimbo if you have high fashion clothes and wear lots of makeup. Agree?*

If you know there are people in the group who have very different views on this, or if there are people in the group with very different clothes and makeup styles, this could be a contentious starter.

(Note that in other instances, it may be a simple, fun starter designed to produce some light-hearted humor. Not everyone will have the same reaction to a topic; some people may not see it as contentious at all. The meaning of something depends on the context.)

Fears

- What's your biggest fear?
- What fears did you have when you were younger?
- Do you have a niggling doubt that's always there?
- Do you have any phobias?
- Are you afraid of getting old / older?

(G) Listening skills: I-listening vs. You-listening

Be a "You-listener" rather than an "I-listener."

I-listeners are people whose aim is to turn everything round so they can talk about themselves, while You-listeners are more interested in hearing what the other person has to say. People like to be listened to, and you will be seen as a much better conversation partner if you are a You-listener.

Example

Topic: Fears

Starter: *Do you have any phobias?*

Person A: *Since I was a child, I've always been terrified of bees and wasps.*

Person B (I-listener): *Me too, I hate the way they always seem to fly round my head, especially when I'm out at a picnic. There was one time when …*

Person C (You-listener): *Poor you. Do you know how this started?*

- Are you afraid of dying?
- What is something that most people are afraid of, but you aren't?
- Which of these would you be most afraid of and why:
  - o Having a spider crawl on your face
  - o Getting lost in a foreign country where you can't speak the language
  - o Walking across a swing bridge one hundred meters high over a river
  - o Spending a night in a haunted house?
- What's a good way to banish a fear?

(Q) Problem solving questions

A problem solving question asks for action, ideas, and suggestions.

Example

Topic: Fears

Starter: *What's a good way to banish a fear?*

Flirting

- Do you flirt, or have you ever flirted?
- Do you notice if someone flirts with you?
- Do you like it when someone flirts with you?
- Does your husband or partner flirt?
- If someone attractive started flirting with you today, what would you do?

(G) Avoid excluding others (2)

If in a group, be aware of spending time having an open conversation with one other person, when it should be a topic for a conversation for just the two of you. For example discussing plans with another person, when the topic isn't relevant to anyone else.

- How did you start your current or most recent relationship?
- Do you get jealous if someone flirts with your partner?
- Who's the most flirtatious person you know?
- What's a subtle way to flirt?
- Is harmless flirting okay?

Food and Drink

- If someone were to describe you as a great cook, what would you say?
- Are TV cooking programs of any use? I don't think anyone would make the food those TV chefs make!
- Are cola drinks safe to drink?
- Did you learn any useful cooking skills at school?
- Do you like wine?

(Q) Saying something you don't believe

If you say something you don't believe, and know that others are likely to agree, it's a good way to energize the conversation when done in a humorous way. Say it with a smile and a twinkle in your eye!

Example

Topic: Food and Drink

Starter: *Are TV cooking programs of any use? I don't think anyone would make the food those TV chefs make!*

- What are your top five favorite drinks?
- If you had invited friends or family for a special meal, what would you make?
- What kind of food could you not eat, no matter what?
- Fast food or slow food—which is better?
- The Western world wastes so much food, yet there are people who are starving. Should we do anything about it?

(G) Criticism and encouragement

People who are skilled at criticism will also be capable of putting others down and making them feel demotivated and unhappy. It's hard to maintain a good quality of relationship when criticism is present.

If you identify with this, consider the alternative: encouragement. Even a few words of encouragement can build people's energy and motivation, and will lead to much happier and strengthened relationships.

Friendships

- Who is your longest standing friend?
- Do you make friends easily?
- Tell us about someone who was a friend but who is now an ex-friend. What happened?
- Who do you know who has an unlikely friendship, and why do they seem mismatched?
- What are your husband's or partner's friends like?

(G) Open vs. closed questions (5)

Open questions give the other person a chance to give more than one word answers. Being able to use open questions to keep the conversation going is a good conversational skill to have. Specifically practice using them in conversation, for example *"Tell me about . . ." "How did that happen?" "And what did your boss say about that?" "And then you . . . ?"*

- What makes for a good friendship?
- Are there boundaries to a friendship?
- Do you think that your husband or partner should also be your best friend?
- Can an animal be equally suitable as a friend?
- What's the difference between a friend and an acquaintance, and what needs to happen for an acquaintance to become a friend?

(Q) Good communicators ask questions

Good communicators are interested in other people and their lives. They are not nosy, they are genuinely interested in others, and so they ask questions to find out about the person and build a greater understanding of them.

They create a base of knowledge about the person so that they have a wider range of topics to talk about, and consequently build a greater rapport.

To build these skills, try asking one additional question each time you are in conversation with someone. Just one.

Fun

- If you could live for a week as someone completely different to you, such as an explorer in the wilds of Indonesia, a housewife with ten children, or a pop star, what kind of person would you like to be?
- If you were in an improvised play and had to chat someone up, what's the most ridiculous line you could come up with?
- What's the most fun you've had with your clothes on?
- Tell us about an event that was supposed to be serious but ended up being lots of fun.

(G) Tell stories (I)

People love to listen to stories, especially funny or self-deprecating ones. Making people laugh with a story about the time you got something majorly wrong, for example, is a guaranteed winner.

It's good to introduce stories in the natural flow of the conversation by saying something like *"Speaking of unusual experiences..."* or *"I know what you mean; something like that also happened to me last week..."*

Don't rush your story, and especially remember to have a dramatic pause at appropriate moments.

- What's your idea of a fun night out?
- What's your idea of a fun night in?
- If you were asked to organize a Family Fun Day at the local community center, what would you include?
- Tell us your funniest incident.

(G) Punch lines

Do you jump in to deliver other people's punch lines? Stop!

No one likes to have their thunder stolen, and it doesn't do *you* any favors either.

- You are holding a party and want to invite someone who will liven things up. Who would you invite and what do you expect they would they do?
- What's the funniest practical joke you've been involved in?
- Tell us some material from your favorite comedian.
- Think of something you attend that isn't usually fun, but could be, such as a staff meeting, committee meeting or family get-together. How can you bring some fun into it?

(Q) Feel free to make amendments

If you can't or don't want to answer the question in the way it has been asked, it's okay to make changes and answer on a slightly different tack.

Example

Topic: Fun

Starter: *Tell us some material from your favorite comedian.*
"Actually the funniest person I know is my brother, and there was a time when he had us rolling on the floor laughing when he ..."

Health

- Which do you prefer, alternative or traditional medicine?
- What is your parents' and grandparents' health history like?
- What's been the worst health issue you've had to cope with?
- Are you a hypochondriac?
- If you had a significant health issue and a new drug had been created to treat it, would you be a guinea pig in the drug trials?

(G) What else is going on for people?

Issues that are happening in people's lives may have an impact on what people say or how they say it, and may not be typical of how they would normally converse.

For example if the other person speaks very negatively of the education system, it may be because their child is having difficulties at school. If they give an antagonistic answer to the question *"Are you a hypochondriac?"* they may have recently had a health scare. If they sound overly enthusiastic and extremely talkative regarding the question about their best vacation ever, they may have just come back from the holiday of a lifetime.

We don't always know the background information so we may have to give some leeway, or simply ask.

- If you had to give one piece of advice on staying healthy, what advice would you give?
- Have you had to nurse anyone through ill health?
- Has disability played a part in your, or your family's, life?
- What Old Wives' Tale do you believe in?
- Does being happy keep people healthier?

Hobbies and Interests

- Is there something you've been interested in all your life?
- What's the most unexpected interest you have?
- If you were stranded on a desert island, which of your hobbies would you miss the most?
- Have you got time in your life for another hobby?

(G) Interrupting (1)

There are different types of interruption, some positive and some not so positive.

If you want to add, in a positive way, to what's being said, it's okay to interrupt someone while they are talking, the polite way being to acknowledge your interruption. For example *"Sorry, can I interrupt for a moment? I've just heard that there will be three extra people coming."*

When you have finished speaking, invite them to continue what they were saying *"Thanks, please carry on."*

- Which person most closely shares one of your hobbies?
- Do you collect anything?
- Is there a hobby you'd like to do, but don't or can't?
- Are your hobbies expensive?
- Could you, or do you, make money by doing your hobby?

House and Home

- Tell us about the house(s) you were brought up in.
- If you could have an additional home somewhere else, where would you choose?
- Whose house do you most admire?

(G) It's okay to talk about yourself

Some people don't like to talk about themselves because they feel it's not polite. They aren't interesting enough, or because they're reluctant to share details about themselves. Their tendency is then to inundate the other person with questions, or say very little.

However it's okay to open up and share something of yourself, as that is how real connections are made. You don't need to share very personal details, but enough that the other person feels they are connecting with you. Remember that most people are interested in other people.

- If you could have one major addition to your house, free of charge, what would you have?
- How did you choose the place you are now living in?
- Which is your favorite room in your house?
- Describe your housekeeping style.

(G) It's not okay to talk about yourself all the time!

If you are the kind of person who likes to have the limelight all the time and talk about yourself, remember that balance is important in a conversation, and that other people have things to say too. A conversation is a dialogue, not a monologue.

- What are your favorite pieces of furniture and how did you acquire them?
- Do you look forward to going home after you've been away?
- What makes a house a home?

In my Wildest Dreams!

*Let your imagination run wild! What would happen in your wildest dreams if there were no boundaries and no repercussions? What would you **really** do?*

- In my wildest dreams this is how I would spend my perfect twenty-four hours . . .
- In my wildest dreams, where I had as much money as I wanted, I would . . .
- In my wildest dreams this is what I would look like . . .

(G) Two ears, one mouth

Epictetus, Greek sage and philosopher, said in the first century AD. *"We have two ears and one mouth so that we can listen twice as much as we speak."*

It's not uncommon for people to feel that they are not adequately listened to, that they are interrupted, that their views are ignored, or that people are not listening to the *essence* of what they are saying.

Epictetus's words are equally as valid today as they were two thousand years ago. Being a good listener is a highly beneficial conversational skill.

- In my wildest dreams this is how my love life would be . . .
- In my wildest dreams this is the seduction scenario . . .
- In my wildest dreams this is what my house would be like . . .
- In my wildest dreams my day-to-day life would involve . . .

(G) Smile!

People like smiley people. Some people are fortunate and are naturally smiley, while others may need to make a little effort. Smiling must be genuine; people can tell a non-genuine smile.

Smiling can show the other person that you are interested in what they are saying. Smiling helps encourage the conversation. Smiling will make people warm to you.

- In my wildest dreams these are the people I would spend time with ...
- In my wildest dreams I would be able to ...
- In my wildest dreams I would be ...

International Issues

- Given that the United States has a huge influence on the rest of the world, is there an argument for people other than Americans having a say in the election of the president?
- How has the issue of the world's response to Syria's chemical warfare shown the relative importance and influence of the United States, Russia, Great Britain, France, and the United Nations?
- Nelson Mandela endured twenty-seven years of imprisonment, subsequently going on to become one of the world's most respected leaders. Was the overall effect of his being in prison a positive or negative one with regard to what he went on to achieve?
- Choose a war you are familiar with and explain what it was *really* about.
- What have been the numerous effects of sending foreign forces to Afghanistan?

(G) Balance of focus

It will make most people feel ill-at-ease if all of the conversation is focused on them or all of the conversation is focused on you. It doesn't have to be 50/50, but it does need to have some balance.

- Is international airport security too strict?
- It is a known fact, when it comes to international trade issues, that some of the goods produced for export to the United States involve the use of child laborers or forced labor. What should the US response be?
- When children attend international schools in a different country to their own, what could be the benefits for their own country when they return?
- When children attend international schools in their own country, what could be the benefits for the country?

Irritations

- What is the most annoying minor irritation *ever*?
- Is there a minor irritation that you could easily sort out but haven't gotten around to?
- Imagine you lived in an apartment and the woman in the apartment above had music playing all day long, even during the night and when she went out. How would you deal with it?

(G) Look when you listen

When people are speaking it's important that they know where the listener is looking. Some people, for example, can't carry on a conversation with someone who is reading the newspaper or looking at a screen. They think you are not giving them your full attention and feel uncomfortable about continuing to speak. Look at people to show you are listening and to show respect.

- What has been one of your success stories in dealing with an irritation?
- Which kinds of people irritate you?
- How would you finish this off: I don't let myself get irritated by ...
- The thing that irritates me most about the media is ...

(G) Interrupting (2)

It's okay to interrupt if you need clarification *"I'm sorry, can you explain that again?"* or if something significant needs to be said *"The cafe closes in ten minutes so we'll need to finish soon."*

- The thing that irritates me most about work is ...
- The thing that irritates me most about my house is ...
- The thing that irritates me most about myself is ...

Is it Appropriate ...?

- Is it appropriate for mothers to do the school run in designer clothes, high heels and makeup?
- Is it appropriate to ask your ex to your wedding?
- Is it appropriate for the man to pay for everything while a couple is dating?
- Is it appropriate to omit a previous job you didn't like from your resume?
- Is it appropriate to take a face cloth from a hotel if you need it?

(Q) Starting with a contentious topic (2)

If you want to have a harmonious conversation, especially with people you don't know well, it's best to avoid contentious issues.

Example

Topic: Is it Appropriate ...?

Starter: *Is it appropriate for the man to pay for everything while a couple is dating?*

If you know that people in the group have very different views on this, it could be a contentious topic, and best avoided.

- Is it appropriate to eat meat in front of a vegetarian?
- Is it appropriate not to tip restaurant staff if the service wasn't very good?
- Is it appropriate to explain to your partner how they could kiss better?
- Is it appropriate to say grace before a meal if there are non-religious people there?
- Is it appropriate to swear in front of your teenage children?

(G) Different cultures

If someone is from a different culture, be aware that different conversation rules may apply. Some languages are influenced by their culture's views on the world, so that words and expressions may have different meanings for people from those cultures, and there may be topics of conversation that are taboo.

Some cultures, for example, see arguments as a positive and essential part of communication while others regard public disagreements as offensive.

However please be aware of stereotyping people, and remember that there are many types of people within every culture.

It's the Little Things

Sometimes we do things that are only small but make life easier;
for example preparing breakfast the night before, or buying under-
wear a size too big so that it's comfortable, or setting a weekly
reminder on your phone to put the garbage out.

- What is the first thing that comes to mind? What is
  something you do that makes life a bit easier?
- Do you do anything to make your morning routine
  easier?
- Do you do anything to make dealing with the laundry
  easier?
- Do you do anything to make dealing with other household chores easier?

(Q) Ask genuine questions

People don't like it when someone asks a question for the sole purpose of
being able to show how superior they are. For example:

"Have you been there before?"

"No I haven't."

"Oh haven't you? We've been many times, twice in the last month, in
fact."

If this is your purpose, it's best not to ask. Ultimately this way of communicating won't do you any favors as it works against building close
relationships.

- Do you do anything regarding your clothing or underwear to make it more comfortable or easier to deal
  with?
- Do you do anything to make finding things in your bag
  or purse easier?
- Do you do anything to stop yourself losing things?
- Do you do anything to help you remember things?

- Do you do anything to make things easier when dealing with your children?
- Do you do anything to make things run more smoothly in the kitchen?

Leaving this World

NOTE: Please be considerate when using this topic; it may be a sensitive area for some women. Check if it's okay to talk about these issues.

- Are you afraid of dying?
- How big an impact has religion had on shaping your thoughts about life after death?
- Some people plan early: they work out the place(s) they would like to live, should they become restricted in their mobility or mental capability, and they also plan their funeral, so that others don't have to make the decisions for them. Have you thought this far ahead? What would you like to happen?
- If you knew, from an early age, exactly when you were going to die, how would this impact on your life?

(G) Physical touch

Some people are very "touchy" people, and like to touch others on the arm or give them a hug as a way of connecting with them. Some people are not "touchy" and don't feel comfortable if someone comes into their personal space. There are no specific rules around this, simply be aware of the differences between people and respect it. If you like personal touch but the other person doesn't, maybe lessen or stop doing it. If you don't like being touched, try not to feel offended, it's just the other person's way of showing they like you and are trying to form a bond.

- If you knew you were dying, would you have any regrets about your life?

- How do you want to be remembered?
- What is the price of life? Should people be kept alive no matter what?
- Why do some people leave this world at a very early age?
- When people have a loved one who is dying, it's said that they don't want to talk about their feelings, they simply want to express them—shock, sorrow, grief. Who could help people deal with this?
- What are your thoughts on:
  - o Passive euthanasia: bringing about a person's death more quickly by changing a form of life support and letting nature take its course.
  - o Indirect euthanasia: causing the death of a person, for example through administering strong pain medication, in response to a request from that person.
  - o Assisted suicide: providing information or the means to commit suicide so that the person can end their own life.
  - o Active euthanasia: causing the death of a person, for example by administering a lethal injection.

Let's Guess!

How well do others know you? Let them guess what you're like by asking them these questions:

- How do you think I behaved when I was a young child at school?
- What types of pictures or posters did I have on my bedroom wall I was a teenager?
- What would make me laugh till I cry?
- Am I an early riser, a night owl, or something else?

(G) Interrupting (3)

A less positive way to interrupt is to try to take over or change the direction of, and not add to, the conversation. If you do this, you are signalling to the other person that what you have to say is more important than what they have to say. It's likely to have an adverse effect on the conversation and on the other speaker, and doesn't paint you as a respectful person.

Some people are chronic interrupters, and it has become a speaking pattern for them. If this is you, don't worry, there are ways around it! The first step is to recognize you are doing it. You could ask someone to let you know when you're doing it, by giving a small cough for example. Once you're aware of it, the next step is to train yourself to wait, and let the other person finish. You may even find that they end up saying what you were going to say. It may take you a while, and you may need some strategies like biting your lip or making a note of what you want to say and adding it at the end, but it will work.

This doesn't mean to say that you should never interrupt, just that you shouldn't interrupt too much.

- If I was given enough money to buy a designer outfit, have a short vacation or get a new gadget, which would I choose?
- Do I wear sensible underwear?
- The worst kind of entertainment event someone could take me to would be ...
- Do I like cleaning, tidying and ironing?
- I chose my current or last partner because ...
- A skill I have that I don't tend to tell people about is ...

Love

- Who loved you the most when you were a child?
- Did you experience puppy love?
- Who has been the greatest love of your life?

- What has been the greatest love of your life?
- How do you know when love is the real thing?

(A) If you are uncomfortable talking about a topic (1)

If it's a topic you'd prefer not to talk about then you don't have to. You could say something like *"I'd prefer not talk about that,"* or *"I only talk about those issues with my partner,"* or *"Can we move on to another topic?"*

Do it with respect, so the other person doesn't feel offended.

- If people have more than one child, is it possible to love them equally?
- Think of a relationship you have with your partner or a family member. What could you do to bring more love into the relationship?
- When it comes to a loving relationship, are you usually quite reserved or can you love easily?
- Has anyone suffered unrequited love for you?
- Some people don't experience any love in their life. What effect do you think this would have on them?

(G) Interrupting (4)

If you find yourself regularly being interrupted, one way of dealing with it is to make a comment *"I haven't quite finished,"* or speak slightly louder and carry on, or not leave too many pauses so that people can jump in. Or, once the interrupter has finished, you can say, preferably in a light hearted way, *"As I was saying . . ."*

Marriage

- Should it be accepted practice to live together before getting married?

- What are the advantages and disadvantages of getting married vs. living together?
- Did your husband propose to you? If so, how? If not, what happened?
- Tell us about your wedding preparations.
- Tell us about your wedding day.

(G) S.T.A.Y. Stop Thinking About Yourself (1)

Often what makes us nervous in communication situations is that we worry about ourselves, how we look, what we say, and so on.

To reduce nerves, don't worry about what the other person thinks of you: Stop Thinking About Yourself! The more you focus on the other person and what they are saying, the more relaxed you will feel, and the better conversation you'll have.

This won't happen overnight; it will take some time, but is an effective way of reducing nervousness.

- When you were walking down the aisle, did you have any doubts at all?
- Did you use traditional marriage vows in your wedding?
- Did you go on honeymoon?
- Many women change their surname to their husband's. Do you like this custom?
- Many marriages end in divorce. Why?

Meeting with Friends

- How often do you meet up with friends?
- Where do you tend to meet up?
- Who usually suggests that you get together?
- What do you do when you get together?
- Do you prefer to meet with friends one-to-one or do you prefer to meet in a group?

- What kinds of activities would you and your friends *never* do?

(G) Paraphrasing

Paraphrasing is where you reword what's been said in a much shorter way.

You can paraphrase something you've said in order to summarize the main points, or you can paraphrase something the other person has said to check that you understand.

Asking for something to be paraphrased can be very useful when you don't understand—or when you have forgotten what the other person has said!

- How long have you known your longest-standing friend?
- Do you prefer to have all-female or mixed get togethers?
- If you have a male partner, does he feel uncomfortable about you meeting up with your girl friends?
- Tell us about the best night out you've ever had with friends.

Men

- Do they drive you crazy?
- What would your perfect man be like?
- Are there *real* differences between men and women?
- Some people say that men and women will never be equal. Agree?

(G) Develop in-jokes

For example take something funny that someone has said and refer to it again. If it works, use it again at a later date with them.

- Can heterosexual women have genuine platonic friendships with heterosexual men?
- What are the challenges of being a man in today's society?
- Why do some men get "man flu"?
- Share one of your thoughts on gay males.

(G) Use inside jokes respectfully

Please don't use inside jokes in order to exclude other people. If you do use them, explain it to the others.

- Male egos!
- It's said that gender falls on a continuum, with some men being at the masculine end of the male continuum and some at the feminine end. Think of the men in your life. Where do they fall on this continuum?

Mixed Bag

- Look at the clothes you are wearing now. If your clothes could tell a story, what story would they tell?
- Would you, or have you, proposed to someone?
- A distant relative has died, leaving you their savings of $100,000 on condition that you live in very basic accommodation for the coming year—leaving your family, job and house if necessary—doing voluntary work amongst homeless people, before you get the money. Would you do it?
- Do you swear?

(G) Swearing. To swear or not to swear?

Swearing can be a great way to build rapport ... or it can alienate you from others. It all depends on the context.

One of the main issues is to be aware of is what the group norms are: Is it generally accepted that swearing is okay? What level of reciprocity is there? How often do people swear? What degree of swearing is acceptable, from mild through to strong?

Note that swearing is more acceptable in informal rather than formal conversation.

In instances when you are repeating what someone has said where swearing is included, you don't have to repeat the words, you can say something like *"...and then he said 'You bleep bleepbleep, how dare you...'"*

- Could you kill a turkey and prepare a meal with it?
- Would you rather live in a tropical or a temperate climate?
- Is a person's character determined by nature or nurture?
- Do you think all twins have a special bond?
- What will happen if people who have been cryogenically frozen are brought back to life in fifty years' time?
- Are there too many people in the world?

(G) Incorrect paraphrasing

Misparaphrasing is when someone incorrectly rewords what you have said. For example they may say *"So, it appears that you don't agree with it at all then"* when what you said was that you hadn't made your mind up.

It may be a genuine misparaphrase, or it may be done deliberately in order to irritate you. The best way to approach this is to deal with it calmly, avoid arguing, and simply state the correct viewpoint.

Money

- If you look back over your life and were to draw a graph of the ups and downs of your finances, how would the graph look?
- Have the times when you have had the most money equated to the times when you have been the happiest?
- Do you give money to worthy causes?
- If someone could completely guarantee that you would be very wealthy if you spent the next five years working twelve hours a day, six days a week, without any vacations, would you do it?

(Q) If you are uncomfortable talking about a topic (2)

You may not trust the questioner, as you may think they are asking questions to probe, be nosy or get you to reveal information so they can gossip or respond with a put down. In these instances, you could politely refuse to answer; change the focus back to them, or move onto a different topic.

Example

Topic: Money

Starter: *If you look back over your life and were to draw a graph of the ups and downs of your finances, how would the graph look?*

If you were wary of giving a response, you could begin with a non-specific answer and then ask the same question of them: *"That's an interesting question. I wouldn't know off the top of my head and would need to think about that one. What would your graph look like?"*

Or you could begin with a non-specific answer and then amend the topic. *"That's an interesting question. I wouldn't know off the top of my head and would need to think about that one. What I have noticed though, is that the time I was earning the most was when I was in a job I was passionate about. Have you found that too?"*

- Other than the essentials of general living costs, what do you spend most money on?
- If you won a million dollars what would you do?
- Who is the biggest miser you know?
- On a scale of zero to ten for being financially savvy, where would you place yourself?
- When choosing a partner, how important is their level of income to you?
- Is it possible to have too much money?

(Q) Impolite questions (2)

Be wary of phrasing questions in a way that implies that you know better than they do as to what they should be doing.

Phrases such as "Don't you think you should" may be seen as antagonistic. For example if they answered the question "*If you won a million dollars what would you do?*" with "*I'd share it with my family members,*" and you respond with "*Don't you think you should give some of it to charity?*" this may indicate that their answer isn't as good as yours.

Movies

- Would you rather rent a movie at home or go to the cinema?
- Which movie has had the biggest emotional impact on you?
- Which is your favorite movie of all time?
- If you had a day off sick and were snuggled up on the couch, would you rather watch movies or read a book?

(Q) Add an option

You don't necessarily have to choose from the options people give you; you can choose a different option.

Example

Topic: Movies

Starter: *If you had a day off sick and were snuggled up on the couch, would you rather watch movies or read a book?*
"I don't think I'd do either of those; I'd probably spend the day doing lots of crossword puzzles."

- Is there a movie sequel that shouldn't have been made?
- Think of a good movie that doesn't have a sequel. Tell us what the sequel should be about.
- Can you watch a movie several times?

(G) S.T.A.Y. Stop Thinking About Yourself (2)

Dale Carnegie said *"You can make more friends in two months by becoming interested in other people than you can in two years by trying to get other people interested in you."*

The goal isn't to show how interesting you are, the goal is to become more interested in the other person than you are in yourself. Interesting people are people who are interested.

- Do you like to watch sad movies?
- Who are your top three movie actors or actresses?
- If you could play any part you liked in a movie of your choice, which role would you choose?

Music

- How important is music in your life?
- What kind of music do you listen to?
- What kind of music don't you like?
- When and how do you listen to music? For example, on the radio in the car, via headphones while out running ... ?

(G) S.T.A.Y. Stop Thinking About Yourself (3)

Think about the other person's needs and feelings. For example, is your conversation making them feel bored, ill-at-ease, embarrassed, offended, angry, belittled? Or might it be making them feel appreciated, recognized, happy, amused, inspired?

Don't focus solely on what you want to say, be aware of the likely effect it will have on the other person.

- Do you play a musical instrument?
- Can you sing? In tune?
- Who is your favorite singer or group?
- What kind of music did your parents listen to?
- Do you use music to create a romantic atmosphere?
- Is there a particular song that has significance for you?

Names and Numbers

- Do you have a name for your car or any other inanimate object?
- If you could change your name or add another name, what name would you choose, sensible or otherwise?
- Do you have, or did you used to have, a nickname?

(Q) Listen and learn: Asking questions

Listen to how others ask questions and take note of the techniques they use. You'll begin to notice which ones produce good responses, which produce one word answers, which make people feel at ease, smile and laugh, or feel ill-at-ease, antagonistic and so on. Make mental notes of the techniques you like and can use.

- How did you choose the names for your children?
- How did you choose the names for your pets?
- Do you constantly forget pin numbers and passwords or do you have a strategy for remembering them?
- How fast can you think in numbers? Quickly—tell me your partner's age; the number of the house you grew up in; the license plate of your first car; your previous phone number; how many days until your next birthday?

(A) Listen and learn. Answering questions

Listen to how others answer questions and take note of the techniques they use. They may for example, pause before answering; ask a question to clarify; give a detailed answer; give a vague answer on purpose; make it into a humorous situation and so on. Make mental notes of what works well and what doesn't, and build up your toolkit of answering techniques.

- What's the most ridiculous name you've ever heard?
- Do you have a lucky number?
- Is the number thirteen an unlucky number?

Other Women

- Which woman has had the biggest influence on your life?
- Which woman would you most like to be like?
- Have you been jealous of other women?
- How would you finish this off: I can't stand women who ...
- What are the women in your family like?

(G) Show you can relate to what people are talking about

People like to feel that you understand what they are talking about and can relate to what they are experiencing, or that you have had the same experience yourself. Show that you can relate to what they are talking about, though only if you can; don't fake it.

Example

Topic: Other Women

Starter: *Have you been jealous of other women?*
If they answer *"Yes"* you could say *"Me too! It's hard to cope with isn't it? What happened for you?"*

- Who do you know, or who have you met, who is the most similar to you?
- Do you have female friends who are significantly younger or older than you?
- If you were stranded on a desert island with one other woman, who would you like it to be?
- Has there been an "other woman" in any of your relationships, or have you ever been the other woman?"
- Within your society, what level of acceptance is there for gay females?

(Q) Pay people a compliment

Paying people a compliment is a great way to make people feel good about themselves and create rapport. Noticing positive aspects about a person is always beneficial.

Example

Topic: Other Women

Starter: *Do you have female friends who are significantly younger or older than you?*

If, for example, they explain that they do, you may say *"I'm not surprised; you have a great knack of getting on with everyone you meet."*

Paranormal

- Have you had a paranormal experience?
- What are UFOs?
- Do alien life forms exist?
- Do you believe that there are people who have been abducted by aliens?

(G) Disagreeing (3)

When you don't agree with what someone else is saying, always treat them with respect. It's okay to disagree with their views without slighting them. Acknowledge any areas where you are in agreement, and aim to avoid using the word "but" as it can be seen as antagonistic; use a non-negative phrase instead if possible.

Example

"I think we both agree that there are a number of flaws in their line of reasoning. How does your suggestion work in practice?"

OR *"I think we both agree that there are a number of flaws in their line of reasoning. Regarding your suggestion, we need to take into account that . . ."*

NOT *"I think we both agree that there are a number of flaws in their line of reasoning, but your suggestion is wrong."*

- What are your thoughts about Area 51?
- Is there a paranormal aspect to the pyramids?
- Can dreams predict the future?
- Can buildings be haunted by ghosts?
- Would you use a Ouija board?
- Can people be possessed?

(G) Respecting differences and fears

People have many and varied fears, and what may seem trivial to one person may be of significance to someone else.

Example

Topic: Paranormal

Starter: *Can buildings be haunted by ghosts?*

If, for example, they say they have a ghost in their house and are terrified of it, it's best to avoid saying something like *"Oh yes, we had a ghost in our last house, it was nothing, there was no point getting upset about it."*

A good rule of thumb when showing respect is to aim to see it from the other person's point of view and understand how their emotions have come about. Avoiding making judgments and asking gentle questions instead when you are not sure can lead you in the right direction.

Personality

- Which of these personality types is most like you:
    - o   Impulsive, likes to talk and have fun
    - o   Ambitious, likes to lead
    - o   Kind, people-focused, likes harmony
    - o   Thoughtful, cautious, likes perfection

- Is your husband or partner the opposite personality type to you?
- Do your main friends have a similar personality to you?

(Q) Bring in humor by saying something incorrect

Say something that's the opposite of what's true. Very amusing when people know the true answer.

Example

Topic: Personality

Starter: *Is your husband or partner the opposite personality type to you? "Absolutely! He's very noisy, never stops talking and always laughs way too loud!"* (When this is really how you are).

- Are you an introvert, an extrovert or a combination?
- Describe the different personalities of the family members you were brought up with.
- What can personality tests show?
- Is it possible to change your personality?
- What kind of people do you have a personality clash with?
- Which personality trait do you wish you had?
- Is it okay to use your personality traits as an excuse?

(Q) If you are uncomfortable talking about a topic (3)

If you feel the question requires specific information about you that you don't want to reveal, you can change the focus of your answer by making it general rather than personal.

Example

Topic: Personality

Starter: *What kind of people do you have a personality clash with?*
You could widen the focus by talking about people in general. *"You know, I was thinking about that issue recently and I've noticed that people who have the same type of personality are the ones who generally clash . . ."*

Physical Appearance

- Which part(s) of your body do you most like?
- Are you happy about how tall you are?
- Do you do anything to deal with your weight?
- Boobs!

(G) Please do not ever . . .

. . . ask a question that involves someone opening up and revealing something personal about themselves, and then treat it with disrespect later on in the conversation or at a later date. Being able to trust someone is one of the fundamentals in a relationship, and if someone exposes a vulnerability only to have it treated without respect, it can cause significant emotional hurt.

For example if the topic were *"Do you do anything to deal with your weight?"* and someone shares the struggles they've had to cope with, it would be inappropriate to bring it up later in a hurtful way *"How can you give advice on that, you couldn't even manage to control your weight?"*

- Do you like having your photo taken?
- Which do you find the most attractive skin color?
- Has your physical appearance ever been an advantage to you?

- Has your physical appearance ever been a disadvantage to you?
- Which famous person would you most like to look like?
- Be honest: do you scrutinize women's appearance and find faults?

(A) Supportive feedback

If the feedback you want to give is not positive, despite being kind, find a way to say it that provides a positive option.

For example, if you were asked *"Does this hairstyle make me look older?"* instead of simply saying *"Yes, it does make you look older"* how about saying *"If you don't feel comfortable about your hairstyle, how about we look through some magazines and see if there are any you like better?"*

Pleasure

- Can you share one of your guilty pleasures?
- What is something that you find intellectually pleasing?
- What is something that is an emotional pleasure for you?
- What is one of the most pleasurable physical sensations?
- What is your favorite sexual pleasure?
- What could or should be pleasurable but isn't?

(G) Being interested

Great conversationalists are genuinely interested in what others say, and are enthusiastic in their questioning and in their listening. When you feel that someone is genuinely interested in what you are saying, it raises the level of energy in the conversation and increases the feeling of connectedness to that person. Ask yourself if you could improve how interested you are in others and what they talk about.

- What was your greatest pleasure when you were a child?
- How can one thing cause someone so much pleasure, such as a lovely meal or beautiful music, but have no effect on someone else?
- What was something that didn't used to be a pleasure for you, but now is? What has changed?
- Some people seem to get pleasure out of hurting others. Is this "pleasure"?

Politics

- How often do you have conversations about politics?
- How would you describe your level of interest in politics?
- Would you like to be, or are you, involved in local politics?
- What should children be taught about politics in school?
- Who has been the greatest political leader?

(A) Pause before you start answering

Take a couple of seconds before you reply, especially before a weighty question. This will give you time to think through what you are going to say, and will give the impression that you are giving a considered opinion.

See the technique: *Pause—Work out your end point—Go in a straight line* from the section "How to avoid rambling" page 17.

You don't need to do it every time though, it's also okay to answer straight away when you know what you want to say.

- For the average person's daily life, does it make much difference which political party is in power?
- Which factors are important when deciding who to vote for?
- Are politicians to be trusted?
- Will a female ever be president of the US?
- Should politicians have any say in religious issues?

(Q) Use quotes

Sometimes it's useful to bring in a suitable quote to liven up your answer. It's a good idea to learn a few short ones, including humorous ones, and build them up over time.

Example

Topic: Politics

Starter: *Are politicians to be trusted?*

"I agree with Henry Kissinger who once said "Ninety percent of the politicians give the other ten percent a bad reputation."'

Possessions

- Are you a hoarder?
- If your house was on fire and you could go in and save one of your possessions, what would you save?

- What's the possession that you've lost and would dearly love to have back again?
- Tell us about a special piece of jewelry.
- Which is your most treasured photo?
- Do you have any of your parents' possessions?

(G) Do you finish other people's ...

... sentences?

Don't do it! People don't like it.

You can think faster than others can speak, so sometimes you may have worked out what the other person is going to say before they've finished. However, if you finish off someone's sentence, firstly you might get it wrong, and secondly it gives the rather impolite impression that what they are saying is so obvious that you can't be bothered waiting for them to get it out!

- If you were stranded on a desert island and could have a spare set of clothes, an item of special importance, and something to keep you occupied, what would you choose?
- Would it interest you to live with very few belongings, where you had the bare minimum of (though enough) possessions?
- Do you have possessions stored away that you haven't seen for years? If so, why do you keep them?
- If a friend or family member said you were welcome to take one of their possessions and keep it as a gift, what would you take?

(G) Meaning is contextual

You obtain the meaning of what people say from the context. Some contexts are obvious. Let's say someone came in wearing a bright red hat and said *"I got it at the thrift shop for five dollars,"* you wouldn't need to ask what they were referring to as the meaning is obvious.

However, some contexts are less obvious. Imagine you said to a friend, *"I'm thinking of going to a movie tomorrow, want to come?"* and they snap at you *"Of course I don't want to come."* In this instance your context may be a simple request for a social night out. Their context may be that they've just had some bad news they are trying to cope with; or perhaps they've had an argument with someone; or they have just been asked to work late tomorrow by a boss they don't get on with.

There are many types of "invisible"contexts that can have an effect on what people are saying which may make the true meaning difficult to grasp.

In situations where someone has communicated something that doesn't feel right, before jumping to conclusions consider that there may be an invisible context you aren't aware of. You may need to gently ask.

Pregnancy

NOTE: Please be considerate when using this topic; it may be a sensitive area for some women. Check it's okay to talk about these issues.

- Was it easy for you to conceive?
- How easy was your pregnancy / pregnancies?
- Did you put on much weight when you were pregnant?
- Did you enjoy being pregnant?

(G) When not to interrupt

If someone is talking about an emotional topic or a topic that's very important to them that they need to share, the typical conversational mode of turn-taking may not apply while you let them say what they need to.

- Did you have any cravings while you were pregnant?
- Describe the birth(s).
- Were you thoroughly prepared for when the baby arrived?
- How long did it take you to lose the weight after giving birth?
- Would you like to have, or would you have liked to have, more children?
- If you are planning to have a child, are you doing anything to get your health and body ready?

Previous Relationships

- Tell us about one of your exes.
- Have you suffered from unrequited love?
- Have you been a good judge of character?
- Has infidelity featured in your previous relationships?
- How have your relationships ended?

(Q) If you are uncomfortable talking about a topic (4)

If you feel a question is inappropriate, deal with it by deflecting and giving a vague answer. Always be pleasant while you are doing so.

Example

Topic: Previous Relationships

Starter: *How have your relationships ended?*
"Oh goodness, I've been married for fifteen years now, and it's such a long time since I had another partner that I'm afraid I can't remember the specifics. I think we just grew apart."

- Do you regret ending any of your previous relationships?
- Were you deceived by any previous partners?
- Are you happy with how you behaved in your previous relationships?
- Could you go back to any of your previous partners?
- If you are divorced, do you regret marrying?

Problems

- What's the biggest problem you've had to deal with?
- What problems are you dealing with at the moment?
- Who do you call on for help?
- Who causes you the most problems?
- Do you know someone who has a problem that you would love to help them with?

(Q) Be aware of "leading" questions

Leading questions are questions where you direct the other person towards answering in a certain way, or put words into their mouth.

Example

Topic: Problems

Starter: *Who causes you the most problems?*
NOT: *Who causes you the most problems? Is it your husband?*

- Has being a woman ever been a problem for you?
- When a problem arises, what's usually your initial reaction?
- Which of your problems are you most proud of having solved?
- What kinds of problems are you skilled at helping others with?
- Some people make a mountain out of a molehill. Can you give an example of this?

Quotes about Women

Give your thoughts on these quotes:

- On the whole, I think women wear too much and are too fussy. You can't see the person for all the clutter. (Julie Andrews)
- Speaking very generally, I find that women are spiritually, emotionally, and often physically stronger than men. (Gary Oldman)
- The connections between and among women are the most feared, the most problematic, and the most potentially transforming force on the planet. (Adrienne Rich)
- A homely face and no figure have aided many women heavenward. (Minna Antrim)
- I always say God should have given women one extra decade at least, especially if you want a family. You're trying to pack a lot in. (Christine Baranski)

> ### (Q) Don't ask a question just to be nosy
>
> Tempting though it may be, using a starters to find out something about the other person simply for the purpose of being nosy (you will know when you are doing this!) isn't the best way to build trust and rapport.

- There are only three things women need in life: food, water, and compliments. (Chris Rock)
- As usual, there is a great woman behind every idiot. (John Lennon)
- It's not fair that women look in the mirror and feel disgust because of what society has made them believe. (Jessica Simpson)
- It's hard to tell how far women's individuality has come in the past twenty years. (Annie Lennox)
- You can find lots of people like you through technology, and women in particular like communities. (Carly Fiorina)

Quotes by Women

Give your thoughts on these quotes:

- Luck? I don't know anything about luck. I've never banked on it, and I'm afraid of people who do. Luck to me is something else: Hard work—and realizing what is opportunity and what isn't. (Lucille Ball)
- The poor give us much more than we give them. They're such strong people, living day to day with no food. And they never curse, never complain. We don't have to give them pity or sympathy. We have so much to learn from them. (Mother Theresa)

(G) Bonding: Have open body language

Keep your body language open and non-threatening and aim to look approachable. You will be perceived in a more positive light and more welcoming if you have open, rather than closed body language.

If you adopt closed body language by sitting hunched up, with arms and legs crossed and an averted gaze, it won't make you look very approachable.

- Giving birth is little more than a set of muscular contractions granting passage of a child. Then the mother is born. (Erma Bombeck)
- Self-pity in its early stages is as snug as a feather mattress. Only when it hardens does it become uncomfortable. (Maya Angelou)
- One never notices what has been done; one can only see what remains to be done. (Marie Curie)
- We do not grow absolutely, chronologically. We grow sometimes in one dimension, and not in another, unevenly. We grow partially. We are relative. We are mature in one realm, childish in another. (Anais Nin)
- I say to the young: "Do not stop thinking of life as an adventure. You have no security unless you can live bravely, excitingly, imaginatively." (Eleanor Roosevelt)
- Though the sex to which I belong is considered weak you will nevertheless find me a rock that bends to no wind. (Elizabeth 1 of England)

(G) The TV

If you are in a room with a TV, be careful that it doesn't cause a distraction. Consider switching the volume down, or switching it off altogether. If you are out somewhere that has a TV screen, think about moving to different seats where it won't be a distraction.

- When I buy cookies I eat just four and throw the rest away. But first I spray them with Raid so I won't dig them out of the garbage later. Be careful, though, because Raid really doesn't taste that bad. (Janette Barber)
- I have flabby thighs, but fortunately my stomach covers them. (Joan Rivers)

Reactions

How would you react if these scenarios happened to you?

- You are walking around a department store when the store detectives approach you and accuse you of shoplifting. Somehow there is a piece of jewelry in your bag or purse and the CCTV shows someone who appears to be you, taking a piece of jewelry.
- You get a phone call from a friend who has recently moved to live two hundred miles away. She is crying and says she is very unhappy and can't see the point of living until tomorrow.

(G) Mirroring

Mirroring is when your speech or body language mirrors the other person's. You can do it consciously, or it may happen subconsciously. Mirroring done well can create rapport, understanding and trust. It will also put the other person at ease.

If the person you're speaking to leans forward, you can too; if they have a fast speaking pace, you can match it; if they cross their legs, try crossing yours, and so on. It's very useful for building connections if done subtly, but don't overdo it and make it look obvious.

- You come home and find a huge bouquet of 100 roses outside your front door and an anonymous note in the mailbox telling you how precious you are.
- You were very close to your grandmother and miss her now that she is gone. She left you a picture she used to have in her living room, which you have had hanging in pride of place for many years in your living room. You have recently discovered that the picture is worth a lot of money. Finances are pretty tight at the moment and you would appreciate some extra income.
- You discover that several years before you moved into your home, a previous owner used the basement to make illegal drugs. Police think the owner buried the equipment in the garden and would like to dig up your lawn to investigate.
- You find that a number of neighbors who don't know you well start calling you by a different name, even though they know your name. When you ask them why, they say you look exactly like another woman, and ask if you have a twin sister.

(G) Put away anything that distracts

Do you get easily distracted? Are you always checking an electronic gadget, fiddling with something such as your keys, or sitting with headphones on listening to music? Put them away! If you can't see them they will be less of a distraction to you.

Letting yourself be distracted is seen as rude and gets in the way of good conversation and good connections. Give people your full attention.

- You discover that the person who performed your wedding ceremony was not qualified to do so, and so you are not officially married.
- You receive an invite in the mail from the school you went to, asking you to come and give a talk to the students as they deem you to be the most successful person they have had at the school.
- You walk into a café. There are several people sitting with parrots on their heads.
- A TV news crew comes up to you as you are walking down the street. They say they have heard that your town contains the highest number of musically-minded people in the country and ask if you would sing into the microphone.

Relationships

- Do other people interfere in your relationships?
- If your partner suggested you have separate vacations this year, how would you feel?
- Are you usually the dominant one in a relationship?
- Which is your most important platonic relationship?

(G) Sensitive information

Be aware that some people may not want their sensitive information shared with others. Saying something like *"Margaret's thinking of leaving her husband, aren't you?"* when Margaret doesn't want people to know, will cause upset and embarrassment. If in doubt, it's best to say nothing.

- Could you be 100 percent happy living the rest of your life not in a relationship?
- Is it reasonable to expect two people to stay in love forever?
- Is being in love the best reason to get married?
- What part does arguing play in a healthy relationship?
- If a couple chooses not to have children, are they missing out on anything?

(G) Turn taking

The accepted norm for conversation is that people take turns, the rationale being that conversation runs more smoothly this way. There are different ways to indicate a change of turn. These include directly asking for a contribution, for example *"What does everyone else think?"*; making a movement such as a change in sitting position; or having a falling intonation to indicate you have finished what you are saying.

A very common way to indicate your turn has finished is to look at another person to show that they can now speak.

- Can polygamy (a marriage of more than two partners) or polyamory (having more than one relationship at a time with the knowledge and agreement of all concerned) work?

Romance

- Are you romantic?
- Could you be more romantic?
- How many "true" romances have you had?
- Who has been your most romantic partner, and what romantic things did they do?

(G) Avoid excluding others (3)

You can inadvertently give the impression you want to exclude someone by sitting with your chair slightly turned away from them; with your back partly turned towards them; or by having eye contact with everyone in the group except them.

- Do you read romantic novels or watch romantic movies?
- Could you be happy in a non-romantic relationship?
- Describe a romantic surprise you gave your husband or partner.
- What's the most romantic gift you've ever received?

(G) Enthusiasm (2)

If someone looks and sounds bored while they are speaking, other people aren't going to be inspired or energized.

If the conversation covers a topic you're not particularly interested in, it's polite to try to find an aspect you can muster some enthusiasm for. Alternatively, and if appropriate, you may like to steer the conversation towards another topic.

- Is it possible to have romance without sex?
- Do women's magazines place too much emphasis on the romantic notion of a perfect life and not enough on day-to-day life?

School

- Tell us about your first day at school or your earliest memory of school.

- Which of your teachers is the most memorable and why?
- What was the funniest incident that happened at school?
- What was the worst incident that happened at school?
- What are your memories of learning to read, write or do math?

(G) Facial expression and meaning

As well as your words, your face also communicates meaning.

Ideally your words and facial expression communicate the same meaning, though not always. It's perfectly possible, for example, to say *"That's very interesting, tell me more,"* while looking thoroughly bored.

When there is a mismatch, people will believe what they see before they believe what they hear. So if your facial expression says one thing and your spoken words say another, they will believe what your face is communicating.

- Who was your best friend at school?
- Did you like school?
- When you were a young child, what happened at the end of the school day? Did someone pick you up from school and take you home?
- Do you have any school photos?
- What did you learn from being at school, over and above the academic aspect?

Secrets

- What secrets did you have as a child?
- Did you have a secret hiding place when you were young?

- Can you keep a secret?
- Have you kept a secret for someone that felt like a burden?

(Q) Don't ask a question then start answering it yourself

This may sound simple enough, though sometimes it's tempting to do it. Once you've asked a question, leave space for the other person to answer.

Example

Topic: Secrets

Starter: *Can you keep a secret?*

NOT: *Can you keep a secret? I'm sure you can. You know, I usually can, but there was a time when . . .*

- Is there a secret you've never shared with anyone that you feel it's okay to share now?
- Do you have a secret stash of chocolate (or similar) in your house?
- Have you ever kept a relationship secret from others?
- Some people are very secretive and give little away about themselves, even ordinary stuff. Why are they like this?
- What would you say is the world's best kept secret?
- What secrets does the government keep from us?

Sex

- Were you brought up to believe that sex before marriage was unacceptable?
- On a scale of zero to ten, how important is sex to you?

- Do you remember the first time you had sex?
- Would you have sex on a first date?
- Do you use sex toys?

(G) Emotions

If someone has opened up on an emotional topic, make sure they are given enough time to finish what they need to say. Please don't rush and change the topic before time. Once they are finished, it's then good to move onto a lighter topic to bring about a mood change.

- If your husband or partner suggested a threesome, how would you feel?
- Have you ever faked it?
- What's the difference between having sex and making love?
- How do you feel about prostitution?
- Is there too much sex on TV?
- Is there enough, and appropriate, sex education at school?

Shopping

- What has been your best bargain?
- How much online shopping do you do?
- What would be your perfect shopping spree?
- Do you spend too much?

(G) Helping those who ramble

Sometimes people can't help themselves losing focus and going off on lengthy tangents. Interjecting and asking good questions that keep people on track is a great way to keep a satisfactory conversation going.

For example, if you ask *"Would you like to go to the market tomorrow?"* and the other person starts to go off on a tangent *"I would love to, but I'll have to call the electrician first because—would you believe it?—the stove blew up as I was making breakfast this morning! I only bought it last year and didn't expect . . ."* You can either let them continue with the story and ask questions about the stove, or you can wait for a suitable break and gently steer the person back on track. *"I'm planning to leave at ten o'clock. Will that give you enough time?"*

- Do you prefer shopping on your own or with someone else?
- Do you ever go out to just window shop and not buy anything?
- If you want an expensive purchase, would you save up for it, get it on credit or choose another way?
- Do you enjoy grocery shopping?
- Are you tempted by a special offer even when it's something you don't need?
- Do you like to buy the latest gadgets?

Situations

These are real situations that people have found themselves in. Is there anything wrong with them? Do we laugh them off, or should something change?

- A professional couple with a family hire a cleaner to come weekly. She turns up in a better car than the couple have.
- It's a young woman's twenty-first birthday. Her boyfriend is at medical school and offers to take her out at lunch time to celebrate. He takes her to the university to watch an operation, saying he hopes she'll find it as enthralling as he does.

(G) Understanding control

Sometimes when people are feeling insecure they try to establish control over the other person. They may do this by calling people names and making derogatory put downs such as "That's a stupid thing to do." If this happens to you, understand that it's their insecurity driving this.

It may help to remember the words of Eleanor Roosevelt: "No one can make you feel inferior without your consent."

- A daughter leaves home at age nineteen. She goes to university, gets a job, buys a house, gets married and has a child. Twenty years later a lot of her stuff is still stored at her parents' house as she says she doesn't have room for it.
- A couple in their sixties still have their forty-four year old son living at home. He has a good job but says he sees no need to move out.
- A professional man in his thirties splits from his wife. He doesn't feel he can afford to rent a place so stays in a tent in his friend's garden.
- A woman attends a training course to learn a new computer package. She is the only person who turns up. The tutor is out sick, so one of the non-teaching staff members offers to teach her what he knows about the package.
- A man working at a company calls up an electrician to do a small rewiring job. The electrician turns up with few tools and asks to borrow a drill and a hammer.
- A woman goes for a job interview at an all-male organization. They tell her they would like to offer her the job but can't as there are no female restrooms.

(G) Listening to stories

When someone tells a story—and it's usually prefaced by an indicator that it will be a story—the usual turn-taking nature of conversation stops and it's expected that you will listen to the whole story. Once it's finished normal turn-taking resumes.

- A woman goes to a local branch of her bank. It's closed. She calls them up later and is told that they have to close at lunchtime because too many customers turn up then.
- A sprightly woman in her eighties goes to the supermarket. She can't find what she needs, so asks for help. Later on she goes to see her granddaughter saying she wants to complain to the supermarket "because they treat me like an eighty year old."

Spiritual

- Are you spiritual?
- When people say they are "spiritual" and not "religious," what does this mean?
- Do you believe in angels and spirits?
- Have you been for a spiritual reading?
- What's the difference between spiritual and supernatural?

(G) Explain things simply

People will lose interest if there is a long drawn-out explanation. A short explanation in easy-to-understand language is the best way to help people grasp what you are saying. The mark of a good communicator is if people have understood their message.

- What are psychic powers?
- What happens when we die / pass over?
- Can mediums connect with people who have died / passed over?
- Can we manifest what we want?
- What are your views on spiritual healing?

Star Signs

Whether you agree with star signs or not, it can be interesting to look at the descriptions of personality traits to see if there is any correlation with who you feel you are, or the kind of person other people present as. Look at the descriptions given below and see if you identify with your star sign or can recognize the qualities in others.

- Aries, The Ram, March 21–April 19. This is a fire sign and Aries people can be fiery, opinionated, quick to anger, impulsive, driven and strong willed. They can also be creative, intuitive and passionate, as well as loyal friends and good family people with a sense of humor.
- Taurus, The Bull, April 20–May 20. Taurus people can be strong and stubborn although they can also be faithful, loving and generous. They are efficient, effective teachers, dependable and decisive.
- Gemini, The Twins, May 21–June 20. Gemini people may have a dual side to their nature and can be prone to mood swings. They like variety, have lots of interests and many talents. They like to talk and think, are inspirational, and have lots of charisma.

(G) If things get heated

In a quote from Rose Macaulay she says, "So they left the subject and played croquet, which is a very good game for people who are annoyed with one another ..."

If the conversation gets heated, have a break. Change the topic or do something different like going to the kitchen and making a cup of tea.

- Cancer, The Crab, June 21–July 22. Cancerians can be loving and family oriented, favoring a traditional home-centered life. They are good friends, faithful and kind, like to have time on their own but can be moody and over-reactive. They enjoy history.
- Leo, The Lion, July 23–August 22. Leos can be power-ful and vocal. They may be inflexible, brave and head strong. However they tend to make good judgments, are good leaders, and are generous and charitable. They may keep their emotions hidden but usually operate from the principle of doing good.
- Virgo, The Virgin, August 23–September 22. Virgos can be good conversationalists, analytical and inquisitive with a sharp mind. They are socially adept and good at working in teams. However they may be opinionated, short-tempered and self-absorbed if out of balance.
- Libra, The Scales, September 23–October 22. Librans like balance, stability and justice. They are concerned about relationships and like communicating, although they may appear introverted and lacking in confidence. They can be kind, caring, and supportive.

(G) Make people feel good

It's said that people won't remember the words you say, they won't remember the things you do, but what they will remember is how you make them feel.

Making people feel good about themselves is a skill you can learn, and one that is a fundamental of excellent communication.

After an interaction, people will generally feel positive, neutral or negative about their communication with you. Aim to leave people feeling positive.

- Scorpio, The Scorpion, October 23–November 21. Although Scorpio people can be secretive, insensitive and stubborn, they can also be calm, collected and capable of great undertakings. They are determined, pay attention to detail and are not easily swayed.
- Sagittarius, The Centaur, November 22–December 21. Sagittarius people can be extroverted, generous and honest. They like life to be big. However they can be impatient, uncontrolled and intense and may undertake too many activities. They take setbacks in their stride but do not like to be tied down.
- Capricorn, The Goat, December 22–January 19. Capricorn people can be intelligent, instinctive and good at organizing. They do not like criticism but will accomplish well if they follow a plan. Faithful and sensual, they are good at helping others with their problems.
- Aquarius, The Water Bearer, January 20–February 18. Aquarians like to find new ways of doing things, and may do so in an unpredictable and flamboyant way. They can be intellectual, artistic and compassionate, taking on humanitarian causes.

(G) If you know A LOT about a topic ...

When you are very knowledgeable about a topic and others aren't, how much do you tell people? Be considerate in how much you share, unless others are equally interested. They may not want to know every tiny detail.

You could give an overview or summarized version of your knowledge in order to gauge the level of interest, and if people are keen to know more they will ask questions.

- Pisces, The Fish, February 19–March 20. Pisceans may come across as quiet and unassuming, though they can be highly knowledgeable and generous. People may take advantage of their kind and trusting nature. They can be loving and trustworthy, a great supporter of family and friends.

Stay at Home Mom

If you are or have been a Stay at Home Mom:
- How did you make the decision to become a Stay at Home Mom?
- Did you ever regret your decision?
- What are or were the most challenging issues?
- Was it the best decision for your child / children?
- Was there any pressure for you to go back to work?

(G) Balance

Conversations generally work better when they are balanced, and people have a similar amount of speaking time. It doesn't need to be equal, but if one person dominates the speaking time, it won't be a satisfactory exchange for those who feel their views are deemed to be unimportant.

If you haven't been a Stay at Home Mom:

- What do you imagine are the benefits of being a Stay at Home Mom?
- What do you imagine are the disadvantages of being a Stay at Home Mom?
- Is it the best thing for the child?
- What would be the difference between having a Stay at Home Mom or a Stay at Home Dad?
- Is it in employer's best interests to keep the woman's job open for a period of time?

Stories

Sometimes making up a continuous imaginary story can be a fun part of conversation. Try making some of them outlandish for more effect. One person starts the story; the next person carries it on, and so on until everyone has had a go.

- I was looking online at travel deals and saw a bargain that was too good to be true ...
- It had been a very tough day. I came home, opened the front door and ...
- When I answered the phone my friend yelled, "You'll never believe what's happened!"
- There was a loud commotion in the shopping mall. When I went over to see what was happening ...

(G) Intonation and meaning

You can sometimes give a different meaning by changing the word you stress, and / or the tone you use. Try saying this seven-word sentence in seven different ways by placing the stress on a different word each time you say it: *"Martha didn't say I broke the vase."*

Now try saying the sentence *"I love the works of Shakespeare"* with the emphasis on the word *"love"* in a genuine tone then in a cynical tone. Now try saying it as if there were a question mark at the end of the sentence.

You can give a range of meanings to what you say, not just by the words you choose, but by how you choose to say them.

- Deciding to treat myself, I went into the lingerie store ...
- It was Saturday night, the last night of our vacation. We were having a meal and I thoroughly expected him to propose to me ...
- Out of the blue I got a phone call from the local radio station, live on air. "You've won!" they announced ...
- In the dead of the night I heard the bedroom window being opened from the outside ...

(G) Count on your fingers

If you have a small number of points you want to talk about, hold up the corresponding number of fingers. Then touch one finger until you've talked about the first point then fold it down, then touch the next finger while you talk about the second point, and so on. It will reduce the likelihood of interruptions. Be aware of not going on for too long about any of the points. This will only work if you have a small number of points.

- I went to meet a friend at a café. When I got there I saw someone at the next table I'd been at school with many years ago ...
- I was extremely shocked when I discovered that ...

Strangers

- Have you ever been on the receiving end of a random act of kindness from a stranger?
- Have you ever carried out a random act of kindness for someone you didn't know?
- If a beggar approached you, smiled and politely asked you for just enough money to buy a simple meal, what would you do?
- Have you had any dealings with tramps?

(G) Words to help continue the conversation

If you have asked a question, the other person has given a reply and you're not sure what to say next, try using a question starting with one of the Five W's and One H: What, When, Who, Why, Where, and How.

Example

Topic: Strangers

Starter: *Have you ever been on the receiving end of a random act of kindness from a stranger?*
If they reply "Yes I have," your next question could be, for example "What happened?" "When was that?" "How did it happen?"

- Think of a female you don't know that you've seen recently, for example working at the local library, at the checkout at the supermarket, or living in the same street as you. Try describing the kind of person you think she is and how she lives. For example what are her hobbies? Where would she go on vacation? What's in her refrigerator? What magazines does she read?
- Think of a male you don't know that you've seen recently, for example working at the local library, at the checkout

at the supermarket, or living in the same street as you. Try describing the kind of person you think he is and how he lives. For example is he married? What pictures does he have on his living room wall? What are his political views? Would he have a tattoo?

- A friend of yours sponsors a child in Africa. She shares details of the child's brother, a four year old boy who is also in need of a sponsor, and asks if you could help. Would you sponsor him?

(G) Explaining who people are

If you talk about people that others don't know, it's respectful to explain who they are. Saying *"Celeste is coming with me tonight"* and carrying on the conversation when people don't know her relationship to you, is not as helpful as saying *"Celeste, my colleague from work, is coming with me tonight."*

- Have you ever stopped to help a stranger?
- You get on a long-journey bus, train or coach and there are two empty seats. One is next to a nun in her thirties and the other is next to a teenage boy holding a bird in a small cage. Who would you sit next to and why?
- You are out with a friend when she bumps into one of her male friends, and you all go for coffee. Her friend is a part time art lecturer at the university and a part time artist. He says he finds your facial features interesting and invites you to his studio so he can paint you. Would you go?

Stress

- Is stress a modern day phenomenon?
- Do you use any strategies to avoid stress?
- What's the most effective way you've found to deal with stress once it's happened?
- When things go wrong, do you have a tendency towards anger or towards depression?
- Do you tend to panic?
- Imagine that you have been invited to write a magazine article or record a podcast on "How to keep calm when everything around you is falling apart." What would you say?

(G) Laugh!

Laughter, surprisingly, isn't so much about humor; it's more about relationships. Fundamentally, people like to laugh because it makes them feel they belong, are accepted, and have a good bond with others.

This, fortunately, means you don't *have* to be good at telling jokes or even telling humorous stories (though those are very useful skills), because ordinary comments are capable of producing laughter if said in a happy, light-hearted or mischievous way. People love to laugh; it's contagious, it's universal, and it has many benefits. It makes you feel better, it helps you remember things, it stimulates and makes you more alert, it helps you relax, and people will warm to you if you make them laugh.

It's important to have genuine laughter—people can tell when it's not—and to laugh *with* others, not laugh *at* others. Laughing *with* shows inclusion, laughing *at* indicates exclusion.

It's also okay to laugh at something you've said yourself; that's very common, and people appreciate it.

- What is the main thing that causes you to feel stressed?
- Who is the main person that causes you to feel stressed?
- Laughter is said to be a good antidote to stress. How much laughter is in your life?
- Which of the following would cause you to feel the most stress and why:
  - o Getting caught in traffic and being late for a job interview
  - o Having your purse stolen
  - o Being wrongly accused of shoplifting
  - o Being trapped in an elevator

Support

- If you need emotional support, who or what would be your first port of call?
- If you were having financial difficulties, what would be your preferred form of support?
- One of your female friends is starting out on a new business venture and asks for any support you can give. What is the main type of support you could offer?
- Do you use books or other forms of written material when you need help over a personal issue?

(G) Bonding: Use eye contact to create a connection with others

It's very hard to create a connection with someone else if you don't look at them. All you need to do is hold the other person's gaze for a few seconds at a time, every now and then. Don't hold their gaze for too short a time that you come across as shy and uneasy in conversation, or for too long a time that they feel you are staring at them.

- Which member of your family generally needs the most support?
- Do you provide support to people other than your family or friends?
- What could be the benefits of having a mentor?
- If you were asked to be a mentor, what type of life issues do you feel most qualified to help others with?
- Who is a person you wouldn't go to for support?
- If you are part of a group of female friends, what happens when one of the group is going through a challenge and needs support?

Technology

- What kind of cell phone do you have and why did you choose it?
- Are items such as cars, ovens, washing machines and microwaves becoming too complex to easily operate or repair?
- I couldn't live without my . . .
- Do you have a favorite technology brand?
- Some women feel that technology companies "dumb down" their marketing to women and make it a bit "pink." Agree?

(G) Matching emotions

People like to feel that there is some sharing of emotions, particularly when the topic is an emotional one for them. If you look distanced from their feelings it will make it hard for them to open up or relate to you.

In order to create rapport, make your facial expressions, body language and way of speaking tie in with their emotions. If they are excited look happy, perhaps lean forward; if they are upset look sympathetic and make comforting sounds such as "oh dear," or maybe touch their arm; and so on.

- It's said that when it comes to games consoles, women from mid-twenties to mid-thirties play more games than men. What's the attraction?
- The dangers of technology for teenage girls.
- Should technology stores have more female assistants? Or at least male assistants who understand how to deal with women?
- What has been the greatest technology advancement in recent years?
- What has been the least useful technology advancement in recent years?

Teenage Years

- What happened when you hit puberty?
- Tell us about the highs and lows of your life as a teenager.
- Learning to deal with periods—how was it for you?
- Skin problems!
- Did you get into any trouble during your teenage years?

(G) Exaggeration

Obvious exaggeration is a great way to bring in humor.

Example

Topic: Teenage years

Starter: *Skin problems!*
"Wow, did I have skin problems. The geography teacher would use my face as a map of the Rockies!"

Use exaggeration sparingly though; if you overdo it, it will wear thin after a while.

- Did your parents like the friends you had?
- Who were your heartthrobs?
- Did alcohol and drugs feature in your teenage years?
- If you could go back in time to when you were a teenager, what advice would you give yourself?
- What's the difference between teenagers these days and teenagers in your day?

Temptation

- What's the temptation you can't resist?
- Is food a temptation for you?
- Is alcohol a temptation for you?
- Is there a person you can't resist?
- Have you ever been tempted to run away and start a new life?

(Q) Say something outrageous or humorous

If it's not a serious topic and you want to make the conversation livelier, say something ridiculous, and not necessarily true!

Example

Topic: Temptation

Starter: *What's the temptation you can't resist?*
"I love going round my local supermarket and secretly putting expensive items into people's shopping cart when they're not looking. Anyone else like doing this?"

- What is the one thing you would never be tempted to do, no matter what?
- Have you gained strength from things you've managed to resist?

- Think of something that's a temptation for you. What could you do to plan ahead in order to reduce the risk of giving in?
- Looking back, which temptation do you really, really wish you hadn't given in to?
- George Orwell said that "Many people genuinely do not want to be a saint." Agree?

The Common Good

The common good is a concept that looks at setting society up in such a way that the conditions are to everyone's advantage, rather than supporting individuals or groups selfishly fighting to meet their own needs. Although not everyone will agree on what constitutes the common good, it's generally agreed that with some simple sacrifices, positive steps are possible.

- What can be done to make forward movements towards an affordable, good quality health care system?
- What can be done to make forward movements towards reducing the carbon footprint?
- What can be done to make forward movements towards having clean air and an unpolluted environment?
- What can be done to make forward movements towards litter-free environments?

(G) Focus on what people are saying!

If you are an I-listener (page 68) it's going to be useful to learn to listen to what others are saying *without* focusing on what *you* want to say. Try some You-listening!

Yes, there will be occasions when there is something you are bursting to say and so don't listen to everything that the other person is saying. That's fine. What's needed is a greater proportion of You-listening than I-listening.

- What can be done to make forward movements towards a more effective education system?
- What can be done to make forward movements towards better public safety?
- What can be done to make forward movements towards reducing poverty?
- What can be done to make forward movements towards a fair and unbiased legal system?
- What can be done to make forward movements towards the issue of working women and suitable child care?
- What can be done to make forward movements towards caring for elderly people?

The Future

- Are you looking forward to the future or are you concerned about what the future may bring?
- If you were able to find out what would happen in your future, would you?
- Are you an optimist or a pessimist?
- Malcolm X said "Tomorrow belongs to the people who prepare for it." Have you been sowing any seeds to harvest in the future?
- When is the future ... when does it start?

(Q) Vulnerability

Displaying a level of vulnerability and talking about something that may be perceived as a weakness can indicate that you trust the other person to respect this aspect of you. It can be a very powerful technique for building a strong level of rapport between people, if used well.

However, be careful to use this technique wisely. Don't use it too much and avoid using it too early on.

Example

Topic: The Future

Starter: *Are you looking forward to the future or are you concerned about what the future may bring?*
"To be honest, I'm quite worried about the immediate future as I've just taken on a big mortgage and now I'm not sure that my job is safe. What on earth will I do if I lose my income?"

- Have we been visited by people or beings from the future?
- When it comes to people, would you say that the best predictor of their future behavior is their past behavior?
- How would you finish this: A year from now ...
- For society as a whole, is the future looking more promising than the past?
- Give your prediction for what the world will be like 100 years from now.

Time

- What is your biggest time stealer?
- Are you an early, on-time, or late person?
- Do you procrastinate? And if so, when?
- A quote from Doug Larson states, "For disappearing acts, it's hard to beat what happens to the eight hours supposedly left after eight of sleep and eight of work." Agree?

(G) Body language

The signals sent by a person's body language do not have a fixed meaning. The meaning for each signal will depend on the context. For example someone who is yawning may not be bored, they may be genuinely tired or on medication that causes drowsiness. Someone who has their arms crossed may be very cold rather than closed or defensive. Different cultures may give different meanings to body language aspects.

When trying to understand what someone's body language means, it's best not to rely on just one clue, but to use several clues to get a sense of the real meaning.

- Do you find it easy to give of your time to other people?
- In your life at the moment, is time passing slowly or quickly?
- What time of the day do you function best?
- Do you ever get so absorbed in something that you don't notice time passing?
- Is there going to be enough time left in life to accomplish everything you want?
- Is time a great healer?

Treating Yourself

- Do you spend time and money on giving yourself a treat?
- What do you do when you want to totally relax?
- You've been given some money as a birthday present in order to treat yourself. How would you spend it?
- A friend has offered to treat you to a meal at a restaurant of your choice. Where would you go and what would you like to order?

(G) Be careful with "why" questions

If you ask too many, or ask them in an insensitive way, "why" questions can sound confrontational or hostile. "why" questions have the potential to put people on the defensive. There are times when they are not the friendliest way to ask a question, and there may be a kinder alternative.

Example

Topic: Treating Yourself

Starter: *Do you spend time and money on treating yourself?*
If the person says *"No, I don't tend to treat myself,"* and you respond with *"Why don't you?"* it may sound rather harsh, even if it is a genuine question.

A kinder way could be *"And would you like to?"* or *"Oh dear, what can we do about that?"*

- It's your birthday and you've taken the day off work. How are you going to spend it?
- Would you view spending money on furthering your education as a "treat?"
- Do you put yourself last after your husband or partner, the children, and maybe even the family pet?
- Are you good to yourself? Do you treat yourself as well as you would treat a friend?
- If you've made a mistake do you berate yourself or treat yourself with compassion? Could you treat yourself more lovingly?
- Do you worry that if you give yourself a break and accept your imperfections that you might become self-indulgent?

(Q) Obvious questions

Sometimes questions seem so obvious that you wonder why people ask them. For example if someone is sneezing, blowing their nose and looks full of a cold, they ask *"Are you okay?"* or if someone has a very obvious new outfit they ask *"New outfit?"*

If someone asks you an obvious question, note that these are not questions as such even though they are phrased that way. They are simply a means of connecting with you, introducing a topic of conversation and giving you a way to start talking about it.

Truth and Lies

- What has been the most hurtful lie someone has ever told you, and how did you deal with it?
- Has there been a time when telling the truth got you into trouble?
- If you were with a couple, both of whom were friends of yours, and the wife told a lie about where she was the previous evening—she was with another man— would you say anything?
- Is there an issue you've buried your head in the sand about because you don't want to know the truth?

(G) Etiquette

The fundamentals of etiquette, no matter the culture, are to respect others' point of view and treat people the way you would like to be treated. This means that if you wouldn't like to be on the receiving end, then don't do it yourself. Aim to behave in a way that is comfortable to others, while understanding that most people are simply seeking friendship, kindness, and peaceful relationships.

- Would you believe a newspaper with a tagline "Truth every day"?
- When is telling a lie the best thing to do?
- Sometimes something is a lie, sometimes something is the truth, and sometimes it's neither of these. Give an example of this.
- When is it a good idea to use a lie detector?
- At what age do children become capable of telling a lie? Why would they start to tell lies?
- Given that a lot of history wasn't well documented, how true can we assume most history books are?

Understanding Behaviour

People behave in certain ways, possibly because of their beliefs, or past experiences, or in an attempt to meet their needs. Read about these people and say what may be underpinning their way of behaving:

- A couple who get married and want to have a large family, at least twelve children if not more.
- A woman who fills in her diary with many, many activities. If there is a blank space she fills it with another activity.
- A man who has reached a high level in a company and who enjoys the work. A new CEO starts whose ideas and philosophy the man doesn't agree with, so he leaves his job without another to go to.

(G) Using your phone

Do you use your phone when you are with others? It's seen as impolite to spend a lot of time on your phone while you are having a conversation. It gives the impression that the person on the end of the phone is more important than the people you are with.

If there is a genuine reason and it's important to check, for example, that the children are all right, that's seen as different to having a casual phone conversation with a friend when you are with someone else.

- A couple with two children, where the wife wants another child and the husband doesn't. They can't come to an agreement.
- A jealous husband who thinks his wife is up to no good during her lunch break. He hires a private investigator to follow her every lunch time for a fortnight. The investigator finds that the wife simply goes shopping, to the library or to a café for lunch.
- A single woman who moves into a new house, who is happy and content with her life situation. The neighbor, whom she doesn't know, comes round to warn her to "keep away from my husband."

(G) Personal space

There are socially agreed norms in societies as to the amount of personal space that is acceptable when conversing with others. For example the space for family and friends is around 18 inches to 4 feet (45cm to 120cm); while the space for intimacy is much closer, and the social distance space is around 4 to 8 feet (1.2 m to 2.4 m). If you sit or stand too close or too far away, it will make people feel uneasy.

- A grandfather who is babysitting his young grandson. The grandson loves to watch the same DVD over and over, but the grandfather gets annoyed and says he can watch it only once.
- The parents of a twenty year old female who check on her every movement, even though she gives them no cause for concern. They check her cell phone, her email and even how many miles she has traveled when she borrows the car.

(G) Accuracy

It's not a good idea to bluff and pretend you know something if you don't. If you're not completely sure of the accuracy of your information, you can add a rider such as *"As far as I know..."* or *"The last I heard* was ..."

- A couple who decide to emigrate, leaving all their family. One of their relatives tells them it is a selfish, stupid thing to do and that they should do what all the other family members have done and stay in the place where they were born.
- A husband who pretends to be happily married. However he is having a relationship with another woman for whom he has bought a house and a car, and spends as much time with her as he can.

Vacations and Travel

- Do vacations play a big part in your life?
- On the continuum from budget vacations through to luxury vacations, which type do you prefer?

- Before you go on vacation, how much planning do you do?
- How much of your country or the world have you seen?

(Q) Choosing questions in a conversation lull

If the conversation dips pick a topic that you know the other person is interested in, even if it's something you don't know anything about. If you show genuine interest, the conversation will liven up. It could be their hobby, family, new job, project they're working on or an association they belong to.

Alternatively, if you don't know them well, choose a generic topic such as *"What are your plans for the weekend?"*

- What has been your best vacation ever?
- Where's the most exotic place you've been to?
- If you could spend a year traveling the world, where would you go?
- Would you rather have a city, beach, camping or adventure vacation?
- Would a vacation in temperatures of over 100 degrees Fahrenheit put you off?
- Are there issues that hinder traveling for you, such as fear of flying or travel sickness?

Weird and Wonderful

- What's the strangest thing that's ever happened to you?
- Who is your most eccentric friend?
- Did you go through a rebellious phase?

- Tell us about the most bizarre outfit you've ever worn.
- If people were to use the word "strange" to describe one of your characteristics, which one would it be?
- What is the most unusual food you've eaten?

(G) Inaccuracy

If someone says something you know isn't accurate, how you deal with it depends on the type of conversation, the level of rapport you have with them, and the importance or otherwise of the inaccuracy. Saying, laughingly *"You haven't got a clue about it, have you?"* may be the best approach for the situation; saying nothing may be suitable for another situation; whereas a more polite version such as *"That may not be accurate"* might be better for a different situation.

In general, bluntly telling people *"That's wrong"* can be seen as antagonistic.

- What is the most bizarre item you possess?
- Tell us about a strange coincidence.
- Which group of people's way of living do you find weird?
- Which group of people's way of living do you find wonderful?

What Would you Do If . . . ?

- What would you do if you opened the front door and one of your exes was standing there?
- What would you do if you found a message in a bottle on a beach, written fifty years ago by someone from another country who wrote their name and address on the note?

- What would you do if you noticed an article in your local newspaper reporting that you had won a million on the lottery, when you hadn't?
- What would you do if you were asked to take part in some research by a female university professor studying women's personal grooming habits?

(Q) Non-answers

Non-answers are replies to a question that don't give any real information. If the other person gives a non-answer, it may be because they feel uncomfortable talking about that particular topic. If you sense this is the case, move on to something else.

However some people give non-answers because they haven't heard the question properly, don't understand what you are asking, don't know very much about the topic, or are not able to express what they want to say. If you sense this is the case, try asking the question another way or move on to another topic.

- What would you do if you found an old camera hidden in the bushes in the local park; took the photos to be developed; and found they were photos of a now-famous person taken before they were famous?
- What would you do if a colleague asked you to look after her pet tarantula while she went away for a few days?
- What would you do if you got a message from a boy you had been at school with at age five, who asked if you would like to meet up?

(G) Ask for advice

People like to be asked their advice on a matter, it makes them feel valued.

If you ask someone's opinion, it may signify that you've already made your mind up no matter what they say, whereas asking for advice gives the impression you haven't yet made your mind up and value their input.

Compare *"I'm going to buy the red one. Do you think it will look okay?"* with *"Which one should I buy, the red one or the pink one?"*

- What would you do if you were asked to model clothes in a local fashion show to raise money for charity?
- What would you do if you were asked to be a model for a life drawing class?
- What would you do if you were asked to be on a radio panel interview to talk about phobias?

Wisdom

Over the years we learn about life aspects, through formal education, and especially through experience. We learn a lot from our successes and failures and by observing what other people do. What wisdom have you gained about the following issues during your life that you could pass on to others?

- Marriage and relationships. What have you learned along the way from relationships that have worked and those that haven't? What advice could you give to young people starting out?

- Friendships. What have you learned about conducting friendships so that all people gain benefit and feel positive about the friendships?

- Health. What do you now know about good health that you didn't know when you were younger? What have you done to maintain or improve your health? What would you recommend?

- Community. Through your experience, what knowledge have you gained about how people can become involved in their community or give back to society?

(G) If you don't understand . . . ask

Sometimes we don't like to interrupt and so we let the other person carry on speaking . . . even though we don't know what they are talking about! They may be talking about something we're not familiar with; we may have missed the start of the conversation; they may use a person's name we don't know; or they may use acronyms we're not aware of. It's probably not a good idea to nod and say *"Mm hm."* It's okay to ask.

- Spiritual. How have you gained spiritual growth throughout your life? Have you noticed different ways that people can access spirituality that work for them, even though they may not work for you?
- Money. People approach the concept of money in different ways. From your own experience and what you have observed in others, what wisdom can you pass on?
- Hobbies and leisure. What have you learned about choosing hobbies and the amount of time to devote to them?
- Work and career. Through analysing your own experiences of working life, career, and career progression, do you have advice for others?

- Education. What would be your recommendations regarding formal education and qualifications? And about life education learned from experience?
- Fun! What is your experience of what fun's all about, how much people need and how they could incorporate it into their lives?

Women Achievers

This is a list of women who have achieved in at least one area of life. What might it have taken for them to get to the level they did, and what is the impact they may have had on others?

- Oprah Winfrey, media proprietor.
- Amelia Earhart, first woman to fly solo across the Atlantic Ocean.
- Marilyn Monroe, actress.

(A) Forgetting the question

Do you ever realize, part way through your answer, that you've forgotten the question? Don't worry, this is fairly common. All you need to do is stop and ask!

- Venus and Serena Williams, tennis players.
- J. K. Rowling, author.
- Michelle Obama, first African American First Lady.
- Lady Gaga, singer, songwriter.
- Angela Merkel, German chancellor.
- Nichelle Nichols, Lieutenant Uhura in Star Trek, first black actress in a main role.
- Indira Ghandi, Prime Minister of India.

Women and Work

- Have you been drawn to female-dominated occupations?
- Have you noticed women being treated differently in the workforce?
- Have you ever felt you've been treated differently in work because you're a woman?

(G) Looking confident

You don't have to *be* confident; you just have to *look* confident.

Three simple ways to help with the look of confidence: a) Have appropriate eye contact (see "Bonding: Use eye contact to create a connection with others," page 131); b) Have open facial expressions and body language; c) Have a relaxed body manner.

If you avoid eye contact, have closed body language and fidget, you'll come across as less confident.

- If you have had children, what effect has this had on your career?
- If you were an employer, how would you feel about employing women who are likely to take time off for maternity leave?
- Have you ever used your "femininity" in a workplace situation?
- Would you be comfortable going to a male practitioner in a female-dominated occupation, for example a male midwife or a male beauty therapist?

(G) Sounding confident

You don't have to *be* confident; you just have to *sound* confident.

Three simple ways to help the sound of confidence: a) Finish many of your sentences with a falling intonation, giving the impression that you are assured in what you are saying and that your contribution has come to a close; b) Avoid fillers such as "er" and simply pause instead while you are thinking of what to say; c) Say your last sentence or the end of a sentence as if it *is* the end, otherwise it will sound like you are questioning yourself.

If you regularly end your sentences with a rising intonation so they sound like a question, use fillers such as "er" or "um" a lot, or let your sentences trail off, you'll come across as less confident.

- Are there any aspects of work that men are naturally better at than women?
- Do men or women make better bosses?
- Is there a glass ceiling for women?

Women Who ...

You have been asked to form a 'Women Who' group. What kind of women would attend, and what would be the purpose of the group?

- Women Who ... love to love.
- Women Who ... feel invisible.
- Women Who ... don't understand men.
- Women Who ... buy too much.
- Women Who ... love to be kids.

(G) Impromptu ... or not

Winston Churchill is famously quoted as saying *"I'm just preparing my impromptu remarks."*

Great conversationalists will, of course, make some great impromptu remarks and tell some great impromptu stories. However, skilled communicators will also continuously work on honing their skills by doing some background preparation.

One of the ways to do this is to think through an anecdote or story you are likely to tell, and work out the best way to tell it to get the most laughs or make the most impact.

- Women Who ... want to be feminine.
- Women Who ... want to say no.
- Women Who ... like midnight snacks.
- Women Who ... can't knit, bake or sew.
- Women Who ... have a lot to give.

Work-Life Balance

- Have you got your work-life balance as you would like it?
- What are you juggling in your life?
- Have you settled for less in some areas of your life in order to improve your work-life balance?
- What is the one thing you could do to improve your work-life balance?

(G) Building on others' ideas

When someone puts forward an idea, helping them think it through or build on it is a good way to enhance a relationship.

Example

Topic: Work-Life Balance

Starter: *What is the one thing you could do to improve your work-life balance?*
   A: *"I've thought about hiring a cleaner once a week so I can have time to go swimming at the weekend instead."*
   B: *"Sounds great, let me know when you do it and I'll come swimming with you."*

- There are 168 hours in a week. How many do you spend on work (time at work, traveling, preparing, etc.) and how many hours do you have available to do as you wish?
- Sometimes success comes at the price of balance. Are you happy to pay this price in order to have success?
- When you can't fit everything in, what is the first thing you let go?
- Do you have help with household chores and / or the children?
- When you are not in work can you completely switch off from it?
- If you work, and are in a situation where financially you could manage without working, why do you work?

(G) Give an outline before you start

If you know you've got a set number of points you want to talk about, outlining them at the beginning will help others understand, and will reduce the likelihood of interruptions.

Example

Topic: Work-life balance

Starter: *If you work, and are in a situation where financially you could manage without working, why do you work?*
"I was thinking about that recently, and came to the conclusion that there are three reasons why I work ..."

Worrying

- Be honest, are you a worrier?
- What are the top three things you worry about?
- If you have a minor health issue, do you blow it out of proportion and imagine it to be a major debilitating disease?
- Is there something you used to worry about in the past, but no longer need to, as you've learned to deal with it or the situation has changed?

(G) Big words and acronyms

Some things get in the way of a good conversation. Using complicated words, sentence structures or acronyms may make it difficult for people to understand.

Example

Topic: Worrying

Starter: *What are the top three things you worry about?*
It's probably not a good idea to say something along the lines of "In the first instance, I find I am predisposed to worrying about feeling less than magnanimous, and for this reason I offered to assist my neighbor organize the upcoming yuletide festivities ..." or "I always worry when I have to contact the CTO of the CFW Corp to discuss their NSP ..."

- Do you get irritated by people who worry about trivialities?
- When you worry, does your health suffer?
- Looking back, were some of your worries in the past not worth the effort of worrying about? Were you making mountains out of molehills?
- Suggest three techniques for reducing or eliminating worrying.
- Which one of the following issues causes you the most worry: your weight; your finances; your appearance; a family member; your work; your health; your level of success; your neighbors; your relationship.

(G) Praise people

People like people who make them feel good about themselves. Finding genuine things to praise people about is a way to make them feel good and build the bonds of friendship.

For example: *"You've done really well, I'm impressed with how you've been coping with all the changes in your life this year."*

- Which of the following are you most concerned about: climate change; the state of the economy; the political situation; the education system; obesity levels; poverty; renewable energy; the health system; crime levels.

Your Call!

Fill in the blanks to make your own customized conversation starters!

- How long have you been _____?

- When was the last time you tried to _____?
- If your husband or partner asked you to _____, would you?
- Would you be surprised if _____ wanted you to go to _____ with him to her?

(G) Tell stories (2)

If it's not a serious conversation, you can tell a story and add to it by exaggerating or embellishing some of the aspects for effect, *"He took so long that I don't know how many cookies I ate while I was waiting for him, but it was in the region of three thousand ..."*

- I'm wondering whether I should _____, and I'd like your advice.
- I once read an article about people who _____. Have you ever done that?
- If you met a gorgeous _____ who wanted you to _____, what would you say?
- Have you ever _____?
- How would you describe your _____?
- I'd like to _____? Will you help?

Your Favorites & Your Starters

Here you can make a note of any of your favorite starters, and compile a list of your own questions and conversation starters.

Notes

Notes

Notes

Notes

Notes

Notes

Notes

Notes